Gatherings of Illumination

In Sending Blessings upon the Best of Creation 

Gatherings of Illumination

In Sending Blessings upon the Best of Creation 

Compiled by
Ustadha Samar al-Asha

Translated by
Feryal Salem

Nur Foundation
FOR SACRED SCIENCES
PUBLICATIONS

First Published in 2012 by
Nur Sacred Sciences Publications, Chicago.
www.nursacredsciences.org

Library of Congress Control Number: 2012952112
ISBN: 978-0-991-64760-6 (hardcover)
ISBN: 978-0-615-71794-4 (paper)

Reprinted with a new cover design (2014)

Printed in the United States of America
16 15 14 3 4 5 6 7 8 9

Set in Minion, Brioso 11/13.5, and Uthman Taha Naskh 14/21

Editor: Valerie Joy Turner
Typesetting: Muhammad Hozien
Cover: Abdallateef Whiteman

Is it not in the remembrance of God
that hearts find tranquility?

[al-Raʿd, 13:28]

Contents

Foreword ix

1 Remembrance among the People of Piety 1

Conditions and Courtesies of Gatherings with the People of Piety 3

Conditions and Actions that Facilitate the Answering of Supplications 4

Times and States in which Supplications are Most Accepted 4

Opening Supplication 5

2 Remembrance Through Sending Prayers on the Messenger ﷺ 7

The Merits of Sending Prayers upon the Prophet ﷺ 7

Supplication upon Seeing the Noble Sanctuary of the Prophet 9

The Supplication of Seeking Permission 10

The Supplication of Entering the Noble Sanctuary 12

The Supplication of Visiting 12

Gatherings of Sending Prayers upon the Prophet ﷺ 23

The Grand Repentance 24

Sending Prayers upon the Prophet 25

The Prayers of the Lovers 25

The Prayers of the Devoted with God's Beautiful Names upon the Prophet Muḥammad ﷺ with his Traditional Praiseworthy Names 44

The Muḥammadan Ode (*al-Qaṣīdat al-Muḥammadiyya*) 60

Ode Sending Prayers upon the Prophet ﷺ 64

Closing Supplication in Gatherings of Prayers upon the Prophet ﷺ 68

3 Remembrance Through the Noble Qurʾān 74
Gatherings to Recite and Complete the Entire Qurʾān 74
Abū ʿAmr al-Dānī's Supplication upon a Complete Reading of the Glorious Qurʾān 74
Additional Supplications 85
Gatherings of Remembrance using Specific Qurʾānic Chapters 87
Sūrat al-Anʿām with Its Supplication 87
Additional Supplications Seeking Divine Assistance 89
Additional Supplications 91
Supplication for Seeking the Fulfillment of Needs 91

4 Seeking Repentance (*Tawba*) and Forgiveness (*Istighfār*) 101
The Merits of Seeking Forgiveness 101
Gatherings of Seeking Forgiveness (*Istighfār*) 102
The Supplication of Repentance 103

5 Remembrance through God's Beautiful Names 109
Formula of Remembrance using God's Beautiful Names 110
Supplication through God's Beautiful Names 115
The Magnificent Ode in Seeking Assistance through God's Beautiful Names 118
Remembrance through the Repetition of *Bismillāh al-Raḥmān al-Raḥīm* 125
The Supplication of the *Basmala* 126
Al-Shādhilī's Litany of Victory (*Ḥizb al-Naṣr*) 131
Remembrance with the Divine Name *Laṭīf* 136
The *Laṭīfiyya* Supplication 138
The Supplication for Divine Assistance and Rain 141

Bibliography 145

FOREWORD

Among the many *ḥadīth*s transmitted regarding the merits of what is known as "Shām," or Greater Syria, is the following report in which the Prophet ﷺ said, "At one point, you will be [split into] standing armies: one army in Shām, one army in Yemen, and one in Iraq." ʿAbd Allāh b. Ḥawāla said, "Choose for me, Messenger of God, in case I live to see that day." The Prophet ﷺ said,

> You must go to Shām. For it is the chosen [land] of God on His earth. He selects for it the chosen ones among His servants. If you decline, then go to Yemen and drink from your springs. [But] God has given me a guarantee regarding Shām and its people.

Truly, the words of the Messenger of God ﷺ in this *ḥadīth* are attested to by fourteen centuries of Islamic history in which this region in general, and Damascus in particular (also known as "Shām" by the Arabs), has been an important center of learning and key to the preservation of the Islamic scholarly and spiritual tradition as inherited by the Prophet ﷺ.

Many of the men and women of spiritual insight have also noted that a great number of the luminaries of Islam have been through Damascus at some point in their lives, either in passing or a sojourn at length; this is yet another indication of the distinction of this city. The likes of Ḥafṣa the wife of the Prophet ﷺ, Ḥasan al-Baṣrī, al-Ghazālī, Rūmī, al-Nawawī, Ibn ʿArabī, al-Mizzī, Ibn Taymiyya, Badr al-Dīn al-Ḥasanī, and countless others have traversed its streets, prayed in its ancient mosques, and inhaled its air. Greater Syria is also honored by being the only land outside the Arabian peninsula where the Messenger of God ﷺ physically set foot, both during his youth as a merchant and during his journey to Jerusalem preceding his Night Ascension (*Miʿrāj*).

Not surprisingly, the blessed city of Damascus has been the center of a revival in women's spirituality and Islamic scholarship in recent decades. Born in 1948 in Damascus, Ustadha Samar al-Asha was privileged to be touched by this revival and, through her distinguished scholarship, to play an important role in its acceleration. After completing a bachelor's degree in biology and a master's degree in education, at a time when it was rare for religious women to pursue a higher education in Damascus, she delved into the study of *ḥadīth* and the Qurʾānic sciences. She studied under the most prominent scholars of her time and was among the first few women to ever receive an *ijāza* (license) in the recitation and mastery of the entire Qurʾān through the late scholar and principal reciter of Damascus, Shaykh Abū l-Ḥasan Muḥyī l-Dīn al-Kurdī. She then followed this by mastering the ten canonical readings and receiving another *ijāza* through Shaykh Abū l-Ḥasan in the ten readings of the Qurʾān. She was deemed so proficient in her mastery of the Qurʾān that Shaykh Abū l-Ḥasan gave her permission, along with a few other women from her circle of peers, to grant the *ijāza* on his behalf in his absence. This was a privilege that was rarely used without necessity, out of courtesy (*adab*) with the Shaykh. Each of these women acquired the title, "al-Muqriʾa l-Ḥāfiẓa l-Jāmiʿa," which means Qurʾānic reciter and master of the ten canonical readings.

With the accomplishments of Ustadha Samar al-Asha and her circle of scholars, the burgeoning of women's spirituality and scholarship in Damascus entered a new phase, in which thousands of women eventually followed their examples in mastering the entire Qurʾān in *tajwīd* (proper recitation) through memorization and earning *ijāza*s which had previously only been obtained by a limited number of men. These women not only acquired a profound spiritual connection to and understanding of God's book through this knowledge, but they also obtained through it the blessings (*baraka*) of a direct connection through twenty-eight generations of reciters to the Prophet ﷺ, the angel Gabriel, and God; with whom the chain of transmission begins.

Ustadha Samar became one of the female Qurʾān specialists in Damascus to devote her days and nights to teaching the book of God to women seeking this important knowledge. Eventually the number of women with *ijāza*s in the Qurʾān for both memorization and *tajwīd*, known as "*ijāza ʿala l-ghayb*," came to number tens of thousands of women from all around the world. In the mid-1990s, efforts were also started to train women in *tajwīd* without memorization; this plan was designed for those women who came to study from abroad and found difficulty memorizing due to their circumstances, such as language barriers or time limitations. During this period, a flood of women came to Damascus from various parts of the world and learned the Book of God under the students of Ustadha Samar and other female Qurʾān specialists among her circle of peers, and took their knowledge back to the women of their diverse countries. Soon, women reciters with the *ijāza* in *tajwīd* (some with and some without memorization), could be found in places as geographically diverse as the Philippines, the United States, Canada, Albania, Pakistan, Germany, France, Malaysia, Indonesia, China, England, Bosnia, Turkey, the Comoros Islands, and many other countries. May the initiators of this beautiful movement be rewarded for each person in the world who learns the Qurʾān through their students and the students of their students.

In addition to this work, Ustadha Samar al-Asha also made critical contributions to the field of Qurʾānic sciences through her writing. In the late 1990s, she published her magnum opus, *al-Bast fī l-qiraʾāt al-ʿashr* (The simplification of the ten readings), a unique reference work that consists of six hefty volumes and details the Qurʾān verse by verse, outlining the ten variant readings of each verse through the use of color coding and charting. This new method of presenting the information of classical poems of great Qurʾānic scholars such as al-Jazarī or al-Shāṭibī has made learning the ten readings (*qirāʾat*) far more accessible to the contemporary student, whose reliance on writing has made visual presentation an integral part of his or her learning process. Ustadha Samar's multi-volume book is regarded as an invaluable contribution to the field of Qurʾānic sciences and many of the most prominent reciters and scholars of the Qurʾān wrote forewords to her work, praising and recommending it; among them are Shaykh Muḥyī l-Dīn al-Kurdī, Shaykh Kurayyim Rājiḥ, Shaykh Ayman Swayd, Shaykh ʿAbd al-Razzāq al-Ḥalabī, and Shaykh Nūr al-Dīn al-ʿItr.

Shaykh ʿAbd al-Razzāq al-Ḥalabī writes, "…I have found this work to be one of its kind in its composition; namely in its structure, organization, and color coding. It is beneficial both for those who specialize in this great science and those who are beginners."

Shaykh Muḥyī l-Dīn al-Kurdī writes:

> I have seen this book from its beginning stages and it was presented to me upon completion. I have seen that much effort has been expended until this book came to its present form, which is new and beneficial, particularly for those who specialize in the canonical readings because it simplifies combining the various transmissions and thus makes it easy for a reciter to read, without straying in any way. This excellent book in this clear presentation benefits both the reciter and the student of recitation by helping them save time and have in front of them the variant evidences from the two *matns* of the Shaṭibiyya and the *Durar*.

Shaykh Kurayyim Rājiḥ writes:

> The esteemed author, sister Samar Diya al-Asha has

> expended an intense amount of effort into this . . . her style is both easy and brilliant. It neither bores the specialist nor overwhelms the beginner. Her efforts are one proof among many proofs of a vast intellectual revival among Muslim women, particularly in the blessed land of Damascus. This revival brings back the learning that the women of the *Ṣaḥaba* (Companions of the Prophet ﷺ), the *Tābiʿīn* (Followers of the Companions), and their followers had during the first [Islamic] centuries, in terms of faith, [proper] creed, enlightened thinking, sophisticated Qurʾānic understanding, constructive knowledge, and work...I recommend this book to be published...because of what is beneficial and accurate in it, as well as what it reveals about the ability of women with proper Islamic training to equal men in their contributions to the Islamic sciences, and possibly even surpass them.

In addition to her mastery of the Qurʾān and her rank as a reciter of the ten canonical readings, Ustadha Samar has also achieved another milestone for women through her scholarship in the field of *ḥadīth* sciences. Ustadha Samar memorized the six canonical *ḥadīth* books of al-Bukhārī, Muslim, al-Tirmidhī, Abū Dāwūd, al-Nasāʾī, and Ibn Māja, along with the *Muwaṭṭa* of Imām Mālik. She also memorized and mastered the knowledge related to each of the transmitters in the chains of transmission (*isnāds*) of each *ḥadīth* in these books. She was then tested and became the first woman known in the contemporary period to receive an *ijāza* of mastery in each of these *ḥadīth* compilations through one of the rare *ḥadīth* transmitters (*muḥaddiths*) left in the world; Shaykh Nūr al-Dīn al-ʿItr, who was the son-in-law and most prominent student of the late *ḥāfiẓ* and *muḥaddith*, Shaykh ʿAbd Allāh Sirāj al-Dīn. Thus, Ustādha Samar herself became a *muḥadditha* (*ḥadīth* transmitter) and later devoted her attention to reviving the legacy of women *ḥadīth* transmitters of early Islamic history by actively training select groups of promising women as *muḥadditha*s and scholars of *ḥadīth*. In the past two decades, due to the efforts of Ustadha Samar and the circle of students she personally trained in *ḥadīth* to work with her, the number of women *muḥadditha*s that she trained is estimated to number in the hundreds.

In 2006, Ustadha Samar opened a unique women's *ḥadīth* training academy in the quarters of old Damascus. After obtaining permission from the Ministry of Endowments for its use, she had a valuable section of abandoned rooms that are a part of the Umayyad Mosque renovated. This new institute became known as, *Madrasat al-Ḥadīth al-Nuriyya li-l-Ināth* or the Nuriyya *Ḥadīth* Institute for Women, which is named after Nūr al-Dīn al-Zanjī, who, in the twelfth century, designated part of this building, among other similar structures he had supported by religious endowments, as a center of learning for students of sacred knowledge. This school is also blessed because it includes in its structure the cell that Imam al-Ghazālī is known to have retreated in during his sojourn in Damascus—the journey which prompted him to write his foundational work, *Iḥyāʾ ʿulūm al-dīn*. Imam al-Ghazālī's cell is currently used as a library in which women aspiring to partake in the spiritual legacy embodied by this great teacher come to study, research, and transmit the words of the Prophet ﷺ. It is also emblematic that this blessed cell is the room in which future *muḥadditha*s who are ready to be tested to receive an *ijāza* in the various books of *ḥadīth* meet with the eminent male *ḥadīth* scholars of Damascus who visit the institute and use this space to assess their mastery of the prophetic tradition. In addition to being a "one of its kind in the world" institute that graduates women *ḥadīth* transmitters after a rigorous five-year program, the Nuriyya Institute also offers a wide array of other less intense programs and classes for women in the sciences of Islam, such as *fiqh*, Arabic grammar, Qurʾānic sciences, theology, and many other subjects.

In the field of *ḥadīth*, Ustadha Samar has thus far written *al-Taysīr fī ḥifẓ al-asānīd: Asānīd ṣaḥīḥ al-imām Bukhārī* (The facilitator in memorizing chains of transmission: The chains of Imām al-Bukhārī). This large two-volume work facilitates the memorization and mastery of the individual transmitters through the use of color codes, symbols representing transmitters, and an illustrated charting system that helps the student of *ḥadīth* visualize and remember individual transmitters and their students in all of the chains of transmission found in al-Bukhārī's compilation of sound traditions. She has also written *al-Madkhal ilā dirāsat al-ḥadīth wa-l-sunna* (An introduction to the study of *ḥadīth* and *sunna*), as well as *Muqtaṭafāt min kutub al-shurūḥ* (Excerpts from books of commentaries). These textbooks are among the many books used in the curriculum of study in the Nuriyya Institute where female students are trained to navigate the classical Islamic texts.

Known simply as "Anse Samar," few would initially assume from her humble down to earth demeanor the erudition of this great scholar who has earned the title of both "Muḥadditha" and "al-Muqriʾa l-Ḥāfiẓa l-Jāmiʿa," while disseminating knowledge of the sacred sciences of Islam among thousands of women. She is a reflection of the upbringing of her own teachers and the spiritual circle of women who have transformed those whose hearts have recognized them without any desire of their own to be recognized or known. The current translation of *Majālis al-nūr fī l-ṣalāti ʿalā l-rasūl* (Gatherings of Illumination in Sending Blessings upon the Best of Creation ﷺ) is Ustadha Samar's most concise book which offers only a passing glimpse into a world of great Muslim women who are giants, both in the breadth of their knowledge as well as their spiritual devotion to God.

Feryal Salem
Chicago, 2012

محمد رسول الله

1

REMEMBRANCE AMONG THE PEOPLE OF PIETY

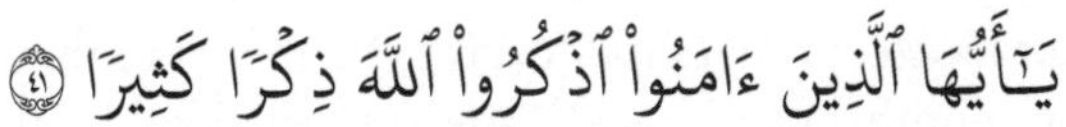

O you who believe, remember God with much remembrance [al-Aḥzāb, 33:41]

God says in the Qur'ān, *And remember the name of your Lord, and devote yourself to Him with [complete] devotion* [al-Muzammil, 73:8]. Spending time in retreat was a tradition of the messengers and extra worship was a mode of devotion by the lovers of God; indeed, gatherings of remembrance have long been the stronghold of people of piety and righteousness (*ṣāliḥīn*). The types of remembrance in these blessed gatherings varied. Some focused on sending prayers upon the Prophet ﷺ or the recitation and study of the Qur'ān, while others devoted themselves to repentance (*istighfār*) and seeking forgiveness or supplicating through God's beautiful names, some or all of them (e.g., the repetition of *Bismillāh al-Raḥmān al-Raḥīm, Yā Lāṭīf, Yā Mughīth*). The fruits of these gatherings are many, including a combination of the purification of hearts, the rectification of the soul, and the elevation of the spirit to the heights of perfection. In addition, these gatherings lead to the removal of troubles and the fulfillment of needs (*qaḍā l-ḥawāʾij*). This is all accomplished while igniting in the hearts of the worshiper the fire of divine love that obliterates attachments to all other than the Beloved.

Since the lowest rank of divine love is the possession of a sound heart, it is essential to free one's heart of any grudges, anger, envy, and jealousy toward one's fellow Muslims in general and the members of one's gathering in particular. Hence, it is recommended that individuals greet one another before the gathering begins by shaking hands without kissing or hugging. It is reported on the authority of Barāʾ ﷺ that the Messenger of God ﷺ said: "There are no two Muslims who meet and shake hands except that God forgives them before they depart [from one another's presence]."[1] Also reported on the authority of Barāʾ saying,

> I entered [into the presence of] the Prophet ﷺ. He welcomed me and took my hand and then said, "O Barāʾ do you know why I took your hand?"
>
> I said: "No, O Prophet of God."
>
> He said, "No Muslim meets a Muslim and is then cheerful with him, greets him, and takes him by the hand except that the sins fall between them the way leaves fall from a tree."[2]

Anas b. Mālik ﷺ reported:

> A man said: "O Messenger of God, if a man from us meets his brother or friend should he bow to him?"
>
> He [the Prophet] said: "No."
>
> He said: "Should he hug him or kiss him?"

1 Abū Dāwūd, *Sunan*, Kitāb al-adab: Bāb fī l-muṣāfaḥa, no. 5212.

2 al-Bayhaqī, *Shuʿab al-īmān*, vol. 6, Bāb 61, no. 8957.

He [the Prophet] said: "No."

He said: "Should he take his hand and shake it?"

He [the Prophet] said, "Yes."[3]

Conditions and Courtesies of Gatherings with the People of Piety

There are numerous manners (*ādāb*) one should maintain in order to gain the full spiritual benefits of attending gatherings with the people of piety and righteousness (*ṣāliḥīn*). Among them are the following.

1. To make *ghusl* before attending the gathering.
2. To have a pure intention. One can say at the beginning of the gathering, "This is my place of worship and I intend to retreat in it" (*hādha masjidi wa-nawaytu al-iʿtikāf bihi*).
3. To have ritual purity of one's body, clothes, and place of gathering.
4. To avoid speaking, except in the remembrance of God or out of necessity. Also, to completely avoid joking and frivolous behavior.
5. To fast if possible; some of the pious have said, "Worship is a craft and its tool is fasting."
6. To pray two *rakaʿas* with the intention of retreating (*iʿtikāf*) or seeking the fulfillment of one's needs (*qaḍāʾ ḥāja*).
7. To sit in a circle or in orderly rows without being overcrowded. The key to benefit in such gatherings is to maintain a state of dignified seriousness (*waqār*) and serenity (*sakīna*).

3 Ibn Māja, *Sunan*, Kitāb al-istiʾdhān: Bāb mā jāʾa fī l-muṣāfaḥa, no. 2728.

Conditions and Actions that Facilitate the Answering of Supplications

1. Begin by thanking God (*ḥamd*) and praising Him (*thanāʾ*), then send prayers upon the Prophet and also end in this way.
2. Be resolute and persist in what one is asking, and be certain of God's response without impatience.
3. Have presence of heart in one's supplication while keeping one's voice at a moderate tone, without it being completely silent or excessively loud. Also refrain from excessiveness or exaggeration in the eloquence of one's words (so as to maintain a spiritual state of intimacy and humility with God).
4. Supplicate in both times of ease and hardship and ask from none other than God Himself.
5. Acknowledge one's sins and ask for their forgiveness. Also, realize one's blessings and thank God for them.
6. Rectify any harm one may have caused others and have a sincere inner state of repentance while being vigilant that one's food, drink, and clothes are from lawful earnings.
7. Supplicate three times and face the *qibla* when possible.
8. Refrain from praying for anything that is sinful or breaks blood relations, and refrain from supplicating against one's family, property, progeny, or oneself.

Times and States in which Supplications are Most Accepted

The times and circumstances in which supplications are more likely to be accepted include: The night of mid-Shaʿbān, the Night of Power (*laylat al-qadr*), the last third of the night, after each obligatory prayer, between the *adhān* and *iqāma*, an unspecified hour from each night, at the time of the call to prayer for each of the obligatory prayers, during rainfall, when preparing to set out in combat for the sake of God, an unspecified hour during Friday, during prostration (*sajda*), during the prescribed supplication when one wakes from sleep at night, during the last sitting of the prayer (*tashahhud al-akhīr*), the supplication of a Muslim for another Muslim without his knowledge, during the month of Ramaḍān, during a gathering of Muslims, during gatherings of remembrance, the prayers of the oppressed, the prayer of the traveler, the prayer of the one fasting until he breaks his fast as well as while breaking his fast, the prayer of a person in dire need, the supplications of a righteous leader of the Muslims (*imām*), and the prayers of a child devoted to his parents.

Opening Supplication

دُعَاء الافْتِتَاح

إِلَهِي تَعَرَّضَ لَكَ المُتَعَرِّضُوْنَ، وَقَصَدَكَ القَاصِدُوْنَ، وأَمِلَ مَعْرُوفَكَ الطَّالِبُوْنَ، وَلَكَ فِيْ هَذَا المَجْلِس نَفَحَاتٌ وَجَوَائِزُ وَعَطَايَا وَ مَوَاهِبُ، تَمُنُّ بِهَا عَلَى مَنْ تَشَاءُ مِنْ عِبَادِكَ، وَتَمْنَعهَا مِمَّن لَم تَسْبق لَهُ العِنَايَة مِنْكَ، وَهَا أَنَاْ ذَا عَبْدُكَ الفَقِيْرُ إِلَيْكَ، المؤملُ فَضْلِكَ وَمَعْرُوفِكَ، فَإِن كُنْتَ يَا مَولَاي تَفَضَّلْتَ فِي هَذِهِ الجَلْسَة عَلَى أَحَدٍ مِنْ خَلْقِكَ، وَجُدْتَ عَلَيْهِ بِعَائِدَةٍ مِن عَطْفِكَ، فَصَلِّ عَلَى سَيِدِنَا مُحَمَّدٍ وَعَلَى آلِهِ وَصَحْبِهِ، وَجُدْ عَلَيَّ بِطَوْلِكَ وَمَعْرُوفِكَ، يَا رَبَّ العَالَمِيْن.

Ilāhī ta'arraḍa laka al-muta'rriḍūn. Wa-qaṣadaka al-qāṣidūn. Wa-amila ma'rūfaka al-ṭālibūn wa-laka fī hadha al-majlis nafaḥātūn wa-jawā'iz, wa-'aṭāyā wa-mawāhibu, tamunnu bihā ʿalā man tashāʾu min ʿibādika wa-tamnaʿhā mimman lam tasbiq lahu l-ʿināyata minka. Wa-hā ana dhā ʿabduka al-faqīru ilayka al-muʾmalu faḍlika wa-maʿrūfika. Faʾin kunta yā mawlay tafaḍḍalta fī hādhihi al-jalsa ʿalā aḥadin min khalqika wa-judta ʿalayhi bi-ʿāʾidatin min ʿaṭfika, fa-ṣalli ʿalā sayyidinā Muḥammadin wa-ʿalā ālihi wa-ṣaḥbihi wa-jud ʿalayya bi ṭawlika wa-maʿrūfika yā rabb al-ʿālamīn.

My God, the petitioners have beseeched You, those who pursue have sought You, and the seekers hope for Your benevolence. You grant in this gathering sweet breezes of mercy, rewards, provisions, and gifts which You bestow upon whom You desire and avert from whomever does not obtain Your attention. Here I am, your poor servant in dire need of You and desiring Your favor and kindness. If You have, my Lord, favored any one of Your creation in this gathering and have bestowed on him part of Your affection, then send prayers upon Muḥammad, his family, and Companions, and bestow Your bounty and favors upon me, O Lord of the worlds.

2

Remembrance Through Sending Prayers on the Messenger 

The Merits of Sending Prayers upon the Prophet ﷺ

We are infinitely grateful to the One who has blessed us with guidance and faith. As we are ever grateful to the One who honored us by linking us to His Chosen Messenger ﷺ, whom He selected to relay His clear signs, empowered with momentous miracles, gave us attention by virtue of our following him, and crowned us through his blessings with divine acceptance in this life and the next. God commanded us in His Book to send prayers upon him as He does and as do the noble angels. He has bestowed upon us, in return for our prayers upon the Messenger ﷺ, immense reward and forgiveness.

God says in the Qurʾān, *God and His angels send prayers upon the Prophet. O you who believe, invoke prayers upon him and greet him with a salutation of peace* [al-Aḥzāb, 33:56]. The Prophet ﷺ said, "Whoever sends one prayer upon me, God sends upon him ten prayers and records for him ten rewards."[1]

1 al-Tirmidhī, *Sunan*, vol. 2., Kitāb abwāb al-ṣalāh; Bāb mā jāʾa fī faḍl

He also said, "Be abundant with sending prayers upon me on Fridays; for there is no one who sends prayers upon me on Friday, except that his prayers are presented to me."[2]

Prayers upon the Prophet ﷺ repel the influences of evil and the harms of tribulations. They also relieve anxieties, alleviate troubles, bring about forgiveness for mistakes, and erase sins. The stingy person is the one who hears the Prophet ﷺ mentioned and does not send prayers upon him. The Prophet said, "The miser is he in whose presence I am mentioned and he does not send prayers upon me."[3] Sending prayers upon the Prophet ﷺ will also cause one's prayers to be answered. Hence, after praising God, one should send prayers upon the Prophet ﷺ in the beginning, middle, and end of one's supplication. Through this, God's mercy descends and one's prayers are answered. Indeed, God says in the Qurʾān, *Call upon Me and I will answer* [al-Ghāfir, 40:60].

The one who sends prayers and blessing upon the Prophet ﷺ is also honored with having their prayers answered by God the Exalted and Most High.

> It is reported that,"The Messenger of God ﷺ came one day with joy on his noble face.
>
> So he [the narrator] said, 'O Messenger of God we see joy on your face!'
>
> He ﷺ said, 'An angel approached me and told me, 'O Muḥammad, God says that no one sends prayers upon you from your community except that I send ten prayers upon him. Neither does anyone from your community send blessings upon you except that I send ten blessing upon him.'"[4]

---

al-ṣalāh ʿala al-nabī ﷺ, no. 484.

2 al-Ḥākim, *al-Mustadrak ʿalā al-Ṣaḥīḥayn*, vol. 2., Kitāb al-tafsīr; Tafsīr Sūrat al-Aḥzāb, 741/3577.

3 al-Ḥaythamī, *Majmāʿ al-zawāʾid*, vol. 10, p. 164. Transmitted by al-Ṭabarānī.

4 al-Nasāʾi, *Sunan*, vol. 3, Kitāb al-sahw: Bāb faḍl al-taslīm ʿalā

Similarly, the Messenger of God ﷺ said, "There is no person who sends greetings of peace upon me, except that God brings my soul back so that I return to him his greetings of peace."[5]

Truly, one's sense of closeness and attachment to the Messenger ﷺ intensifies after visiting the Prophet's ﷺ mosque and standing in front of his blessed grave. In addition, one is granted the privilege of his intercession, as in accordance with his words, "Whoever visits my grave, my intercession will be guaranteed for him."[6] For this reason, it is fitting to begin this compilation of prayers upon the Prophet ﷺ with supplications to be said when visiting his grave.

Supplication upon Seeing the Noble Sanctuary of the Prophet

It is recommended, when first seeing the sanctuary in which the Prophet's grave is enclosed, that one say the following supplication.

دُعَاء رُؤْيَة الحَرَم النَّبَوِي الشَّرِيف

اللهُمَّ هَذا حَرَمُ رَسُولِ الله ﷺ الَّذِي حَرَّمْتَهُ عَلَى لِسَانِه، وَدَعَاكَ أَنْ تَجْعَلَ فِيْهِ مِنْ الخَيْرِ والبَرَكَةِ مِثْلَمَا فِي حَرَمِ البَيْتِ الحَرَامِ، فَحَرِّمْنِي عَلَى النَّار، وَآمِنِّي مِنْ عَذابِكَ يَوْمَ تَبْعَثُ عِبَادَك، وارْزُقْنِي مِنْ بَرَكَاتِكَ، وَوَفِّقْنِي لِحُسْنِ الأَدَبِ وَفِعْلِ الخَيْرَاتِ وَتَرْكِ المُنْكَراتِ.

Allāhumma hādha ḥaramu rasūlillāh ﷺ alladhī ḥarramtahu 'alā lisānih, wa-da'āka an taj'ala fīhi min al-khayri wa-l-barakati

al-nabī ﷺ, no. 1283.

5 Abū Dāwūd, *Sunan*, Kitāb al-Manāsik (al-ḥajj), Bāb ziyārat al-qubūr, no. 2041.

6 al-Dāraquṭnī, *Sunan*, Kitāb al-ḥajj, Bāb al-mawāqit, no. 244.

mithlamā fī ḥarami al-bayti al-ḥaram, fa-ḥarrimnī ʿalā l-nār, wa-āminnī min ʿadhābika yawma tabʿathu ʿibādak, warzuqnī min barakātika, wa-waffiqnī li-ḥusnī l-adabi wa-fiʿli al-khayrāti wa-tarki al-munkarāti.

O God, this is the sanctuary of the Messenger of God ﷺ which You sanctified upon his own tongue, and he prayed to You for goodness and blessings as long as he is in the abode of his sanctuary. Protect me from Hellfire and grant me amnesty from Your punishment the day You raise Your servants. Bestow upon me blessings, grant me excellence in courtesy (*adab*), the performance of good actions, and the abandonment of what You prohibit.

The Supplication of Seeking Permission

The visitor to the Prophet's ﷺ sanctuary should then stand at the door and say:

دُعَاء الاسْتِئْذَان

اللَّهُمَّ إِنِّي وَقَفْتُ عَلَى بَابٍ مِنْ أَبْوَابِ مَسْجِدِ نَبِيِّكَ ﷺ، وَقَدْ مَنَعْتَ النَّاسَ أَنْ يَدْخُلُواْ إِلَّا بِإِذْنِهِ، فَقُلْتَ:يَـٰٓأَيُّهَا ٱلَّذِينَ ءَامَنُواْ لَا تَدْخُلُواْ بُيُوتَ ٱلنَّبِيِّ إِلَّآ أَن يُؤْذَنَ لَكُمْ (سُورَةُ الأَحْزَابِ :٥٣) اللَّهُمَّ إِنِّيْ أَعْتَقِدُ حُرْمَةَ صَاحِبِ هَذَا المَقَامِ الشَّرِيْفِ فِي غَيْبَتِهِ كَمَا أَعْتَقِدُهَا فِي حَضْرَتِهِ، وَأَعْلَمُ أَنَّ رَسُوْلَكَ حَيٌّ عِنْدَكَ يُرْزَقُ، يَسْمَعُ كَلَامِي، وَيَرُدُّ سَلَامِي، وَأَنَّكَ حَجَبْتَ عَنْ سَمْعِي كَلَامَهُ، وَفَتَحْتَ بَابَ فَهْمِي بِلَذِيْذِ مُنَاجَاتِهِ، وَإِنِّي أَسْتَأْذِنُكَ يَارَبِّ أَوَّلاً، وَأَسْتَأْذِنُ رَسُولَكَ وَ آلِهِ ﷺ ثَانِياً، وَأَسْتَأْذِنُ المَلَائِكَةَ المُوَكَّلِيْنَ بِهَذِهِ البُقْعَةِ المُبَارَكَةِ ثَالِثاً، اللَّهُمَّ فَأْذَنْ لِي فِيْ الدُّخُوْلِ أَفْضَلَ مَا أَذِنْتَ لِأَحَدٍ مِنْ خَلْقِكَ، فَإِنْ لَمْ أَكُنْ أَهْلاً لِذَلِكَ فَأَنْتَ أَهْلٌ لِذَلِكَ.

Allāhumma innī waqaftu ʿalā bābin min abwābi masjidi nabiyyika, wa-qad manaʿta al-nāsa an yadkhulū illā bi idhnih, fa-qulta: "*Yā ayyuha alladhīna āmanū lā tadkhulū buyūta al-nabiyyi illā an yuʾdhana lakum.*" Allāhumma innī aʿtaqidu ḥurmata ṣāḥibi hādha al-maqāmi al-sharīfi fī ghaybatihi kamā aʿtaqiduhā fī haḍratihi, wa-aʿlamu anna rasūlaka ḥayyun ʿindaka yurzaqu, yasmaʿu kalāmī, wa-yaruddu salāmi, wa-annaka ḥajabta ʿan samʿī kalāmahu wa-fataḥta bāba fahmī bi-ladhīdhi munājātihi. Wa-innī astaʾdhinuka yā rabbi awwalan, wa-astaʾdhinu rasūlaka wa-ālihi thāniyan, wa-astaʾdhinu al-malāʾikata al-muwakkilīna bi hādhihi al-buqʿati al-mubārakati thālithan. Allāhumma faʾdhan lī fī l-dukhūli afḍala mā adhinta li aḥadin min khalqika, fa-in lam akun ahlan li-dhālika fa-anta ahlun li-dhālik.

O God, I stand at the door of the doors of the mosque of Your Prophet. You have forbidden people to enter except with permission in Your words, *O you who believe, do not enter the chambers of the Prophet, except that he has granted you permission* [al-Aḥzāb, 33:53]. O God, I believe in the sanctity of the owner of this noble place in his absence as I do in his presence. I know that the Messenger of God is alive in Your presence and is granted provision, hears my words, and replies to my greetings. And that you have veiled me from hearing his words but You have opened my understanding to receive the sweetness of his call. First, I seek permission from You, O God. Second, I seek permission from Your Messenger and his family. Third, I seek permission from the angels assigned to this holy place. O God, grant me permission to enter with the most favored permission which You have granted anyone from Your creation. If I am not worthy of this, You [certainly] possess the power to be generous with me beyond what I deserve.

The Supplication of Entering the Noble Sanctuary

The visitor should then enter in a state of calmness, dignity, presence of heart, and humility while giving preference to the people on his right over his left in entering and saying the following words.

دُعَاء الدُّخُول إِلَى الحَرَمِ الشَّرِيْف

بِسْمِ اللهِ وَبِاللهِ وَفِي سَبِيْلِ اللهِ وَعَلَى مِلَّةِ رَسُولِ اللهِ صَلَّى اللهُ عَلَيْهِ وَآلِهِ، اللَّهُمَّ اغْفِرْ لِي ذُنُوبِي وَافْتَحْ لِيْ أَبْوَابَ رَحْمَتِكَ، رَبِّ أَدْخِلْنِي مُدْخَلَ صِدْقٍ وَأَخْرِجْنِي مُخْرَجَ صِدْقٍ وَاجْعَل لِي مِن لَدُنْكَ سُلْطَاناً نَصِيْراً، وَتُبْ عَلَيَّ إِنَّكَ أَنْتَ التَّوَّابُ الرَّحِيْمُ.

Bismi-llāhi wa-bi-llāhi wa-fī sabīli-llāhi wa-ʿalā millati rasūli-llāhi ṣalla Allāhu ʿalayhi wa-ālihi. Allāhumma ighfir lī dhunūbī waftaḥ lī abwāba raḥmatika. Rabbi adkhilnī mudkhala ṣidqin wa-akhrijnī mukhraja ṣidqin wajʿal lī min ladunka ṣulṭānan naṣīran. Wa-tub ʿalayya innaka anta al-tawwābu al-raḥīm.

In the name of God, with God, for the sake of God, and for the nation of the Messenger of God ﷺ. O God, forgive my sins and open for me the doors of Your mercy. My Lord, grant me an entrance of sincerity and grant me an exit of sincerity. And grant me from You a power which is victorious. And turn toward me, for You are indeed the Accepter of Repentance and the Merciful.

The Supplication of Visiting

When one is approaching the grave of the Prophet ﷺ he should say the following supplication.

دُعَاءُ الزِّيَارَة

السَّلَامُ عَلَيْكَ يَا رَسُولَ اللهِ، السَّلَامُ عَلَيْكَ يَا نَبِيَّ اللهِ، السَّلَامُ عَلَيْكَ يَا مُحَمَّدُ بنِ عَبْدِ اللهِ، السَّلَامُ عَلَيْكَ يَا خَاتَمَ النَّبِيِّينَ، السَّلَامُ عَلَيْكَ يَا سَيِّدَ المُرْسَلِينَ، السَّلَامُ عَلَيْكَ يَا إِمَامَ المُتَّقِينَ وَيَا قَائِدَ الغُرِّ المُحَجَّلِينَ، السَّلَامُ عَلَيْكَ يَا صَفْوَةَ اللهِ، السَّلَامُ عَلَيْكَ يَا حَبِيْبَ اللهِ، السَّلَامُ عَلَيْكَ يَا أَمِيْنَ اللهِ، السَّلَامُ عَلَيْكَ يَا نَبِيَّ الرَّحْمَةِ، السَّلَامُ عَلَيْكَ يَا شَفِيْعَ الأُمَّةِ، السَّلَامُ عَلَيْكَ وَعَلَى آلِ بَيْتِكَ الطَّاهِرِيْنَ، السَّلَامُ عَلَيْكَ وَعَلَى سَائِرِ الأَنْبِيَاءِ وَالمُرْسَلِينَ، وَعَلَى عِبَادِ اللهِ الصَّالِحِينَ.

Al-salāmu ʿalayka yā rasūl Allāh! Al-salāmu ʿalayka yā nabiyya Allāh! Al-salāmu ʿalayka yā Muḥammad bin ʿAbdillāh! Al-salāmu ʿalayka yā khātama al-nabiyyīn! Al-salāmu ʿalayka yā sayyid al-mursalīn! Al-salāmu ʿalayka yā imāma al-muttaqīn wa-yā qāʾida al-ghurri al-muḥajjalīn! Al-salāmu ʿalayka yā ṣafwata Allāh! Al-salāmu ʿalayka yā ḥabīb Allāh! Al-salāmu ʿalayka yā amīn Allāh! Al-salāmu ʿalayka yā nabiyya al-raḥma! Al-salāmu ʿalayka yā shafīʿa al-umma! Al-salāmu ʿalayka wa-ʿalā āli baytika al-ṭāhirīn! Al-salāmu ʿalayka wa-ʿalā sāʾiri al-anbiyāʾi wa-l-mursalīn wa-ʿalā ʿibādillāh al-ṣāliḥīn!

Peace be upon you, O Messenger of God! Peace be upon you, O Prophet of God! Peace be upon you, O Muḥammad the son of ʿAbd Allāh! Peace be upon you, O last of the prophets! Peace be upon you, O master of the messengers! Peace be upon you, O guide of the pious and leader of the radiant marked ones (*al-ghurr al-muḥajallīn*).[7] Peace be upon you, O distinguished

7 The Prophet ﷺ said that he would recognize his community on the Day of Judgment by the radiance of the limbs they used to

one of God! Peace be upon you, O beloved of God! Peace be upon you, O trustworthy one of God! Peace be upon you, O Prophet of mercy! Peace be upon you, O intercessor of the Muslim community! Peace be upon you and upon your pure family! Peace be upon you and all of your Companions in their entirety! Peace be upon you and the rest of the prophets and messengers, and your upright servants!

Then one should stand in front of the grave of the Prophet ﷺ and say:

أَشْهَدُ أَنْ لا إِلَهَ إِلَّا اللهُ وَحْدَهُ لا شَرِيْكَ لَهُ، وَأَشْهَدُ أَنَّ مُحَمَّداً عَبْدُهُ وَرَسُوْلُهُ، وَأَشْهَدُ أَنَّكَ رَسُوْلُ اللهِ، وَأَنَّكَ مُحَمَّدُ ابنُ عَبْدِ اللهِ، وَأَشْهَدُ أَنَّكَ قَدْ بَلَّغْتَ رِسَالاَتِ رَبِّكَ، وَنَصَحْتَ لِأُمَّتِكَ، وَجَاهَدْتَ فِي سَبِيْلِ اللهِ، وَعَبَدْتَ اللهَ مُخْلِصاً حَتَّى أَتَاكَ اليَقِيْنُ، وَدَعَوْتَ إِلَى سَبِيْلِ رَبِّكَ بِالحِكْمَةِ وَالمَوْعِظَةِ الحَسَنَةِ، وَأَدَّيْتَ الَّذِي عَلَيْكَ مِنَ الحَقِّ، وَأَنَّكَ قَدْ رَئِفْتَ بِالمُؤْمِنِيْنَ وَغَلُظْتَ عَلَى الكَافِرِيْنَ، الحَمْدُ للهِ الَّذِي اسْتَنْقَذَنَا بِكَ مِنَ الشِّرْكِ وَالضَّلَالَةِ،

Ashhadu an lā ilāha illa Allāh waḥdahu lā sharīka lahu, wa-ashhadu anna Muḥammadan ʿabduhu wa-rasuluh, wa-ashhadu annaka rasūlullāhu, wa-annaka Muḥammadu ibnu ʿAbdillāh, wa-ashhadu annaka qad balaghta risālāti rabbika. Wa-naṣaḥta li-ummatika. Wa-jāhadta fī sabīli-llāhi, wa-ʿabadta Allāh mukhliṣan ḥattā atāka al-yaqīn, wa-daʿawta ilā sabīli rabbika bi-l-ḥikmati wa-l-mawʿiẓati al-ḥasanati. Wa-addayta alladhī ʿalayka min al-ḥaqqi, wa-annaka qad

wash during the ritual washing, or *wuḍū*. The word *ghurr* means radiant. The word *muḥajallīn* is related to the word *taḥjīl*, which relates to the white marks that can sometimes be found on all four or at least three legs of a horse. Hence, the believers who made ritual ablutions regularly will have a similar radiant and distinguishing mark according to the Prophet ﷺ.

ra'ifta bi-l-mu'minīna wa-ghaluẓta ʿalā l-kāfirīn. Alḥamduli-llāhi alladhī istanqadhnā bika min al-shirki wa-l-ḍalālati.

I testify that there is no god but God, the single One who has no partners. And I testify that Muḥammad is his servant and messenger. I testify that you are the Messenger of God, and that you are Muḥammad the son of ʿAbd Allāh. I testify that you have delivered the messages of your Lord, advised your community, struggled in the way of God, worshipped God with sincerity until you reached certainty, called people to the path of your Lord with wisdom and good advice, delivered [the responsibility] that was upon you in truth, and that you were gentle with the believers and harsh with those who rejected the truth. [We give] thanks to God who saved us through you from polytheism and misguidance.

اللَّهُمَّ فَاجْعَل صَلَوَاتِكَ وَصَلَوَاتِ مَلَائِكَتِكَ المُقَرَّبِينَ، وَأَنْبِيَائِكَ المُرْسَلِينَ، وَعِبَادِكَ الصَّالِحِيْنَ، وَأَهْلِ السَّمَوَاتِ وَالأَرَضِيْنَ، وَمَنْ سَبَّحَ لَكَ يَا رَبَّ العَالَمِيْنَ مِنَ الأَوَّلِيْنَ وَالآخِرِيْنَ، عَلَى مُحَمَّدٍ عَبْدِكَ وَرَسُولِكَ وَنَبِيِّكَ وَأَمِيْنِكَ وَنَجِيِّكَ وَحَبِيْبِكَ وَصَفِيِّكَ وَخَاصَّتِكَ وَصَفْوَتِكَ وَخِيْرَتِكَ مِنْ خَلْقِكَ،

Allāhumma fajʿal ṣalawātika wa-ṣalawāti malāʾikatika al-muqarrabīna, wa-anbiyāʾika al-mursalīn, wa-ʿibādika al-ṣaliḥīn, wa-ahli al-samawāti wa-l-araḍīna, wa-man sabbaḥa laka yā rabba al-ʿālamīna min al-awwalīna wa-l-ākhirīn, ʿalā Muḥammadin ʿabdika wa-rasūlika wa-nabiyyika wa-amīnika wa-najiyyika wa-ḥabībika wa-ṣafiyyika wa-khāṣṣatika wa-ṣafwatika wa-khīratika min khalqika.

O God, make Your prayers and the prayers of the close angels, the sent messengers, Your upright servants, the inhabitants of the heavens and the earth, and those who praise You from the first to the last upon Muḥammad, Your servant, messenger, prophet, trustworthy one, savior [to humanity], beloved, distinguished, special [one], perfected, and the best of Your creation.

اللَّهُمَّ أَعْطِهِ الدَّرَجَةَ الرَّفِيْعَةَ، وَآتِهِ الوَسِيْلَةَ مِنَ الجَنَّةِ، وَابْعَثْهُ مَقَاماً مَحْمُوداً يَغْبِطُهُ بِهِ الأَوَّلُونَ وَالآخِرُونَ، اللَّهُمَّ إِنَّكَ قُلْتَ: وَلَوْ أَنَّهُمْ إِذ ظَّلَمُوٓاْ أَنفُسَهُمْ جَآءُوكَ فَٱسْتَغْفَرُواْ ٱللَّهَ وَٱسْتَغْفَرَ لَهُمُ ٱلرَّسُولُ لَوَجَدُواْ ٱللَّهَ تَوَّابًا رَّحِيمًا ﴿٦٤﴾ (سُورَةُ النِّسَاءِ) وَإِنِّي أَتَيْتُكَ مُسْتَغْفِراً تَائِباً مِنْ ذُنُوبِي وَإِنِّي أَتَوَجَّهُ بِكَ إِلَى اللهِ رَبِّي وَرَبِّكَ لِيَغْفِرَ لِي ذُنُوبِي.

Allāhumma aʿṭihi al-darajata al-rafīʿata, wa-ātihi al-wasīlata min al-jannati, wa-abʿathhu maqāman maḥmūdan yaghbiṭuhu bihi al-awwalūna wa-l-ākhirūn. Allāhumma innaka qulta, *"wa-law annahum idh ẓalamū anfusahum jāʾūka fastaghfarū Allāha wa-astaghfara lahumu al-rasūlu la-wajadū Allāha tawwāban raḥīman."* Wa-innī ataytuka mustaghfiran, tāʾiban min dhunūbī wa-innī atawajjahu bika ilā Allāh rabbi wa-rabbika li-yaghfira lī dhunūbī.

O God, grant him an exalted rank, a means to Paradise, and a praiseworthy status that is desired by the first and the last. O God, You have said: *And if, when they wronged themselves, they had come to you [O Muḥammad], and asked forgiveness of Allah and the Messenger had asked forgiveness for them, they would have found God accepting of repentance and Merciful* [al-Nisāʾ, 4:64]. And I have come to You in repentance asking for forgiveness for my sins and I turn with you to Your Lord and my Lord that He may forgive my sins.

It is also recommended that one say:

أَتَيْتُكَ يَا رَسُوْلَ اللهِ مُهَاجِراً إِلَيْكَ، مُؤْمِناً بِمَا أَوْجَبَهُ اللهُ عَلَى مَنْ

قَصَدَكَ، وَإِذْ لَمْ أَلحَقْكَ حَيّاً فَقَدْ قَصَدْتُكَ بَعْدَ مَوْتِكَ، عَالِماً أَنَّ حُرْمَتَكَ مَيِّتَاً كَحُرْمَتِكَ حَيّاً. فَكُنْ بِذَلِكَ عِنْدَ اللهِ شَاهِداً.

Ataytuka yā rasūl Allāh muhājiran ilayk, muʾminan bimā awjabahu Allāh ʿalā man qaṣadaka, wa-idh lam alḥaqka ḥayyan faqad qaṣadtuka baʿda mawtika, ʿāliman anna ḥurmataka mayyitan ka ḥurmatika ḥayyā. Fakun bi dhālika ʿinda Allāhi shāhidan.

I have come to you, O Messenger of God, emigrating to you, believing in what God has commanded of me of seeking you. If I was unable to meet you while you were alive, I have sought you after your death with the awareness that your noble rank with God is the same in your death as it was in your life. So be a witness to this in front of God.

اللَّهُمَّ اجْعَلْ ذَلِكَ بَيْعَةً مَرْضِيَّةً لَدَيْكَ وَعَهْداً مُؤَكَّداً عِنْدَكَ تُحْيِيْنِي مَا أَحْيَيْتَنِي عَلَيْهِ، وَعَلَى الوَفَاءِ بِشَرَائِطِهِ وَحُدُودِهِ وَحُقُوقِهِ وَأَحْكَامِهِ، وَتُمِيتُنِي إِذَا أَمَتَّنِي عَلَيْهِ، وَتَبْعَثُنِي إِذَا بَعَثْتَنِي عَلَيْهِ. اللَّهُمَّ كَمَا نَوَّلْتَنَا فِي الدُّنْيَا زِيَارَتَهُ، فَنَوِّلْنَا فِي الآخِرَةِ شَفَاعَتَهُ يَا أَرْحَمَ الرَّاحِمِيْنَ.

Allāhumma ijʿal dhālika bayʿatan marḍiyyatan ladayka wa-ʿahdan muʾakkadan ʿindaka tuḥyīnī mā aḥyaytanī ʿalayh. Wa-ʿalā l-wafāʾi bi-sharāʾiṭihi wa-ḥudūdihi wa-ḥuqūqihi wa-aḥkāmihi, wa-tumītunī idhā amattanī ʿalayh, wa-tabʿathunī idhā baʿathtanī ʿalayhi. Allāhumma kamā nawwaltanā fī l-dunyā ziyāratahu, fa-nawwilnā fī l-ākhirati shafāʿatahu yā arḥam al-rāḥimīn.

O God, make this pledge of loyalty to be a pledge which You are pleased with. And an oath that is verified by You. [Enable] me to live whatever lifespan I have by its loyalty, bounds, limits, rights, and laws. When you take my life [enable me] to die upon it and be raised [on the Day of Resurrection] upon it. O God, the way You have bestowed upon us the honor of visiting him, grant us his intercession in the next life, O Most-Merciful of those who show mercy.

Afterward, one should convey the greetings of whoever asked him to relay their greetings to the Messenger of God ﷺ. This is said in the following way:

> Al-salāmu ʿalayka yā rasūl Allāh min . . . so and so the son/daughter of so and so . . . yusallimu ʿalayka wa-yastashfiʿu bika ilā rabbika fashfaʿ lahu wa-lijamīʿ al-muslimīn.

Peace be unto you, O Messenger of God from so and so the son/daughter of so and so (one should name the person sending their greetings here). He sends greetings to you and seeks your intercession to Your Lord so intercede on his behalf and on behalf of all of the Muslims.

One should then give greetings to Abū Bakr, saying:

السَّلَامُ عَلَيْكَ يَا خَلِيفَةَ رَسُولِ اللهِ، السَّلَامُ عَلَيْكَ يَا صَاحِبَ رَسُولِ اللهِ فِي الغَارِ، السَّلَامُ عَلَيْكَ يَا رَفِيقَهُ فِي الأَسْفَارِ. السَّلَامُ عَلَيْكَ يَا أَمِينَهُ عَلَى الأَسْرَارِ، جَزَاكَ اللهُ عَنَّا أَفْضَلَ مَا جَزَى إِمَاماً عَن رَعِيَّتِهِ، فَلَقَدْ خَلَفْتَ رَسُولَ اللهِ ﷺ أَحْسَنَ خَلَف، وَسَلَكْتَ طَرِيْقَهُ وَمِنْهَاجَهُ خَيْرَ سُلُوك، وَقَاتَلْتَ أَهْلَ الرِّدَّةِ وَالبِدَعِ وَنَصَرْتَ الإِسْلَامَ، وَكَفَلْتَ الأَيْتَام، وَوَصَلْتَ الأَرْحَام، وَلَمْ تَزَلْ قَائِماً بِالحَقِّ نَاصِراً لِأَهْلِهِ حَتَّى أَتَاكَ اليَقِيْن، فالسَّلامُ عَلَيْكَ وَرَحْمَةُ اللهِ وَبَرَكَاتُهُ. اللَّهُمَّ أَمِتْنَا عَلَى حُبِّهِ وَلا تُخَيِّبْ سَعْيَنَا فِي زِيَارَتِهِ، يَا أَرْحَمَ الرَّاحِمِيْن. اللَّهُمَّ أَرْضَ عَنْهُ، وَأَرْفَعْ دَرَجَتَهُ وَأَ كْرِمْ مَقَامَهُ، وَأَجْزِلْ ثَوَابَهُ بِفَضْلِكَ وَكَرَمِكَ.. آمين.

Al-salāmu 'alayka yā khalīfata rasūlillāh! Al-salāmu 'alayka yā ṣāḥiba rasūlillāh fī l-ghār! Al-salāmu 'alayka yā rafīqahu fī l-asfār! Al-salāmu 'alayka yā amīnahu 'alā l-asrār! Jazāka Allāhu 'annā afḍala mā jazā imāman 'an ra'iyyatihi, fa-laqad khalafta rasūl Allāhi ﷺ aḥsana khalaf. Wa-salakta ṭarīqahu wa-minhājahu khayra sulūk. Wa-qātalta ahla al-riddati wa-l-bida'in wa-naṣarta al-islām, wa-kafalta al-aytām, wa-waṣalta al-arḥām, wa-lam tazal qā'iman bi-l-ḥaqqi nāṣiran li-ahlihi ḥattā atāka al-yaqīn. Fa-l-salāmu 'alayka wa-raḥmatu-llāhi wa-barakātuhu. Allāhumma amitnā 'alā ḥubbihi wa-lā tukhayyib sa'yanā fī ziyāratihi, yā arḥam al-rāḥimīn! Allāhumma arḍa 'anhu wa-arfa' darajatahu wa-akrim maqāmahu wa-ajzil thawābahu bi-faḍlika wa-karamika. Amīn!

Peace be upon you, O representative of the Messenger of God! Peace be upon you, O Companion of the Messenger of God in the cave! Peace be upon you, O friend of his in travels! Peace be upon you, O keeper of secrets [of the Prophet ﷺ]! May God reward you on our behalf with the best of rewards that a leader is rewarded for his followers! You have followed the Messenger of God ﷺ in the best way and you have followed his path and his method in perfection. You fought the people of *ridda*[8] and innovation. You gave victory to Islam, you took care of the orphans, you kept blood ties, and you did not cease to stand for the truth and strive for its people until the end of your life. Peace, blessings, and mercy be unto you. O God, make us die loving him and reward our efforts in visiting him, O Most Merciful of those who show mercy. God be pleased with him, raise him in his rank, ennoble his status, and increase him in his reward through your favor and generosity. *Āmīn!*

After this, one greets the leader of the believers, ʿUmar b. al-Khaṭṭāb رضي الله عنه and says the following.

8 Tribes in the Arabian Peninsula who refused to pay *zakāt* after the Prophet's ﷺ death.

السَّلَامُ عَلَيْكَ يَا أَمِيْر المُؤْمِنِيْنَ، السَّلَامُ عَلَيْكَ يَا مُظْهِرَ الإِسْلَام، السَّلَامُ عَلَيْكَ يَا مُكَسِّرَ الأَصْنَامِ، السَّلَامُ عَلَيْكَ يَا سِرَاجَ أَهْلِ الجَنَّةِ، السَّلَامُ عَلَيْكَ يَا فَارُوْق، السَّلَامُ عَلَيْكَ يَا مَنْ نَطَقَ بِالصَّوَابِ، يَا أَبَا الفُقَرَاءِ وَ الضُّعَفَاءِ، السَّلَامُ عَلَيْكَ يَا مَنْ وَافَقَ قَوْلُهُ مُحْكَمَ الكِتَابِ. جَزَاكَ اللهُ عَنَّا أَفْضَلَ الجَزَاء، وَرَضِيَ عَمَّن اسْتَخْلَفَكَ، فَلَقَدْ نَظَرَ إِلَى الإِسْلَامِ وَالمُسْلِمِيْنَ حَيّاً وَمَيِّتاً، فَكَفِلْتَ مِثْلَهُ الأَيْتَام، وَوَصَلْتَ الأَرْحَامَ، وَقَوِيَ بِكَ الإِسْلَامُ، وَكُنْتَ لِأَهْلِ الإِسْلَامِ هَادِياً، جَمَعْتَ شَمْلَهُم، وَأَغْنَيْتَ فَقِيْرَهُم، وَجَبَرْتَ كَسْرَهُم، فَالسَّلَامُ عَلَيْكَ وَرَحْمَةُ اللهِ وَبَرَكَاتُه.

Al-salāmu ʿalayka yā amīr al-muʾminīn! Al-salāmu ʿalayka yā muẓhira al-islām! Al-salāmu ʿalayka yā mukassira al-aṣnām! Al-salāmu ʿalayka yā sirāja ahli al-jannati! Al-salāmu ʿalayka yā Farūq! Al-salāmu ʿalayka ya man naṭaqa bi-al-ṣawāb, yā abā l-fuqarāʾi wa-ḍuʿafāʾi! Al-salāmu ʿalayka yā man wāfaqa qawluhu muḥkama al-kitāb! Jazāka Allāhu ʿannā afḍala al-jazāʾ wa-raḍiya ʿamman istakhlafaka. Fa-laqad naẓara ilā l-islāmi wa-l-muslimīna ḥayyan wa-mayyitan fa-kafilta mithlahu al-aytām, wa-waṣalta al-arḥām, wa-qawiya bika al-islām, wa-kunta li-ahli al-islāmi hādiyan. Jamaʿta shamlahum, wa-aghnayta faqīrahum, wa-jabarta kasrahum, fa-l-salāmu ʿalayka wa-raḥmatu-llāhi wa-barakātuh.

Peace be unto you, O leader of the believers! Peace be unto you, O one who openly proclaimed Islam! Peace be unto you, O breaker of idols! Peace be unto you, O guiding light to the people of Paradise! Peace unto you, O Fārūq! Peace be unto you, O one who spoke in truth! O father of the poor and the weak! Peace be unto you, O whose words were confirmed by the ruling of the Book! May God reward you on our behalf with the best of rewards and be pleased with those who followed you. You have taken care of the Muslims both in their life and after their death by sponsoring the orphans and keeping blood ties. Islam was strengthened by you and you were a guide to the people of Islam. You united their factions, enriched their poor, and mended their broken hearts. Peace be unto you, and the mercy and blessings of God.

Then one stands in front of both of their heads رضي الله عنهما and says:

السَّلَامُ عَلَيْكُمَا يَا ضَجِيْعَي رَسُول الله وَرَفِيْقَيْهِ وَوَزِيْرَيْهِ، وَمُشِيْرَيْهِ،
وَمُعَاوِنَيْهِ عَلَى القِيَامِ فِي الدِّيْنِ، جَزَاكُما الله تَعَالَى عَنَّا أَفْضَلَ الجَزَاءِ.

Al-salāmu ʿalaykumā yā ḍajīʿay rasūl Allāh wa-rafīqayhi wa-wazīrayhi wa-mushīrayhi wa-muʿāwinayhi ʿalā l-qiyāmi fī l-dīni. Jazākumā Allāh taʿālā ʿannā afḍala al-jazāʾ.

Peace unto you, O two noble ones lying beside the Messenger of God ﷺ, [you were] his companions, his advisers, and helpers in upholding the faith. May God reward the both of you with the best of rewards.

Afterward, one returns to the noble sanctuary (*rawḍa*) and faces the direction of prayer. He then thanks God, praises Him, and sends prayers upon the Prophet ﷺ and says the following supplication:

اللَّهُمَّ إِلَيْكَ أَلجَأْتُ أَمْرِي، وَإِلَى قَبْرِ نَبِيِّكَ مُحَمَّدٍ ﷺ أَسْنَدْتُ
ظَهْرِي، وَالقِبْلَةَ الَّتِي رَضِيْتَ لِرَسُولِكَ مُحَمَّدٍ ﷺ اسْتَقْبَلْتُ، اللَّهُمَّ
إِنِّي أَصْبَحْتُ لَا أَمْلِكُ لِنَفْسِي خَيْرَ مَا أَرْجُو لَهَا، وَلَا أَدْفَعُ عَنْهَا شَرَّ مَا
أَحْذَرُ عَلَيْهَا، وأَصْبَحَتِ الأُمُورُ كُلُّهَا بِيَدِكَ، وَلَا فَقِيرَ أَفْقَرُ مِنِّي، رَبِّ
إِنِّي لِمَآ أَنزَلْتَ إِلَيَّ مِنْ خَيْرٍ فَقِيرٌ ﴿٢٤﴾ (سُورَةُ القَصَصِ) اللَّهُمَّ اردُدْنِي

مِنْكَ بِخَيْرٍ وَلَا رَادَّ لِفَضْلِكَ، اللَّهُمَّ إِنِّي أَعُوذُ بِكَ مِنْ أَنْ تُبَدِّلَ إِسْمِي، وَتُغَيِّرَ جِسْمِي أَوْ تُزِيلَ نِعْمَتَكَ عَنِّي، اللَّهُمَّ زَيِّنِّي بِالتَّقْوَى، وَجَمِّلْنِي بِالنِّعَمِ، وَاغْمُرْنِي بِالعَافِيَةِ، وَارْزُقْنِي شُكْرَ العَافِيَةِ.

Allāhumma ilayka aljaʾtu amrī, wa-ilā qabri nabiyyika Muḥammadin ﷺ asnadtu ẓahrī, wa-l-qiblata allatī raḍīta li-rasūlika Muḥammadin ﷺ astaqbalt. Allāhumma innī aṣbaḥtu lā amliku li-nafsī khayra mā arjū lahā, wa-lā adfaʿu ʿanhā sharra mā aḥdharu ʿalayhā, wa-aṣbaḥati al-umūru kulluhā bi-yadika wa-lā faqīra afqaru minnī. *"Rabbī innī limā anzalta ilayya min khayrin faqīrun."* Allāhumma ardidnī minka bi-khayrin wa-lā rādda li-faḍlika. Allāhumma innī aʿūdhu bika min an tubaddila ismī, wa-tughayyira jismī aw tuzīla niʿmataka ʿannī. Allāhumma zayyinnī bi-l-taqwā, wa-jammilnī bi-l-niʿami, wa-aghmurnī bi-l-ʿāfiya, wa-arzuqnī shukra al-ʿāfiya.

O God, I have submitted my affairs to You. I have placed my back against the grave of the Messenger of God ﷺ and have turned my face to the direction of prayer which You have chosen for Your Messenger Muḥammad ﷺ. O God, I do not have in my possession the goodness that I wish for myself. Nor am I able to repel the harms I fear for it. All of my affairs are in Your hands. There is no poor person poorer than me. *My Lord, indeed I am, for whatever good You would send down to me, in need* [al-Qaṣaṣ, 28:24]. O God, grant me goodness. There is nothing that can turn away Your favor. O God, I seek refuge from Your changing my name, altering my body (from health to illness), or that blessings upon me should disappear. O God, ornament me with fear [of You], embellish me with Your bounty, and envelop me in well-being.

This supplication is to be followed by general supplications for one's parents, teachers, relatives, brothers, sisters, and those who requested individual prayers.

Gatherings of Sending Prayers upon the Prophet 

Some mosques in Damascus hold gatherings on a regular basis to send prayers upon the Prophet ﷺ after the dawn prayer, out of love for the Messenger of God ﷺ and with the intention of seeking the fulfillment of their needs (*qaḍāʾ al-ḥawāʾij*). Afterward, food is distributed to the poor thus spreading joy, soothing hearts, alleviating troubles, relieving anxieties, and having one's sins forgiven.

Ubayy b. Kaʿb said, "I said, 'O Messenger of God I send prayers upon you abundantly. What portion of my prayers should be devoted to sending prayers upon you?'

He replied, 'Whatever you wish.'

I said, 'One quarter?'

He said, 'As you wish but if you increase this it would be better for you.'

I said, 'Half?'

He said, 'As you wish and if you increase this it will be better for you.'

I said, 'Two-thirds?'

He said, 'As you wish and if you increase this it will be better for you.'

I said, 'Should I make all of it for your sake?'

The Messenger of God ﷺ said, 'In this case your concerns will be relieved and your sins will be forgiven.'"[9]

These gatherings usually consist of the following: The recitation of the *Fātiḥa* and the Grand Repentance (*al-Istighfār al-Kabīr*).

9 al-Tirmidhī, *Sunan*, Kitāb ṣifat al-qiyāma wa-riqāq wa-l-rawʿ, no. 2457.

The Grand Repentance

الإِسْتِغْفَار الكَبِير

أَسْتَغْفِرُ اللهَ العَظِيْمَ الَّذِي لَا إِلَهَ إِلَّا هُوَ الحَيَّ القَيُّومَ، غَفَّارَ الذُّنُوْبِ ذَا الجَلَالِ وَالإِكْرَامِ، وَأَتُوبُ إِلَيْهِ مِنْ جَمِيعِ الْمَعَاصِي وَالذُّنُوْبِ وَالآثَامِ وَمِنْ كُلِّ ذَنْبٍ أَذْنَبْتُهُ عَمْداً وَخَطَأً ظَاهِراً وَبَاطِناً قَوْلاً وَفِعْلاً، فِي جَمِيْعِ حَرَكَاتِي وَسَكَنَاتِي وَخَطَرَاتِي وَأَنْفَاسِي كُلِّهَا دَائِماً أَبَداً سَرْمَداً، مِنَ الذَّنْبِ الَّذِي أَعْلَمُ وَمِنَ الذَّنْبِ الَّذِي لَا أَعْلَمُ، عَدَدَ مَا أَحَاطَ بِهِ العِلْمُ وَأَحْصَاهُ الكِتَابُ وَخَطَّهُ القَلَمُ، وَعَدَدَ مَاأَوْجَدَتْهُ القُدْرَةُ وَخَصَّصَتْهُ الإِرَادَةُ، وَمِدَادَ كَلِمَاتِ اللهِ كَمَا يَنْبَغِي لِجَلَالِ وَجْهِ رَبِّنَا وَجَمَالِهِ وَكَمَالِهِ، وَكَمَا يُحِبُّ رَبُّنَا وَيَرْضَى.

Astaghfirullāh al-ʿaẓīm alladhī lā ilāha illa huwa al-ḥayya al-qayyūm, ghaffār al-dhunūbi dhā al-jalāli wa-l-ikrām, wa-atūbu ilayhi min jamīʿ al-maʿāṣī wa-l-dhunūbi wa-l-āthāmi wa-min kulli dhanbin adhnabtuhu ʿamdan wa-khaṭaʾan ẓahiran wa-bāṭinan qawlan wa-fiʿlan fī jamīʿi ḥarakātī wa-sakanātī wa-khaṭarātī wa-anfāsī kullihā dāʾiman abadan sarmadan, min al-dhanb allādhī aʿlamu wa-min al-dhanb alladhī lā aʿlamu, ʿadada mā aḥāṭa bihi al-ʿilmu wa-aḥṣāhu al-kitābu wa-khaṭṭahu al-qalamu, wa-ʿadada mā awjadathu al-qudratu wa-khaṣṣaṣathu al-irādatu, wa-midāda kalimāti-llāhi kamā yambaghī li-jalāli wajhi rabbinā wa-jamālihi wa-kamālihi, wa-kamā yuḥibbu rabbunā wa-yarḍā.

I seek forgiveness from God the Magnificient, there is no god but He, the Living, the Sustainer. I repent to Him from all of my sins in their entirety; and of my wrongdoings and offenses. [I seek forgiveness] from every sin that I have committed both intentionally and unintentionally, publicly and privately, in words, in actions, in all of my motions, silences, thoughts, and breaths, in their entirety forever and continually. [I seek forgiveness] from the sins that I am aware of and the sins that I am unaware of; to the extent which knowledge is expanded, enclosed in the book, and written by pens. And [I seek forgiveness by the extent] of which You brought power into existence, distinguished it by will, and the extent of God's words in a way that is worthy of the essence of the magnificence of our Lord, His majesty, and perfection. [I seek forgiveness] in the way that our Lord loves and is pleased with, in each glance [of the eye], and breath to the extent of God's knowledge.

Sending Prayers upon the Prophet

This is done using the following phrase: *Allāhumma ṣallī ʿalā Sayyidinā Muḥammad wa-ʿalā ālihi wa-ṣaḥbihi wa-sallim* (92,000 times), after which it is ended with the recitation of the *Fātiḥa*.

This is often followed by some religious songs (*inshād*) or poetry (*qasīdas*) in praise of the Prophet. Reciting various prayers on the Prophet is also encouraged, including "The Prayers of the Lovers" or "The Prayers of the Devoted with God's Beautiful Names upon the Prophet Muḥammad with his Traditional Praiseworthy Names."

The Prayers of the Lovers

صَلَوَاتُ الْمُحِبِّيْنَ

اللَّهُمَّ صلِّ عَلَى الذَّاتِ المُحَمَّدِيَّةِ صَلَاةً تَدُوْمُ بِدَوَامِكَ ، وَتَبْقَى بِبَقَائِكَ ، لَا مُنْتَهَى لَهَا دُوْنَ عِلْمِكَ ، صَلَاةً تُرْضِيْكَ وَتُرْضِيْهِ وَتَرْضَى بِهَا عَنَّا يَا رَبَّ العَالَمِيْنَ.

Allāhumma ṣallī ʿalā dhāt al-Muḥammadiyya ṣalātan tadūmu bi-dawāmika wa-tabqā bi-baqāʾika lā muntahā lahā dūna

ʿilmika, ṣalātan turḍīka wa-turḍīhi wa-tarḍā bihā ʿannā yā rabba al-ʿālamīn.

O God, send prayers upon the person of Muḥammad, [prayers] that are perpetuated through Your permanence and are made everlasting through Your eternal attribute. [Send prayers] that do not cease without Your knowledge, prayers that please You and please him and make You, through them (the blessings upon the Prophet), pleased with us, O Lord of the worlds.

اللَّهُمَّ صَلِّ عَلَى سَيِّدِنَا مُحَمَّدٍ عَدَدَ مَا فِي عِلْمِ اللهِ ، صَلَاةً دَائِمَةً بِدَوَامِ مُلْكِ اللهِ.

Allāhumma ṣallī ʿalā sayyidinā Muḥammadin ʿadada mā fī ʿilm illāhi, ṣalātan dāʾimatan bi-dawāmi mulk illāhi.

O God, send prayers upon our master Muḥammad as extensively as God's divine knowledge, and as perpetually as the continuance of God's realm.

اللَّهُمَّ صَلِّ عَلَى سَيِّدِنَا مُحَمَّدٍ صَلَاةً تُنَجِّيْنَا بِهَا مِنْ جَمِيْعِ الأَهْوَالِ وَالآفَاتِ ، وتَقْضِي لَنَا بِهَا جَمِيْعَ الحَاجَاتِ ، وَتُطَهِّرُنَا بِهَا مِنْ جَمِيْعِ السَّيِّئَاتِ، وَتَرْفَعُنَا بِهَا أَعْلَى الدَّرَجَاتِ ، وَتُبَلِّغُنَا بِهَا أَقْصَى الغَايَاتِ مِنْ جَمِيْعِ الخَيْرَاتِ ، فِي الحَيَاةِ وَبَعْدَ الْمَمَاتِ.

Allāhumma ṣallī ʿalā sayyidinā Muḥammadin ṣalātan tunajjīnā bihā min jamīʿi al-ahwāli wa-l-āfāti. Wa-taqḍī lanā bihā jamīʿa al-ḥājāti. Wa-tuṭahhirunā bihā min jamīʿi al-sayyiʾāti. Wa-tarfaʿunā bihā aʿlā l-darajāt wa-tuballighunā bihā aqṣā al-ghāyāti min jamīʿi al-khayrāti, fī l-ḥayāti wa-baʿd al-mamāti.

O God, send prayers upon our master Muḥammad; prayers that will deliver us from all calamities and ailments, and through them fulfill all of our needs, and purify us through them from all sins, raise us through them to the highest of ranks, and enable us to attain through them the foremost aspirations of all [types] of goodness during life and after death.

اللَّهُمَّ صَلِّ عَلَى سَيِّدِنَا مُحَمَّدٍ صَلَاةَ الرِّضَى، وَارْضَ عَنْ أَصْحَابِهِ رِضَاءَ الرِّضَى.

Allāhumma ṣallī ʿalā sayyidinā Muḥammadin ṣalāta al-riḍā, wa-arḍā ʿan aṣḥābihi riḍā l-riḍā.

O God, send prayers upon our master Muḥammad, prayers of divine approval, and be pleased with his Companions with the utmost of divine approval.

اللَّهُمَّ صَلِّ وَسَلِّمْ وَبَارِكْ عَلَى سَيِّدِنَا مُحَمَّدٍ الرَّؤُوفِ الرَّحِيمِ، ذِي الخُلُقِ العَظِيْمِ، وَعَلَى آلِهِ وَ أَصْحَابِهِ وَأَزْوَاجِهِ فِي كُلِّ لَحْظَةٍ عَدَدَ كُلِّ حَادِثٍ وَقَدِيْمٍ.

Allāhumma ṣallī wa-sallim wa-bārik ʿalā sayyidinā Muḥammadin al-raʾūfi al-raḥīm, dhī l-khuluqi al-ʿaẓīm wa-ʿalā ālihi wa-aṣḥābihi wa-azwājihi fī kulli laḥẓatin ʿadada kulli ḥādithin wa-qadīm.

O God, send prayers, salutations, and blessings upon our master Muḥammad, who is of sublime character, and upon his family, his Companions, and his wives, during every moment by the extent of the numbers of all who are contemporary and ancient.

اللَّهُمَّ صَلِّ وَسَلِّمْ وَبَارِكْ عَلَى سَيِّدِنَا مُحَمَّدٍ الفَاتِحِ لِمَا أُغْلِقَ، وَالخَاتِمِ لِمَا سَبَقَ، وَالنَّاصِرِ الحَقَّ بِالحَقِّ، وَالهَادِي إِلَى صِرَاطِكَ الْمُسْتَقِيمِ، صَلَّى اللهُ عَلَيْهِ وَعَلَى آلِهِ وَصَحْبِهِ وَسَلَّم حَقَّ قَدْرِهِ وَمِقْدَارِهِ العَظِيْمِ.

Allāhumma ṣalli wa-sallim wa-bārik ʿalā sayyidinā Muḥammadin al-fātiḥ limā ughliqa wa-l-khātimi limā sabaqa wa-l-nāṣiri al-ḥaqqa bi al-ḥaqqi wa-l-hādī ilā ṣirāṭika al-mustaqīm. Ṣalla Allāhu ʿalayhi wa-ʿalā ālihi wa-ṣaḥbihi wa-sallim ḥaqqa qadrihi wa-miqdārihi al-ʿaẓīm.

O God, send prayers, salutations, and blessings upon our master Muḥammad, the opener of what is closed, the conclusion of what came before, the victor of the truth by the truth, the guide to Your straight path. O God, send prayers upon him, upon his family, and his Companions by the virtue of his rank and exalted status.

اللَّهُمَّ صَلِّ وَسَلِّمْ وَبَارِكْ عَلَى سَيِّدِنَا مُحَمَّدٍ وَعَلَى آلِهِ صَلَاةً تَلِيْقُ بِجَمَالِهِ وَجَلَالِهِ وَكَمَالِهِ، وَصَلِّ وَ سَلِّمْ وَبَارِكْ عَلَى سَيِّدِنَا مُحَمَّدٍ وَعَلَى آلِهِ، وَأَذِقْنَا بِالصَّلَاةِ عَلَيْهِ لَذَّةَ وِصَالِهِ.

Allāhumma ṣalli wa-sallim wa-bārik ʿalā sayyidinā Muḥammadin wa-ʿalā ālihi ṣalātan talīqu bi-jamālihi wa-jalālihi wa-kamālihi. Wa-ṣalli wa-sallim wa-bārik ʿalā sayyidinā Muḥammadin wa-ʿalā ālih, wa-adhiqnā bi al-ṣalāti ʿalayhi ladhdhata wiṣālihi.

O God, send prayers, salutations, and blessings upon our master Muḥammad and upon his family; prayers that are worthy of his majesty, grandeur, and perfection. Also send prayers, salutations, and blessings upon our master Muḥammad and upon his family, and enable us to experience through them the delight of meeting him.

اللَّهُمَّ صَلِّ عَلَى سَيِّدِنَا مُحَمَّدٍ طِبِّ الْقُلُوبِ وَدَوَائِهَا، وَعَافِيَةِ الأَبْدَانِ وَشِفَائِهَا، وَنُوْرِ الأَبْصَارِ وَضِيَائِهَا، وَعَلَى آلِهِ وَصَحْبِهِ وَسَلِّمْ.

Allāhumma ṣalli ʿalā sayyidinā Muḥammadin ṭibbi al-qulūbi wa-dawāʾihā, wa-ʿāfiyati al-abdāni wa-shifāʾihā wa-nūri al-abṣāri wa-ḍiyāʾihā wa-ʿalā ālihi wa-ṣaḥbihi wa-sallim.

O God, send prayers, salutations, and blessings upon our master Muḥammad, the healer of hearts and their treatment, the well-being of bodies and their cure, the light of the eyes and their illuminator; and [send prayers, salutations, and blessings] upon his family and Companions.

اللَّهُمَّ اجْعَلْ عَلَى سَيِّدِنَا مُحَمَّدٍ وَعَلَى آلِهِ مِنْ صَلَوَاتِكَ أَفْضَلَهَا وَأَزْكَاهَا، وَمِنْ بَرَكَاتِكَ أَنْمَاهَا وَأَعْلَاهَا، وَاجْعَلْ صَلَاتَنَا عَلَيْهِ صَلَاةً تَرْضَاهَا.

Allāhumma ajʿal ʿalā sayyidinā Muḥammadin wa-ʿalā ālihi min ṣalawātika afḍalahā wa-azkāhā, wa-min barakātika anmāhā wa-aʿlāhā wa-ajʿal ṣalātanā ʿalayhi ṣalātan tarḍāhā.

O God, send the most excellent and purest of Your prayers upon our master Muḥammad and his family. [Send] Your blessings [upon him] in their most abundant and paramount form. And make our prayers upon him prayers which You are pleased with.

اللَّهُمَّ صَلِّ عَلَى سَيِّدِنَا مُحَمَّدٍ النَّبِيِّ الأُمِّيِّ، وَعَلَى آلِهِ وَصَحْبِهِ وَسَلِّمْ، عَدَدَ مَا فِي السَّمٰوَاتِ وَمَا فِي الأَرْضِ وَمَا بَيْنَهُمَا، وَأَجْرِ يَارَبِّ لُطْفَكَ الخَفِيَّ فِي أُمُوْرِنَا وَالْمُسْلِمِيْنَ أَجْمَعِيْنَ.

Allāhumma ṣalli ʿalā sayyidinā Muḥammadin al-nabī l-ummī wa-ʿalā ālihi wa-ṣaḥbihi wa-sallim, ʿadada ma fī l-samawāti wa-mā fī l-arḍi wa-mā baynahumā. Wa-ajrī yā rabbī luṭfaka al-khafiyya fī umūrinā wa-l-muslimīna ajmaʿīn.

O God, send blessing upon our master Muḥammad the unlettered Prophet, and to his family and his Companions

[send] salutations by the extent of what is in the heavens, what is on the earth, and what is between them. Diffuse Your subtle grace in our affairs and that of all of the Muslims.

اللَّهُمَّ صَلِّ عَلَى سَيِّدِنَا مُحَمَّدٍ فِي اللَّيْلِ إِذَا يَغْشَى، وَالنَّهَارِ إِذَا تَجَلَّى، وَصَلِّ عَلَى سَيِّدِنَا مُحَمَّدٍ فِي الآخِرَةِ وَالأُوْلَى.

Allāhumma ṣallī ʿalā sayyidinā Muḥammadin fī l-layli idhā yaghshā wa-l-nahāri idhā tajallā. Wa-ṣallī ʿalā sayyidinā Muḥammadin fī l-ākhirati wa-l-ūlā.

O God, send prayers upon our master Muḥammad, by the night when it conceals [light], the day when it becomes manifest, and send prayers upon our master Muḥammad in the end and in the beginning.

اللَّهُمَّ صَلِّ عَلَى سَيِّدِنَا مُحَمَّدٍ النَّبِيِّ الأُمِّيِّ الطَّاهِرِ المُطَهَّرِ وَعَلَى آلِهِ وَصَحْبِهِ وَسَلِّمْ.

Allāhumma ṣallī ʿalā sayyidinā Muḥammadin al-nabī l-ummī l-ṭāhir al-muṭahhari wa-ʿalā ālihi wa-ṣaḥbihi wa-sallim.

O God, send prayers upon our master Muḥammad the unlettered Prophet, the pure and the purified, and upon his family and his Companions [send] salutations.

اللَّهُمَّ صَلِّ وَسَلِّمْ وَبَارِكْ عَلَى سَيِّدِنَا مُحَمَّدٍ ذِيْ المُعْجِزَاتِ البَاهِرَةِ، وَصَلِّ وَسَلِّمْ وَبَارِكْ عَلَى سَيِّدِنَا مُحَمَّدٍ ذِيْ الْمَنَاقِبِ الفَاخِرَةِ، وَصَلِّ وسَلِّمْ وَبَارِكْ عَلَى سَيِّدِنَا مُحَمَّدٍ فِي الدُّنْيَا وَالآخِرَةِ، وَصَلِّ وسَلِّمْ وَبَارِكْ عَلَى سَيِّدِنَا مُحَمَّدٍ وَخَلِّقْنَا بِأَخْلَاقِهِ الطَّاهِرَةِ.

Allāmumma ṣalli wa-sallim wa-bārik ʿalā sayyidinā Muḥammadin dhī l-muʿjizāti al-bāhira wa-ṣalli wa-sallim wa-bārik ʿalā sayyidinā Muḥammadin dhī l-manāqib al-fākhira, wa-ṣalli wa-sallim wa-bārik ʿalā sayyidinā Muḥammadin fī l-dunyā wa-l-ākhira, wa-ṣalli wa-sallim wa-bārik ʿalā sayyidinā Muḥammadin wa-khalliqnā bi akhlāqihi al-ṭāhira.

O God, send prayers, salutations, and blessings upon our master Muḥammad, the possessor of splendid miracles. Send prayers, salutations, and blessings upon our master Muḥammad, the possessor lofty attributes. Send prayers, salutations, and blessings upon our master Muḥammad in this world and in the next. Send prayers, salutations, and blessings upon our master Muḥammad and imbibe us with his virtuous character.

اللَّهُمَّ صَلِّ وَسَلِّمْ وَبَارِكْ عَلَى سَيِّدِنَا مُحَمَّدٍ وَأَعْطِهِ الوَسِيْلَةَ وَالفَضِيْلَةَ، وَصَلِّ وَسَلِّمْ وَبَارِكْ عَلَى سَيِّدِنَا مُحَمَّدٍ ذِي المَقَامَاتِ الجَلِيْلَةِ، وَصَلِّ وَسَلِّمْ وَبَارِكْ عَلَى سَيِّدِنَا مُحَمَّدٍ وَخَلِّقْنَا بِأَخْلَاقِهِ الجَمِيْلَةِ.

Allāhumma ṣalli wa-sallim wa-bārik ʿalā sayyidinā Muḥammadin wa-aʿṭihi al-wasīlata wa-l-faḍīla. Wa-ṣalli wa-sallim wa-bārik ʿalā sayyidinā Muḥammadin dhī l-maqāmāt al-jalīla. Wa-ṣalli wa-sallim wa-bārik ʿalā sayyidinā Muḥammadin wa-khalliqnā bi-akhlāqihi al-jamīla.

O God, send prayers, salutations, and blessings upon our master Muḥammad and grant him the privilege of mediation (*wasīla*) and divine favor (*faḍīla*). Send prayers, salutations, and blessings upon our master Muḥammad, possessor of exalted ranks. Send prayers, salutations, and blessings upon our master Muḥammad and imbibe us with his beautiful character.

اللَّهُمَّ صَلِّ وَسَلِّمْ وَبَارِكْ عَلَى سَيِّدِنَا مُحَمَّدٍ وَهَبْ لَنَا قَلْباً شَكُورَا، وَصَلِّ وَسَلِّمْ وَبَارِكْ عَلَى سَيِّدِنَا مُحَمَّدٍ وَاجْعَلْ سَعْيَنَا مَشْكُوراً، وَصَلِّ وَسَلِّمْ وَبَارِكْ عَلَى سَيِّدِنَا مُحَمَّدٍ وَلَقِّنَا نَضْرَةً وَسُرُوْراً، وَصَلِّ وَسَلِّمْ وَبَارِكْ عَلَى سَيِّدِنَا مُحَمَّدٍ وَأَلْقِ عَلَيْنَا مِنْكَ مَحَبَّةً وَنُوراً، وَصَلِّ وَسَلِّمْ وَبَارِكْ عَلَى سَيِّدِنَا مُحَمَّدٍ وَزِدْنَا بِاتِّبَاعِهِ تَوْفِيْقاً وَحُبُوراً.

Allāhumma ṣalli wa-sallim wa-bārik ʿalā sayyidinā Muḥammadin wa-hab lanā qalban shakūra. Wa-ṣalli wa-sallim wa-bārik ʿalā sayyidinā Muḥammadin wa-ajʿal saʿyanā mashkūrā. Wa-ṣalli wa-sallim wa-bārik ʿalā sayyidinā Muḥammadin wa-laqqinā naḍratan wa-surūrā. Wa-ṣalli wa-sallim wa-bārik ʿalā sayyidinā Muḥammadin wa-alqi ʿalaynā minka maḥabbatan wa-nūrā. Wa-ṣalli wa-sallim wa-bārik ʿalā sayyidinā Muḥammadin wa-zidnā bi-ttibāʿihi tawfīqan wa-ḥubūrā.

O God, send prayers, salutations, and blessings upon our master Muḥammad; and endow us with hearts that are grateful. Send prayers, salutations, and blessings upon our master Muḥammad and accept our endeavors. Send prayers, salutations, and blessings upon our master Muḥammad and grant us radiance and bliss. Send prayers, salutations, and blessings upon our master Muḥammad and bestow upon us love and light from You. Send prayers, salutation, and blessings upon our master Muḥammad and increase us in success and felicity, by our following him.

اللَّهُمَّ صَلِّ وَسَلِّمْ وَبَارِكْ عَلَى سَيِّدِنَا مُحَمَّدٍ بِقَدَرِ حُبِّكَ فِيهِ، وَزِدْنَا يَا مَوْلَانَا حُبّاً فِيهِ، اللَّهُمَّ بِجَاهِهِ عِنْدَكَ فَرِّجْ عَنَّا مَا نَحْنُ فِيهِ.

Allāhumma ṣalli wa-sallim wa-bārik ʿalā sayyidinā Muḥammadin bi-qadari ḥubbika fīhi. Wa-zidnā yā mawlānā ḥubban fīhi. Allāhumma bi-jāhihi ʿindaka farrij ʿannā mā naḥnu fīhi.

O God, send prayers, salutations, and blessings upon our master Muḥammad as [great as] the extent of Your love for him and increase us, our Lord, in love for him. O God, by the virtue of his rank with You, relieve us of the difficulties which we are in.

اللَّهُمَّ صَلِّ وَسَلِّمْ وَبَارِكْ عَلَى سَيِّدِنَا مُحَمَّدٍ النَّاطِقِ بِالصِّدْقِ وَالصَّوَابِ، وَصَلِّ وَسَلِّمْ وَبَارِكْ عَلَى سَيِّدِنَا مُحَمَّدٍ أَفْضَلَ مَنْ أُوْتِيَ الحِكْمَةَ وَفَصْلَ الخِطَابِ وَصَلِّ وَسَلِّمْ وَبَارِكْ عَلَى سَيِّدِنَا مُحَمَّدٍ بَابِ الأَبْوَابِ وَلُبَابِ اللُّبَابِ، وَصَلِّ وَسَلِّمْ وَبَارِكْ عَلَى سَيِّدِنَا مُحَمَّدٍ وَأَزِلْ عَنْ قُلُوْبِنَا بِنُوْرِهِ ظُلْمَةَ الحِجَابِ، وَصَلِّ وَسَلِّمْ وَبَارِكْ عَلَى سَيِّدِنَا مُحَمَّدٍ وَأَلْهِمْنَا الحِكْمَةَ وَالصَّوَابَ، وَصَلِّ وَسَلِّمْ وَبَارِكْ عَلَى سَيِّدِنَا مُحَمَّدٍ وَاسْقِنَا مِنْ لَدُنْكَ صَافِيَ الشَّرَابِ، وَصَلِّ وَسَلِّمْ وَبَارِكْ عَلَى سَيِّدِنَا مُحَمَّدٍ وَفَهِّمْنَا أَسْرَارَ الكِتَابِ، وَصَلِّ وَسَلِّمْ وَبَارِكْ عَلَى سَيِّدِنَا مُحَمَّدٍ وَاجْعَلْنَا بِالصَّلَاةِ عَلَيْهِ مِنَ الأَنْجَابِ، وَصَلِّ وَسَلِّمْ وَبَارِكْ عَلَى سَيِّدِنَا مُحَمَّدٍ وَأَدْخِلْنَا حَظِيْرَةَ القُدْسِ فِيْ جُمْلَةِ الأَحْبَابِ، وَصَلِّ وَسَلِّمْ وَبَارِكْ عَلَى سَيِّدِنَا مُحَمَّدٍ وَعَلَى سَائِرِ الأَنْبِيَاءِ وَالأَصْفِيَاءِ وَالآلِ وَالأَصْحَابِ.

Allāhumma ṣalli wa-sallim wa-bārik ʿalā sayyidinā Muḥammadin al-nāṭiqi bi al-ṣidqi wa-l-ṣawāb. Wa-ṣalli wa-sallim wa-bārik ʿalā sayyidinā Muḥammadin afḍala man ūtiya al-ḥikmata wa-faṣl al-khiṭāb. Wa-ṣalli wa-sallim wa-bārik ʿalā sayyidinā Muḥammadin bābi al-abwābi wa-lubābi al-lubāb. Wa-ṣalli wa-sallim wa-bārik ʿalā sayyidinā Muḥammadin wa-azil ʿan qulūbinā bi nūrihi ẓulmat al-ḥijāb. Wa-ṣalli wa-sallim wa-bārik ʿalā sayyidinā Muḥammadin wa-alhimnā l-ḥikmata wa-l-ṣawāb. Wa-ṣalli wa-sallim wa-bārik ʿalā sayyidinā Muḥammadin wasqinā min ladunka ṣāfiya al-sharāb. Wa-ṣalli wa-sallim wa-bārik ʿalā sayyidinā Muḥammadin wa-fahhimnā asrāra al-kitāb. Wa-ṣalli wa-sallim wa-bārik ʿalā sayyidinā Muḥammadin wa-ajʿalnā bi al-ṣalāti ʿalayhi min al-anjāb. Wa-ṣalli wa-sallim wa-bārik ʿalā sayyidinā Muḥammadin wa-adkhilnā ḥaẓīrati al-qudsi fī jumlati al-aḥbāb. Wa-ṣalli wa-sallim wa-bārik ʿalā sayyidinā

Muḥammadin wa-ʿalā sāʾiri al-anbiyāʾi wa-l-aṣfiyāʾi wa-l-āli wa-l-aṣḥāb.

O God, send prayers, salutations, and blessings upon our master Muḥammad; the speaker of the truth and righteousness. Send prayers, salutations, and blessings upon our master Muḥammad who is the most superior of those who have been granted wisdom and discernment in judgment. Send prayers, salutations, and blessings upon our master Muḥammad who is the access to all entries and the essence of cores (*lub al-lubāb*). Send prayers, salutations, and blessings upon our master Muḥammad; and unveil from our hearts the shrouds of darkness through their light. Send prayers, salutations, and blessings upon our master Muḥammad; and inspire us with wisdom and righteousness. Send prayers, salutations, and blessings upon our master Muḥammad; and allow us to drink from Your pure drink. Send prayers, salutations, and blessings upon our master Muḥammad; and grant us discernment of the subtleties of Your Book. Send prayers, salutations, and blessings upon our master Muḥammad; and make us, through sending prayers upon him, from among the elite. Send prayers, salutations, and blessings upon our master Muḥammad; and enable us to enter the divine presence in the company of all of the lovers. Send prayers, salutations, and blessings upon our master Muḥammad; and to the remainder of the prophets, people of purity, his family, and Companions.

اللَّهُمَّ صَلِّ وَسَلِّمْ وَبَارِكْ عَلَى سَيِّدِنَا مُحَمَّدٍ الصَّادِقِ الأَمِيْنِ، وَصَلِّ وَسَلِّمْ وَبَارِكْ عَلَى سَيِّدِنَا مُحَمَّدٍ الَّذِيْ جَاءَ بِالحَقِّ الْمُبِينِ، وَصَلِّ وَسَلِّمْ وَبَارِكْ عَلَى سَيِّدِنَا مُحَمَّدٍ الَّذِيْ أَرْسَلْتَهُ رَحْمَةً لِلْعَالَمِيْنَ، وَصَلِّ وَسَلِّمْ وَبَارِكْ عَلَى سَيِّدِنَا مُحَمَّدٍ وَعَلَى جَمِيْعِ الأَنْبِيَاءِ وَالْمُرْسَلِينَ وَعَلَى آلِهِمْ وَصَحْبِهِمْ أَجْمَعِيْنَ، كُلَّمَا ذَكَرَكَ الذَّاكِرُوْنَ، وَغَفَلَ عَنْ ذِكْرِكَ الغَافِلُوْنَ.

Allāhumma ṣalli wa-sallim wa-bārik ʿalā sayyidinā Muḥammadin al-ṣādiqi al-amīn. Wa-ṣalli wa-sallim wa-bārik ʿalā sayyidinā Muḥammadin alladhī jāʾa bi al-ḥaqqi al-mubīn. Wa-ṣalli wa-sallim wa-bārik ʿalā sayyidinā Muḥammadin alladhī arsaltahu raḥmatan lil-ʿālamīn. Wa-ṣalli wa-sallim wa-bārik ʿalā sayyidinā Muḥammadin wa-ʿalā jamīʿi al-anbiyāʾi wa-l-mursalīn wa-ʿalā ālihim wa-ṣaḥbihim ajmaʿīn, kullamā dhakaraka al-dhākirūn wa-ghafala ʿan dhikrika al-ghāfilūn.

O God, send prayers, salutations, and blessings upon our master Muḥammad, the trustworthy and honest. Send prayers, salutations, and blessings upon our master Muḥammad, who came with the manifest truth. Send prayers, salutations, and blessings upon our master Muḥammad, whom you have sent as a mercy to the worlds. Send prayers, salutations, and blessings upon our master Muḥammad and to the entirety of the prophets, messengers, and to all of their families and Companions; with each instance that those of remembrance remember You and those of negligence neglect Your remembrance.

اللَّهُمَّ صَلِّ عَلَى سَيِّدِنَا مُحَمَّدٍ وَعَلَى آلِ سَيِّدِنَا مُحَمَّدٍ صَلَاةً تَكُوْنُ لَكَ رِضَاءً وَلِحَقِّهِ أَدَاءً، وَأَعْطِهِ الوَسِيْلَةَ وَالْمَقَامَ الَّذِيْ وَعَدْتَهُ.

Allāhumma ṣallī ʿalā sayyidinā Muḥammad wa-ʿalā āli sayyidinā Muḥammad ṣalātan takūnu laka riḍāʾan wa-li-ḥaqqihi adāʾan, wa-aʿṭihi al-wasīlata wa-l-maqām alladhi waʿadtah.

O God, send prayers upon our master Muḥammad and his family, prayers that will be a source of Your pleasure with us and are worthy of the Prophet's right [over us]. Grant him mediation (*wasīla*) and the [honored] station which You have promised.

اللَّهُمَّ صَلِّ عَلَى سَيِّدِنَا مُحَمَّدٍ فِيْ الأَوَّلِيْنَ، وَصَلِّ عَلَى سَيِّدِنا مُحَمَّدٍ فِي الآخِرِينَ، وَصَلِّ عَلَى سَيِّدِنَا مُحَمَّدٍ فِيْ الْمُرْسَلِيْنَ، وَصَلِّ عَلَى سَيِّدِنا مُحَمَّدٍ فِيْ الْمَلَإِ الأَعْلَى إِلَى يَوْمِ الدِّيْنِ.

Allāhumma ṣallī ʿalā sayyidinā Muḥammadin fī l-awwalīn. Wa-ṣalli ʿalā sayyidinā Muḥammadin fī l-ākhirīn. Wa-ṣalli ʿalā sayyidinā Muḥammadin fī l-mursalīn. Wa-ṣalli ʿalā sayyidinā Muḥammadin fī l-malaʾi al-aʿlā ilā yawmi al-dīn.

O God, send prayers upon our master Muḥammad in the beginning and send prayers upon our master Muḥammad in the end. Send prayers upon our master Muḥammad among the prophets. Send prayers upon our master Muḥammad in the highest heaven until the Day of Judgment.

اللَّهُمَّ صَلِّ عَلَى سَيِّدِنَا مُحَمَّدٍ الَّذِي مَلَأْتَ قَلْبَهُ مِنْ جَلَالِكَ وَعَيْنَهُ مِنْ جَمَالِكَ، فَأَصْبَحَ فَرِحاً مَسْرُوْراً مُؤَيَّداً مَنْصُوْراً، وَعَلَى آلِهِ وَصَحْبِهِ وَسَلِّمْ تَسْلِيْماً.

Allāhumma ṣalli ʿalā sayyidinā Muḥammadin alladhi malaʾta qalbahu min jalālika, wa-ʿaynahu min jamālika, fa-aṣbaḥa fariḥan masrūran muʾayyadan manṣūran. Wa-ʿalā ālihi wa-ṣaḥbihi wa-sallim taslīmā.

O God, send prayers upon our master Muḥammad, whose heart You have filled with Your grandeur and whose eyes [you have filled] with Your majesty, upon which he became of the fortunate, blissful, and empowered with victory. Also, to his family and Companions [send] salutations of peace.

اللَّهُمَّ إِنِّي أَسْأَلُكَ بِنُوْرِ وَجْهِ اللهِ العَظِيْمِ، الَّذِيْ مَلَأَ أَرْكَانَ عَرْشِ اللهِ العَظِيْمِ، وَقَامَتْ بِهِ عَوَالِمُ اللهِ العَظِيْمِ، أَنْ تُصَلِّيَ عَلَى مَوْلَانَا مُحَمَّدٍ

ذِي الْقَدْرِ الْعَظِيمِ، وَعَلَى آلِ نَبِيِّ اللهِ الْعَظِيمِ، وَسَلِّمْ عَلَيْهِ وَعَلَى آلِهِ مِثْلَ ذَلِكَ، وَاجْمَعْ بَيْنِي وَبَيْنَهُ كَمَا جَمَعْتَ بَيْنَ الرُّوحِ وَالْجَسَدِ، ظَاهِراً وَبَاطِناً، يَقَظَةً وَمَنَاماً، وَاجْعَلْهُ يَا رَبِّ رُوحاً لِذَاتِي مِنْ جَمِيعِ الْوُجُوهِ، فِي الدُّنْيَا وَالآخِرَةِ يَا عَظِيمُ.

Allāhumma innī as'aluka bi-nūri wajh illāhi al-ʿaẓīm, alladhī mala'a arkāna ʿarsh illāhi al-ʿaẓīm, wa-qāmat bihi ʿawālimu llāhi al-ʿaẓīm, an tuṣalliya ʿalā mawlānā Muḥammadin dhī l-qadri al-ʿaẓīm wa-ʿalā nabiyyi llāhi al-ʿaẓīm. Wa-sallim ʿalayhi wa-ʿalā ālihi mithla dhālika. Wa-ajmaʿ baynī wa-baynahu kamā jamaʿta bayna al-rūḥi wa-l-jasad ẓāhiran wa-bāṭinan, yaqaẓatan wa-manāman. Wa-ajʿalhu yā rabbi rūḥan li-dhātī min jamīʿi al-wujūhi fī l-dunyā wa-l-ākhirati yā ʿaẓīm.

O God, I beseech You by the magnificent light of Your essence that has overflowed the magnificent pillars of God's throne and through it all of God's magnificent worlds stood forth, that You send prayers upon our master Muḥammad, possessor of magnificent stature, and to the magnificent family of the Messenger of God. Send salutations to him and his family in this way, as well. Bond me to him as you have bonded the soul and the body, externally and internally, in wakefulness and in slumber. Make him, my Lord, sustenance for my being from all aspects, in this life and in the next, O Magnificent.

اللَّهُمَّ يَا دَائِمَ الْفَضْلِ عَلَى الْبَرِيَّةِ، يَا بَاسِطَ الْيَدَيْنِ بِالْعَطِيَّةِ، يَا صَاحِبَ الْمَوَاهِبِ السَّنِيَّةِ، صَلِّ عَلَى مُحَمَّدٍ خَيْرِ الْبَرِيَّةِ، وَاغْفِرْ لَنَا يَا ذَا الْعُلَا فِي هَذِهِ الْجَلْسَةِ الْهَنِيَّةِ.

Allāhumma yā dā'im al-faḍli ʿalā l-bariyya, yā bāsiṭa al-yadayni bi-l-ʿaṭiyya, yā ṣāḥiba al-mawāhib al-saniyya, ṣalli ʿalā

Muḥammadin khayri al-bariyya, wa-aghfir lanā yā dha al-ʿulā fī hādhihi al-jalsati al-haniyya.

O God! O Perpetual Bestower of favors upon creation! O You whose hand is always open in giving! O Possessor of spectacular power! Send prayers upon Muḥammad, the best of creation, and forgive [our sins] in this blessed gathering, O Possessor of majesty!

اللَّهُمَّ اجْعَلْ صَلَوَاتِكَ وَرَحْمَتَكَ وَبَرَكَاتِكَ عَلَى سَيِّدِ الْمُرْسَلِيْنَ وَإِمَامِ الْمُتَّقِيْنَ، وَخَاتَمِ النَّبِيِّيْنَ، عَبْدِكَ وَرَسُوْلِكَ إِمَامِ الخَيْرِ وَقَائِدِ الخَيْرِ، وَرَسُوْلِ الرَّحْمَةِ. اللَّهُمَّ ابْعَثْهُ الْمَقَامَ الْمَحْمُوْدَ الَّذِي يَغْبِطُهُ بِهِ الأَوَّلُوْنَ وَالآخِرُوْنَ.

Allāhumma ajʿal ṣalawātika wa-raḥmataka wa-barakātika ʿalā sayyid al-mursalīn, wa-imām al-muṭṭaqīn, wa-khātam al-nabiyyīn, ʿabdika wa-rasūlika imāmi al-khayri, wa-qāʾidi al-khayri, wa-rasūli al-raḥmati. Allāhumma abʿathhu maqāma al-maḥmūda alladhī yaghbiṭuhu bihi al-awwalūna wa-l-ākhirūn.

O God, grant Your prayers, mercy, and blessings upon the master of all the messengers, the leader of those who are God-fearing (*muṭṭaqīn*), the last of the prophets, Your servant, Your Messenger, the head of goodness (*khayr*), the leader of goodness, and the messenger of mercy. O God, grant him the exalted rank that is desired by all who came before and after.

اللَّهُمَّ صَلِّ عَلَى سَيِّدِنَا مُحَمَّدٍ صَلَاةً تُشْرَحُ بِهَا الصُّدُوْرُ، وَتُهَوَّنُ بِهَا الأُمُوْرُ، وَتُنَجِّيْنَا بِهَا يَوْمَ النُّشُوْرِ بِرَحْمَةٍ مِنْكَ يَا عَزِيْزُ يَا غَفُوْرُ، وَعَلَى آلِهِ وَصَحْبِهِ وَسَلِّمْ.

Allāhumma ṣallī ʿalā sayyidinā Muḥammadin ṣalatan tushraḥu bihā l-ṣuḍūr, wa-tuhawwanu bihā l-umūr, wa-tunajjīnā bihā yawm al-nushūri bi-raḥmatin minka yā ʿazīzu yā ghafūr wa-ʿalā ālihi wa-ṣaḥbihi wa-sallim.

O God, send prayers upon our master Muḥammad, prayers through which hearts are expanded, our affairs are facilitated, and with it we are saved on the Day of Resurrection through your mercy. O Almighty and Most-Forgiving! And to his family and Companions send salutations.

يَا حَيُّ يَا قَيُّوْمُ، يَا ذَا الجَلَالِ وَالإِكْرَامِ، صَلِّ عَلَى سَيِّدِنَا مُحَمَّدٍ وَعَلَى آلِ سَيِّدِنَا مُحَمَّدٍ، وَأَحْيِ قَلْبِي، وَأَمِتْ نَفْسِي حَتَّى أَحْيَا بِكَ حَيَاةً طَيِّبَةً فِيْ الدُّنْيَا وَالآخِرَةِ، إِنَّكَ عَلَى كُلِّ شَيْءٍ قَدِيْرٌ.

Yā ḥayyu yā qayyūm, yā dha al-jalāli wa-l-ikrām, ṣalli ʿalā sayyidinā Muḥammadin, wa-ʿalā āli sayyidinā Muḥammadin, wa-aḥyī qalbī wa-amit nafsī ḥattā aḥyā bika ḥayātan ṭayyibatan fī l-dunyā wa-l-ākhira, inaka ʿalā kulli shayʾin qadīr.

O Living and Self-Existent, send prayers upon our master Muḥammad and to the family of our master Muḥammad. Bring life to my heart and death to my ego (*nafs*); so that I may live a virtuous life in this world and the next. You possess full power over everything.

اللَّهُمَّ صَلِّ عَلَى سَيِّدِنَا مُحَمَّدٍ الحَبِيْبِ الْمَحْبُوبِ، شَافِي العِلَلِ، وَمُفَرِّجِ الكُرُوبِ، وَعَلَى آلِهِ وَصَحْبِهِ وَسَلِّمْ.

Allāhumma ṣalli ʿalā sayyidinā Muḥammadin al-ḥabībi al-maḥbūb, shāfī l-ʿilali wa-mufarrij al-kurūb, wa-ʿalā ālihi wa-ṣaḥbihi wa-sallim.

O God, send prayers upon our master Muḥammad the beloved who is cherished, the remedy of ailments, and the resolver of troubles; and to his family and Companions [send] salutations.

اللَّهُمَّ صَلِّ عَلَى سَيِّدِنَا مُحَمَّدٍ النَّبِيِّ الأُمِّيِّ، وَعَلَى آلِهِ وَصَحْبِهِ وَسَلِّمْ، عَدَدَ مَا عَلِمْتَ، وَزِنَةَ مَا عَلِمْتَ، وَمِلْءَ مَا عَلِمْتَ.

Allāhumma ṣalli ʿalā sayyidinā Muḥammadin al-nabī l-ummī, wa-ʿalā ālihi wa-ṣaḥbihi wa-sallim, ʿadada ma ʿalimta wa-zinata mā ʿalimta wa-milʾa mā ʿalimta.

O God, send prayers upon our master Muḥammad the unlettered Prophet, and to his family and his Companions [send] salutations as vast as Your knowledge, the weight of Your knowledge, and the amount of Your knowledge.

اللَّهُمَّ صَلِّ وَسَلِّمْ وَبَارِكْ عَلَى سَيِّدِنَا مُحَمَّدٍ وَعَلَى آلِهِ عَدَدَ كَمَالِ اللهِ، وَكَمَا يَلِيْقُ بِكَمَالِهِ، وَاجْزِهِ عَنَّا مَا هُوَ أَهْلُهُ.

Allāhumma ṣalli wa-sallim wa-bārik ʿalā sayyidinā Muḥammadin wa-ʿalā ālihi ʿadada kamāli llāhi, wa-kamā yalīqu bi-kamālih, wa-ajzihi ʿannā mā huwa ahluhu.

O God, send prayers, salutations, and blessings upon our master Muḥammad and to his family as vast as the perfection of God, and as is worthy of His perfection. Reward him as he is worthy [of being rewarded].

اللَّهُمَّ صَلِّ عَلَى سَيِّدِنَا مُحَمَّدٍ الْمَاحِيْ لِظَلَامِ الجَهْلِ وَالنِّسْيَانِ بِنُوْرِهِ، وَعَلَى آلِهِ وَصَحْبِهِ وَسَلِّمْ.

Allāhumma ṣalli ʿalā sayyidinā Muḥammadin al-māḥī li-ẓalāmi al-jahli wa-l-nisyāni bi-nūrihi, wa-ʿalā ālihi wa-ṣaḥbihi wa-sallim.

O God, send prayers upon our master Muḥammad, the eliminator of the darkness of ignorance and forgetfulness through his light, and to his family and Companions [send] salutations.

اللَّهُمَّ صَلِّ عَلَى سَيِّدِنَا مُحَمَّدٍ مِفْتَاحِ خَزَائِنِكَ، اللَّهُمَّ افْتَحْ لِي بِهِ ﷺ مَا أُغْلِقَ عَلَيَّ، اللَّهُمَّ صَلِّ عَلَى سَيِّدِنَا مُحَمَّدٍ النَّبِيِّ الأُمِّيِّ وَعَلَى آلِهِ وَصَحْبِهِ وَسَلِّمْ تَسْلِيماً.

Allāhumma ṣalli ʿalā sayyidinā Muḥammadin miftāḥi khazāʾinika. Allāhumma iftaḥ lī bihi ﷺ mā ughliqa ʿalayya. Allāhumma ṣalli ʿalā sayyidinā Muḥammadin al-nabī l-ummī wa-ʿalā ālihi wa-ṣaḥbihi wa-sallim taslīmā.

O God, send prayers upon our master Muḥammad, the opener of your treasures. O God, open for me through him ﷺ what has been closed to me. O God, send prayers upon our master Muḥammad the unlettered Prophet and to his family and Companions [send] many salutations.

اللَّهُمَّ صَلِّ عَلَى سَيِّدِنَا مُحَمَّدٍ عَدَدَ مَنْ صَلَّى عَلَيْهِ، وَصَلِّ عَلَى سَيِّدِنَا مُحَمَّدٍ عَدَدَ مَنْ لَمْ يُصَلِّ عَلَيْهِ، وَصَلِّ عَلَى سَيِّدِنَا مُحَمَّدٍ كَمَا تُحِبُّ أَنْ يُصَلَّى عَلَيْهِ، وَصلِّ عَلَى سَيِّدِنَا مُحَمَّدٍ كَمَا أَمَرْتَ أَنْ يُصَلَّى عَلَيْهِ، وَصَلِّ عَلَى سَيِّدِنَا مُحَمَّدٍ كَمَا تَنْبَغِي الصَّلَاةُ عَلَيْهِ.

Allāhumma ṣalli ʿalā sayyidinā Muḥammadin ʿadada man ṣalla ʿalayh. Wa-ṣalli ʿalā sayyidinā Muḥammadin ʿadada man lam yuṣalli ʿalayh. Wa-ṣalli ʿalā sayyidinā Muḥammadin kamā tuḥibbu an yuṣallā ʿalayh. Wa-ṣalli ʿalā sayyidinā Muḥammadin kamā amarta an yuṣallā ʿalayhi. Wa-ṣalli ʿalā sayyidinā Muḥammadin kamā tanbaghī l-ṣalātu ʿalayhi.

O God, send prayers upon our master Muḥammad as

extensive as the numbers of those who have sent prayers upon him. Send prayers upon our master Muḥammad [equal to] the extent of those who have not sent prayers upon him. Send prayers upon our master Muḥammad in the way in which You desire to have prayers sent upon him. Send prayers upon our master Muḥammad in the way in which You have commanded that prayers be sent upon him. Send prayers upon our master Muḥammad in the way in which prayers ought to be sent upon him.

اللَّهُمَّ صَلِّ صَلَاةً كَامِلَةً، وَسَلِّمْ سَلَاماً تَامّاً عَلَى سَيِّدِنَا مُحَمَّدٍ الَّذِي تَنْحَلُّ بِهِ العُقَدُ، وَتَنْفَرِجُ بِهِ الكُرَبُ، وَتُقْضَى بِهِ الحَوَائِجُ، وَتُنَالُ بِهِ الرَّغَائِبُ، وَحُسْنُ الخَوَاتِيمُ، وَيُسْتَسْقَى الغَمَامُ بِوَجْهِهِ الكَرِيمِ وَعَلَى آلِهِ وَصَحْبِهِ وَسَلِّمْ فِيْ كُلِّ لَمْحَةٍ وَنَفَسٍ عَدَدَ كُلِّ مَعْلُوْمٍ لَكَ.

Allāhumma ṣalli ṣalātan kāmilatin, wa-sallim salāman tāmman, ʿalā sayyidinā Muḥammadin, alladhī tanḥallu bihi al-ʿuqadu, wa-tanfariju bihi al-kurabu, wa-tuqḍā bihi al-ḥawāʾij wa-tunālu bihi al-raghāʾib wa-ḥusnu al-khawatīmu, wa-yustasqā l-ghamāmu bi-wajhihi al-karīm wa-ʿalā ālihi wa-ṣaḥbihi wa-sallim fī kulli lamḥatin wa-nafasin ʿadada kulli maʿlūmin laka.

O God, send prayers that are most complete and send salutations that are most extensive to our master Muḥammad; through whom knots are unraveled, troubles are relieved, needs are fulfilled, aspirations are attained, as are the best of ends, and by whose noble countenance the clouds are watered. Also, to his family and Companions [send] salutations in each moment and every breath by the extent of all that is known to You.

اللَّهُمَّ صَلِّ عَلَى سَيِّدِنَا مُحَمَّدٍ وَعَلَى آلِ سَيِّدِنَا مُحَمَّدٍ، وَبَارِكْ عَلَى سَيِّدِنَا مُحَمَّدٍ وَعَلَى آلِ سَيِّدِنَا مُحَمَّدٍ، كَمَا صَلَّيْتَ وَبَارَكْتَ عَلَى سَيِّدِنَا إِبْرَاهِيمَ

وَعَلَى آلِ سَيِّدِنَا إِبرَاهِيْمَ، فِيْ العَالَمِيْنَ إِنَّكَ حَمِيْدٌ مَجِيْدٌ، عَدَدَ خَلْقِكَ وَرِضَا نَفْسِكَ وَزِنَةَ عَرْشِكَ وَمِدَادَ كَلِمَاتِكَ، كُلَّمَا ذَكَرَكَ الذَّاكِرُونَ، وَغَفَلَ عَنْ ذِكْرِكَ الغَافِلُوْنَ.

Allāhumma ṣalli ʿalā sayyidinā Muḥammadin wa-ʿalā āli sayyidinā Muḥammad, wa-bārik ʿalā sayyidinā Muḥammadin wa-ʿalā āli sayyidinā Muḥammad, kamā ṣallayta wa-bārakta ʿalā sayyidinā Ibrāhīm wa-ʿalā āli sayyidinā Ibrāhīm fī l-ʿālamīna innaka ḥamīdun majīd, ʿadada khalqika wa-riḍā nafsika wa-zinata ʿarshika wa-midāda kalimātika kullamā dhakaraka al-dhākirūn wa-ghafala ʿan dhikrika al-ghāfilūn.

O God, send prayers upon our master Muḥammad and to the family of our master Muḥammad as You have sent prayers and blessings upon our master Ibrāhīm and the family of our master Ibrāhīm. You are the most worthy of praise and majestic in all of the worlds. [Send prayers equal to] the [vast] numbers of Your creation, as much as it pleases You, as the splendor of Your throne, and as the eternal nature of Your words, with each time the people of remembrance remember You and the people of negligence neglect Your remembrance.

The Prayers of the Devoted with God's Beautiful Names upon the Prophet Muḥammad ﷺ with his Traditional Praiseworthy Names

صَلَوَاتُ المُقَرَّبِيْن بِأَسْمَاءِ اللهِ الحُسْنَى عَلَى النَّبِي مُحَمَّد ﷺ بِأَسْمَائِهِ المَأْثُوْرَةِ الفَضْلَى

صَلِّ وَسَلِّمْ وَبَارِكْ يَا اللهُ عَلَى مُحَمَّدٍ الدَّاعِيْ بِأَنَّ لَا إِلَهَ إِلَّا اللهُ.

Send prayers, peace, and blessings, O Allāh, upon Muḥammad, the one who calls us to witness that there is no god but God.

صَلِّ وَسَلِّمْ وَبَارِكْ يَا رَحْمَٰنُ عَلَى فَصِيحِ اللِّسَانِ مُطَهِّرِ الجَنَانِ.

Send prayers, peace, and blessings, O Most Compassionate, upon the [one with the] eloquent tongue (*faṣīḥ al-lisān*) and purified heart.

صَلِّ وَسَلِّمْ وَبَارِكْ يَا رَحِيْمُ عَلَى طه كَمَا صَلَّيْتَ عَلَى إِبْرَاهِيْمَ.

Send prayers, peace, and blessings, O Most Merciful, upon Ṭāhā, the way you sent prayers upon Ibrāhīm.

صَلِّ وَسَلِّمْ وَبَارِكْ يَا مَلِكُ عَلَى سَيِّدِ المُرْسَلِينَ وَأَنْبِيَاءِ المَلِكِ.

Send prayers, peace, and blessings, O King, upon the master of the messengers (*sayyid al-mursalīn*) and upon the prophets of the King (God's sent prophets).

صَلِّ وَسَلِّمْ وَبَارِكْ يَا قُدُّوسُ عَلَى مُطَهِّرِ القُلُوْبِ وَالنُّفُوْسِ.

Send prayers, peace, and blessings, O Holy, upon the purifier (*muṭahhir*) of hearts and souls.

صَلِّ وَسَلِّم وَبَارِك يَا **سَلَام** عَلَى الرَّسُوْلِ الدَّاعِيْ إِلَى دَارِ السَّلَام.

Send prayers, peace, and blessings, O Peace, upon the messenger (*al-rasūl*), who called to the abode of peace.

صَلِّ وَسَلِّم وَبَارِك يَا **مُؤْمِن** عَلَى المُنْذِرِ الَّذِيْ كَانَ بِعَذَابِ القَبْرِ مُوْقِن.

Send prayers, peace, and blessings, O Granter of Safety, upon the warner (*al-mundhir*), who had certitude of the punishments of the grave.

صَلِّ وَسَلِّم وَبَارِك يَا **مُهَيْمِن** عَلَى المُدَّثِّرِ الَّذِيْ أُنْزِلَ عَلَيْهِ الكِتَابُ المُهَيْمِن.

Send prayers, peace, and blessings, O Guardian, upon the covered one (*al-muddaththir*), to whom the comprehensive book was revealed.

صَلِّ وَسَلِّم وَبَارِك يَا **عَزِيْز** عَلَى عَلَمِ اليَقِين هَادِيْ الثَّقَلَيْنِ بِالكِتَابِ العَزِيْز.

Send prayers, peace, and blessings, O Eminent, upon the symbol of certainty (*ʿalam al-yaqīn*) and the guide to the humans and jinn (*al-thaqalayn*) through the majestic book.

صَلِّ وَسَلِّم وَبَارِك يَا **جَبَّار** عَلَى رَسُوْلِ المَلَاحِم هَازِمِ الكُفَّار.

Send prayers, peace, and blessings, O Compeller, upon the messenger of battles (*rasūl al-malāḥim*) and subjugator of the disbelievers.

صَلِّ وَسَلِّم وَبَارِك يَا **مُتَكَبِّر** عَلَى المَكِين الَّذِيْ أَوْعَدَ بِالنَّارِ كُلَّ حَلَّافٍ مَهِيْن.

Send prayers, peace, and blessings, O Majestic, upon the firm one (*al-makīn*), who promised Hellfire to everyone who makes false testimony.

صَلِّ وَسَلِّم وَبَارِك يَا **خَالِق** عَلَى العَاقِبِ الَّذِيْ أَرْسَلْتَهُ رَحْمَةً لِلْخَلَائِق.

Send prayers, peace, and blessings, O Creator, upon the last [of the prophets] (*al-ʿāqib*) whom You have sent as a mercy to creation.

صَلِّ وَسَلِّم وَبَارِك يَا **بَارِئ** عَلَى الجَامِعِ الَّذِيْ عَلَّمَهُ اللهُ وَلَيْسَ بِقَارِئ.

Send prayers, peace, and blessings, O Originator, upon the gatherer [of knowledge] (*al-jāmiʿ*) who was taught by God and was not lettered.

صَلِّ وَسَلِّم وَبَارِك يَا **مُصَوِّر** عَلَى مُقِيم السُّنَّةِ الهَادِي المُنَوِّر.

Send prayers, peace, and blessings, O Fashioner, upon the upholder of the *sunna* (*muqīm al-sunna*), which is the guiding light.

صَلِّ وَسَلِّم وَبَارِك يَا **غَفَّار** عَلَى أَبِيْ القَاسِمِ الَّذِيْ سَلَّمَت عَلَيْهِ الحَجَرُ وَالأَشْجَار.

Send prayers, peace, and blessings, O Forever Forgiving, upon Abū l-Qāsim, to whom the rocks and the trees sent greetings of peace.

صَلِّ وَسَلِّم وَبَارِك يَا **قَهَّار** عَلَى نَاصِرِ الحَقِّ قَاهِرِ الفُجَّار.

Send prayers, peace, and blessings, O Subduer, upon the victor of the truth (*nāṣir al-ḥaqq*), the conqueror of the disbelievers.

صَلِّ وَسَلِّم وَبَارِك يَا **وَهَّاب** عَلَى صَاحِبِ المَقَامِ المُثَابِرِ الأَوَّاب.

Send prayers, peace, and blessings, O Bestower, upon the possessor of the rank (*ṣāḥib al-maqām*) and the one continuously turning to God.

صَلِّ وَسَلِّم وَبَارِك يَا **رَزَّاق** عَلَى كَاشِفِ الكُرَبِ الفَيَّاض بِالأَرْزَاق.

Send prayers, peace, and blessings, O Provider, upon the reliever of troubles (*kāshif al-kurab*) and the abundant in provision.

صَلِّ وَسَلِّم وَبَارِك يَا **فَتَّاح** عَلَى مِفْتَاحِ الرَّحْمَةِ الفَتَّاح.

Send prayers, peace, and blessings, O Opener, upon the key to mercy (*miftāḥ al-raḥma*), the opener [of what is closed].

صَلِّ وَسَلِّم وَبَارِك يَا **عَلِيْم** عَلَى المُبَلِّغ مِنْ لَدُنْ حَكِيْمٍ عَلِيْم.

Send prayers, peace, and blessings, O All-Knowing, upon the conveyor (*al-muballigh*) from the All-Wise and All-Knowing.

صَلِّ وَسَلِّم وَبَارِك يَا **قَابِض** عَلَى الكَامِلِ الَّذِيْ قَلْبُهُ بِحُبِّ اللهِ نَابِض.

Send prayers, peace, and blessings, O Constrictor, upon the perfect one (*al-kāmil*), whose heart overflows with the love of God.

صَلِّ وَسَلِّم وَبَارِك يَا **بَاسِط** عَلَى السَّابِقِ الَّذِيْ كَفُّهُ بِالجُوْدِ بَاسِط.

Send prayers, peace, and blessings, O Expander, upon the foremost one (*al-sābiq*) [in good works], the one whose hands are expanded in generosity.

صَلِّ وَسَلِّم وَبَارِك يَا **خَافِض** عَلَى سَعْدِ الخَلْق مَنْ جَنَاحُهُ لِلْمُؤْمِنِيْنَ خَافِض.

Send prayers, peace, and blessings, O Abaser, upon the joy of creation (*saʿd al-khalq*), whose wings [of mercy] were expanded to the believers.

صَلِّ وَسَلِّم وَبَارِك يَا **رَافِع** عَلَى وَاصِل صَاحِبِ العَزْمِ وَ لِلرَّايَةِ رَافِع.

Send prayers, peace, and blessings, O Exalter, upon the connector (*wāṣil*) [of blood ties], a member of [the prophets] steadfastness (*ʿulu al-ʿazm*) and the raisers of [God's] flag.

صَلِّ وَسَلِّم وَبَارِك يَا **مُعِزّ** عَلَى الهَادِي الْمَخْصُوْصِ بِالكَوْثَرِ وَالكَرَامَةِ وَالعِزّ.

Send prayers, peace, and blessings, O Honorer, upon the

guide (*al-hādī*), distinguished by the [spring of] Kawthar, nobility, and dignity.

صَلِّ وَسَلِّم وَبَارِك يَا **مُذِلّ** عَلَى سَيْفِ اللهِ المَنْصُوْرِ بِالرُّعْبِ وَلِلْعَدُوِّ الذُّلّ.

Send prayers, peace, and blessings, O One who humbles, upon the sword of God (*sayf Allāh*), who is victorious through awe and subjugation of the enemy.

صَلِّ وَسَلِّم وَبَارِك يَا **سَمِيْع** عَلَى كَلِيْم اللهِ الَّذِي كَلَّمَ المَوْتَى وَهُوَ لَهُم سَمِيْع.

Send prayers, peace, and blessings, O All-Hearing, upon the one who spoke to God (*kalīm Allāh*) and who spoke to the dead and heard them.[10]

صَلِّ وَسَلِّم وَبَارِك يَا **بَصِير** عَلَى المُنِيْر الَّذِيْ يَرَى مَنْ خَلْفَهُ بِنُوْرِ البَصِيْر.

Send prayers, peace, and blessings, O All-Seeing, upon the illuminator (*al-munīr*), who saw behind him with the light of discernment.

صَلِّ وَسَلِّم وَبَارِك يَا **حَكَم** عَلَى رُوْحِ القِسْطِ خَيْرِ مَنْ عَدَلَ أَوْ حَكَم.

Send prayers, peace, and blessings, O Arbitrator, upon the just soul (*rūḥ al-qisṭ*), the most superior of all who are just or judge.[11]

صَلِّ وَسَلِّم وَبَارِك يَا **عَدْل** عَلَى الوَلِّي الَّذِيْ قَوْلُهُ فَصْلٌ وَحُكْمُهُ عَدْل.

---

10 Referring to the incident in the Battle of Uḥud in which the Prophet ﷺ spoke to the dead from the Quraysh and heard them.

11 This refers to the following incident cited in *Ṣaḥīḥ*s of al-Bukhārī and Muslim. After the Battle of Ḥunayn, the Prophet ﷺ distributed the booty that was acquired from it and a man came saying, "This division is not based on justice and it was not intended to win the pleasure of God." When the news of this was given to the Prophet ﷺ he replied, "Who will do justice if God and his Messenger will not?"

Send prayers, peace, and blessings, O Just, upon the friend (*walī*), whose words are decisive and whose judgments are just.

صَلِّ وَسَلِّم وَبَارِك يَا **لَطِيْف** عَلَى الأَمِين الآمِرِ بِبِرِّ الوَالِدَيْنِ وَالقَوْلِ اللَّطِيْف.

Send prayers, peace, and blessings, O Subtle Benevolent One, upon the trustworthy one (*al-amīn*), who commanded goodness to one's parents and kindness in speech.

صَلِّ وَسَلِّم وَبَارِك يَا **خَبِير** عَلَى الشَّهِيْر مَلَاذِنَا يَوْمَ العَرْضِ عَلَى الخَبِيْر.

Send prayers, peace, and blessings, O All-Aware, upon the famed one (*al-shahīr*), our haven on the Day of Judgment in front of the All-Aware.

صَلِّ وَسَلِّم وَبَارِك يَا **حَلِيْم** عَلَى البَشِيْر المُزَيَّنِ بِالْحِلْمِ مِنْ رَبٍّ حَلِيْم.

Send prayers, peace, and blessings, O Forbearing, upon the bringer of good news (*al-bashīr*), [who has been] ornamented with forbearance from a forbearing Lord.

صَلِّ وَسَلِّم وَبَارِك يَا **عَظِيْم** على المُجِيْبِ الْمَخْصُوْصِ بِالْخُلُقِ العَظِيْم.

Send prayers, peace, and blessings, O Magnificent, upon the answerer (*al-mujīb*), distinguished with lofty character.

صَلِّ وَسَلِّم وَبَارِك يَا **غَفُوْر** عَلَى النَّبِي المُسْتَغْفِرِ لِأُمَّتِهِ الرَّبَّ الغَفُوْر.

Send prayers, peace, and blessings, O Forgiver, upon the Prophet (*al-nabī*), who sought forgiveness for his community from a forgiving Lord.

صَلِّ وَسَلِّم وَبَارِك يَا **شَكُوْر** عَلَى المَوْصُوْل الشَّاكِرِ آلَاءَ رَبِّهِ الشَّكُوْر.

Send prayers, peace, and blessings, O Grateful,[12] upon the

12 This means that God rewards good deeds with even greater rewards. Thankfulness and appreciativeness is to return good with good.

one [who is] connected (*al-mawṣūl*) [to God], grateful for his appreciative Lord's bounties.

صَلِّ وَسَلِّم وَبَارِك يَا عَلِيّ عَلَى الحَفِيّ صَاحِبِ الوَسِيْلَةِ وَالقَدْرِ العَلِيّ.

Send prayers, peace, and blessings, O Most-High, upon the welcoming one (*al-ḥafiyy*), the possessor of the [privilege of] mediation and high status.

صَلِّ وَسَلِّم وَبَارِك يَا كَبِيْر عَلَى المَهْدِي صَاحِبِ القَلْبِ الكَبِيْر.

Send prayers, peace, and blessings, O Great One, upon the guide (*al-mahdī*), possessor of an expansive heart.

صَلِّ وَسَلِّم وَبَارِك يَا حَفِيْظ عَلَى النَّاصِرِ الْمَحْفُوْظِ فِيْ الغَارِ بِحِفْظِ الحَفِيْظ.

Send prayers, peace, and blessings, O Preserver, upon the victor (*al-nāṣir*), [who was] protected in the cave by a protecting Lord.

صَلِّ وَسَلِّم وَبَارِك يَامُقِيْت عَلَى المَدْعُو الَّذِي يَطْعَمُ عِنْدَكَ وَيَبِيْت.

Send prayers, peace, and blessings, O Nourisher, upon the invited one (*al-madʿū*), who is provided provision[13] by You and shelter.

صَلِّ وَسَلِّم وَبَارِك يَاحَسِيْب عَلَى عَبْدِ اللهِ الَّذِي حَسْبُهُ اللهُ وَنِعْمَ الحَسِيْب.

Send prayers, peace, and blessings, O Reckoner, upon the servant of God (*ʿabdillāh*), for whom God was sufficient and He was the best means of sufficiency.

صَلِّ وَسَلِّم وَبَارِك يَا جَلِيْل عَلَى المُبَشَّرِ بِهِ فِيْ التَوْرَاةِ وَالإِنْجِيْل.

---

13 The Prophet used to connect his fasts (*wiṣāl*) for days without breaking it and forbade his Companions from imitating him, saying, "I am not like any of you. I am given food and drink [by God] during the night." See *Ṣaḥīḥ al-Bukhārī*, Kitāb al-ṣawm, Bāb al-wiṣāl, no. 182.

Send prayers, peace, and blessings, O Sublime, upon the one who was foretold (*al-mubashshir*) in the Torah and Bible.

صَلِّ وَسَلِّم وَبَارِك يَا **كَرِيْم** عَلَى أَبِيْ الطَّيِّب مُقْرِي الضَّيْفِ مُكْرِمِ اليَتِيْم.

Send prayers, peace, and blessings, O Generous, upon Abū Ṭayyib, who was generous with guests and treated the orphans well.

صَلِّ وَسَلِّم وَبَارِك يَا **رَقِيْب** عَلَى رَؤُوْفٍ رَحِيْمٍ قَدْ بَايَعَهُ اثْنَا عَشَرَ نَقِيْب.

Send prayers, peace, and blessings, O All-Aware, upon the kind and the merciful one (*raʾūf al-raḥīm*), [who was] given allegiance by twelve chieftains.

صَلِّ وَسَلِّم وَبَارِك يَا **مُجِيْب** عَلَى نَجِيِّ الله الَّذِي هُوَ لِدَعْوَةِ الْمَظْلُوْمِ مُجِيْب.

Send prayers, peace, and blessings, O Answerer, upon the one who called on his Lord secretly (*Najī Allāh*) and who is the answerer of the call of the oppressed.

صَلِّ وَسَلِّم وَبَارِك يَا **وَاسِع** عَلَى العَفُوِّ الَّذِي كَانَ قَلْبُهُ بِالرَّحْمَةِ وَالغُفْرَانِ وَاسِع.

Send prayers, peace, and blessings, O Vast, upon the pardoner (*al-ʿafuww*), whose heart was vast with mercy and clemency.

صَلِّ وَسَلِّم وَبَارِك يَا **حَكِيْم** عَلَى صَفِيِّ الله خَلِيْفَتِكَ فِيْ الحُكْمِ وَالتَّحْكِيْم.

Send prayers, peace, and blessings, O Wise, upon God's chosen one (*ṣafī Allāh*), Your appointed one in governing and arbitration.

صَلِّ وَسَلِّم وَبَارِك يَا **وَدُوْد** عَلَى الدَّاعِي الأَلِفِ رُوْحِ الأَرْوَاحِ سِرِّ الوُجُوْد.

Send prayers, peace, and blessings, O Most-Loving, upon the friendly caller (*al-dāʿī*) of the essence of souls [to God], the secret of existence.

صَلِّ وَسَلِّم وَبَارِك يَا **مَجِيْد** عَلَى خَلِيْلِ الرَّحْمٰنِ الَّذِي أَوْرَثْنَا الْمَجْدَ التَّلِيْد.

Send prayers, peace, and blessings, O Most-Glorious, upon the friend of the Most Compassionate (*khalīl al-raḥmān*) through whom we inherited a glorious continuous [legacy].

صَلِّ وَسَلِّم وَبَارِك يَا **بَاعِث** عَلَى النَّذِيْرِ الْمَبْعُوثِ لِكُلِّ نَاكِث.

Send prayers, peace, and blessings, O Resurrector, upon the warner (*al-nadhīr*), who was sent to every renegade.

صَلِّ وَسَلِّم وَبَارِك يَا **شَهِيْد** عَلَى هَدِيَّةِ اللهِ الْمُنْعِمِ بِالْعَطَاءِ وَالْمَزِيْد.

Send prayers, peace, and blessings, O Witness, upon the gift of God (*hadiyyati-llāh*), bestowed with bounties and more.

صَلِّ وَسَلِّم وَبَارِك يَا **حَقّ** عَلَى نِعْمَةِ اللهِ مُزْهِقِ البَاطِلِ وَمُحِقِّ الحَقّ.

Send prayers, peace, and blessings, O Truth, upon the bounty of God (*niʿmatillāh*), the eliminator of falsehood and the establisher of truth.

صَلِّ وَسَلِّم وَبَارِك يَا **وَكِيْل** عَلَى أَبِي إِبْرَاهِيْم القَائِلِ حَسْبُنَا اللهُ وَنِعْمَ الوَكِيْل.

Send prayers, peace, and blessings, O Trustee, upon Abū Ibrāhīm, who said in God we trust and upon Him we depend.

صَلِّ وَسَلِّم وَبَارِك يَا **قَوِيّ** عَلَى وَجِيْهٍ أَخَذْتَ لَهُ المِيْثَاقَ مِنْ كُلِّ نَبِيّ.

Send prayers, peace, and blessings, O Almighty, upon the honorable one (*wajīh*), who took an oath from every prophet.

صَلِّ وَسَلِّم وَبَارِك يَا **مَتِين** عَلَى شَفِيْعٍ حَنَّ إِلَيْهِ الجِذْعُ الدَّفِيْن.

Send prayers, peace, and blessings, O Firm One, upon the intercessor (*shafīʿ*), whom the rooted trunk longed for.

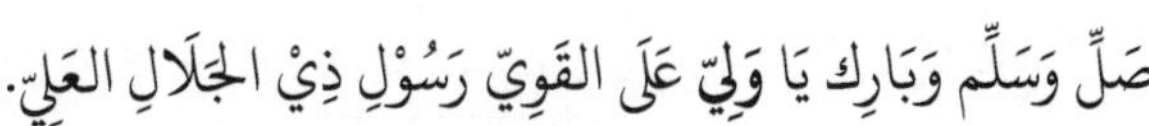

صَلِّ وَسَلِّم وَبَارِك يَا **وَلِيّ** عَلَى القَوِيّ رَسُوْلِ ذِيْ الجَلَالِ العَلِيّ.

Send prayers, peace, and blessings, O Patron, upon the strong one (*al-qawī*), the messenger of the Lord of exalted majesty.

صَلِّ وَسَلِّم وَبَارِك يَا **حَمِيْد** عَلَى مُصْلِح هَلَّلَت لَهُ العَوَالِمُ بِالتَّحْمِيْد.

Send prayers, peace, and blessings, O Praised One, upon the reformer (*muṣliḥ*), [who was] received by the world with praise.

صَلِّ وَسَلِّم وَبَارِك يَا **مُحْصِي** عَلَى صَالِح شَاكِرٍ لأَنْعُمِكَ وَلَا يُحْصِي.

Send prayers, peace, and blessings, O Keeper of Accounts, upon the righteous one (*ṣāliḥ*), grateful for your blessings that cannot be counted.

صَلِّ وَسَلِّم وَبَارِك يَا**مُبْدِئ** عَلَى الأُمِّيِّ الَّذِي كَانَ إِمَامًا لِكُلِّ مُقْرِئ.

Send prayers, peace, and blessings, O Initiator, upon the unlettered one (*al-ummī*), who was a teacher to every scholar.

صَلِّ وَسَلِّم وَبَارِك يَا **مُعِيْد** عَلَى غِيَاثٍ يُغِيْثُ النَّاسَ يَوْمَ الوَعِيْد.

Send prayers, peace, and blessings, O Restorer of Life, upon the rescuer (*ghiyāth*), [who will] save people on the promised day.

صَلِّ وَسَلِّم وَبَارِك يَا **مُحْيِي** عَلَى الْمُحْيِي الَّذِي هُوَ لِلْمَوْتَى يُحْيِي.

Send prayers, peace, and blessings, O Giver of Life, upon the reviver (*al-muḥyī*), who brings life to dead [hearts].

صَلِّ وَسَلِّم وَبَارِك يَا **مُمِيْت** عَلَى العَزِيْزِ الْمَبْعُوثِ بِأَنَّ اللهَ يُحْيِي وَيُمِيْت.

Send prayers, peace, and blessings, O Giver of Death, upon the dignified one (*al-ʿazīz*), [who] came with [the message] that God gives life and causes death.

صَلِّ وَسَلِّم وَبَارِك يَا **حَيّ** عَلَى دَلِيْلِ الخَيْرَاتِ خَيْرَ دَاعٍ بِاسْمِكَ الْحَيّ.

Send prayers, peace, and blessings, O Living, upon the guide to goodness (*dalīl al-khayrāt*), the best caller [to You] by Your name; the Living.

صَلِّ وَسَلِّم وَبَارِك يَا **قَيُّوم** عَلَى الْمُكَرَّم عَابِدِ رَبِّهِ القَيُّوم.

Send prayers, peace, and blessings, O Self-Existing, upon the honorable one (*al-mukarram*), the worshiper of his Lord, the Self-Existing.

صَلِّ وَسَلِّم وَبَارِك يَا **وَاجِد** عَلَى غَيْثٍ نَبَعَ مِنْ أَصَابِعِهِ الْمَاءُ البَارِد.

Send prayers, peace, and blessings, O Resourceful, upon the abundant rain (*ghayth*), from whose fingers flowed cold water.

صَلِّ وَسَلِّم وَبَارِك يَا **مَاجِد** عَلَى الفَاضِلِ الْمُتَقَلِّبِ فِي السَّاجِدِيْنَ الأَمَاجِد.

Send prayers, peace, and blessings, O Glorious, upon the favored one (*al-fāḍil*), whose ancestors were glorious and worshipful.

صَلِّ وَسَلِّم وَبَارِك يَا **وَاحِد** عَلَى الْمُطِيْعِ الْمُتَحَنِّثِ فِي الغَارِ لِلإِلٰهِ الوَاحِد.

Send prayers, peace, and blessings, O Unique One, upon the obedient one (*al-muṭīʿ*), [who] retreated in the cave to worship the One God.

صَلِّ وَسَلِّم وَبَارِك يَا **صَمَد** عَلَى صَاحِبِ العِزَّةِ الْمُبَشِّرِ بِفَضْلِ: قُلْ هُوَ اللهُ أَحَد.

Send prayers, peace, and blessings, O Eternal, upon the possessor of dignity (*ṣāḥib al-ʿizz*), [who] announced glad tidings of the merits of "qul huwa Allāhu aḥad" (Say, He is One God).

صَلِّ وَسَلِّم وَبَارِك يَا **قَادِر** عَلَى الصَّادِقِ الْمُسْتَعِيْذِ بِكَ مِنْ كُلِّ سَاحِر.

Send prayers, peace, and blessings, O All-Powerful, upon the truthful one (*al-ṣādiq*), [who] sought refuge in You from every sorcerer.

صَلِّ وَسَلِّم وَبَارِك يَا **مُقْتَدِر** عَلَى المُصْطَفى حَامِل الكَلّ الَّذِي لَا يَنْتَهِر.

Send prayers, peace, and blessings, O Determiner of All, upon the chosen one (*al-muṣṭafā*), the carrier of the weary, who shows no harshness.

صَلِّ وَسَلِّم وَبَارِك يَا **مُقَدِّم** عَلَى المُجْتَبى سَيِّد المُرْسَلِيْن وَ لَهُ نُعَظِّم.

Send prayers, peace, and blessings, O Promoter, upon the distinguished one (*al-mujtabā*), the master of the messengers and [those] we exalt.

صَلِّ وَسَلِّم وَبَارِك يَا **مُؤَخِّر** عَلَى الكَافِي المُقَدَّمِ وَ غَيْرُهُ مُتَأَخِّر.

Send prayers, peace, and blessings, O Postponer, upon the one who suffices (*al-kāfī*), the forerunner while others are left behind.

صَلِّ وَسَلِّم وَبَارِك يَا **أَوَّل** عَلَى المُقَدَّس الَّذِي عَلَى حُبِّهِ الْمُعَوَّل.

Send prayers, peace, and blessings, O First, upon the holy one (*al-muqaddas*), whose love we depend upon.

صَلِّ وَسَلِّم وَبَارِك يَا **آخِر** عَلَى الشَّهِيْدِ الشَّاهِدِ وَلِلرُّسُلِ آخِر.

Send prayers, peace, and blessings, O Last, upon the testifying witness (*al-shahīd*) and the last of the messengers.

صَلِّ وَسَلِّم وَبَارِك يَا **ظَاهِر** عَلَى السِّرَاج الَّذِي وَجْهُهُ بِالنُّورِ بَاهِر.

Send prayers, peace, and blessings, O Manifest One, upon the source of light (*al-sirāj*), whose face glows with luminosity.

صَلِّ وَسَلِّم وَبَارِك يَا **بَاطِن** عَلَى النَّجْمِ الثَّاقِبِ الَّذِي خَشِيَ رَبَّهُ بِالظَّاهِرِ وَالبَاطِن.

Send prayers, peace, and blessings, O Hidden One, upon the piercing star (*al-najm al-thāqib*), who feared his Lord both publicly and privately.

صَلِّ وَسَلِّم وَبَارِك يَا **وَالِي** عَلَى أَبِي الطَّاهِرِ مُحَمَّد الحَبِيْبِ الغَالِي.

Send prayers, peace, and blessings, O Ruler, upon Abū l-Ṭāhir, Muḥammad, the valuable beloved one.

صَلِّ وَسَلِّم وَبَارِك يَا **مُتَعَالِي** عَلَى مِفْتَاح الجَنَّةِ صَاحِبِ الْمَقَامِ الْمَحْمُودِ العَالِي.

Send prayers, peace, and blessings, O Exalted, upon the key to paradise (*miftāḥ al-janna*), possessor of the exalted praiseworthy rank.

صَلِّ وَسَلِّم وَبَارِك يَا **بَرّ** عَلَى المَخْصُوص بِالعِزِّ مَنْ يَدِيْنُ لَهُ كُلُّ عَبْدٍ وَحُرّ.

Send prayers, peace, and blessings, O Absolute Doer of Good, upon the one distinguished with dignity (*al-makhṣūṣ bi-l-ʿizz*), to whom every free and shackled person is indebted.

صَلِّ وَسَلِّم وَبَارِك يَا **تَوَّاب** عَلَى المُجَابِ الَّذِي رَآكَ وَسَمِعَ مِنْكَ لَذِيْذَ الخِطَاب.

Send prayers, peace, and blessings, O Accepter of Repentance, upon the one whose call is answered (*al-mujāb*), who saw You and heard from You delightful speech.

صَلِّ وَسَلِّم وَبَارِك يَا **مُنْتَقِم** عَلَى المُنْتَقى الْمَنْصُورِ بِالصَّبَا وَالرُّعْبُ مَعَهُ مُنْسَجِم.

Send prayers, peace, and blessings, O Avenger, upon the selected one (*al-muntaqā*), [who was] granted victory by the wind along with the fear [thrown into the hearts of enemies].

صَلِّ وَسَلِّم وَبَارِك يَا **عَفُوّ** عَلَى سَيِّدٍ شِيْمَتُهُ التَّسَامُحُ وَالعَفْو.

Send prayers, peace, and blessings, O Effacer of Sin, upon the master (*sayyid*), whose character was clemency and forgiveness.

صَلِّ وَسَلِّم وَبَارِك يَا **رَؤُوْف** عَلَى الْمَعْلُومِ الَّذِي هُوَ بِالْحِكْمَةِ وَالرَّأْفَةِ مَوْصُوف.

Send prayers, peace, and blessings, O Kind One, upon the known one (*al-maʿlūm*), who is described with wisdom and kindness.

صَلِّ وَسَلِّم وَبَارِك يَا **مَالِكَ الْمُلْك** عَلَى نَبِي الرَّحْمَة الْمُحَذِّرِ أُمَّتَهُ مِنَ الرِّيَاءِ وَالشِّرْك.

Send prayers, peace, and blessings, O King of Absolute Sovereignty, upon the Prophet of mercy (*nabī l-raḥma*), who warned his people to abstain from vanity and polytheism.

صَلِّ وَسَلِّم وَبَارِك يَا **ذَاالْجَلَالِ وَالإِكْرَام** عَلَى مُطَهَّرِ الْجِنَانِ مَنْ اصْطَفَاهُ لَنَا ذُو الطَّوْلِ وَالإِنْعَام.

Send prayers, peace, and blessings, O Lord of Majesty and Honor, upon the one of a purified heart (*muṭahhar al-jinān*), chosen for us by the Possessor of Might and Favor.

صَلِّ وَسَلِّم وَبَارِك يَا **مُقْسِط** عَلَى ذِي الْقُوَّةِ قَاهِرِ الأَحْزَابِ وَلِكَيْدِهِم مُحْبط.

Send prayers, peace, and blessings, O Equitable, upon the strong one (*dhī l-quwwa*), [who] defeated the confederates and unraveled their plot.

صَلِّ وَسَلِّم وَبَارِك يَا **جَامِع** عَلَى عَلَم الهُدَى الْمُنَوِّرِ بُيُوتَكَ وَالْمَجَامِع.

Send prayers, peace, and blessings, O Gatherer, upon the symbol of guidance (*ʿalam al-hudā*), the illuminator of homes and gatherings.

صَلِّ وَسَلِّم وَبَارِك يَا **غَنِيّ** عَلَى كَرِيْم كَفُّهُ بِالخَيْرَاتِ سَخِيّ.

Send prayers, peace, and blessings, O Self-Sufficient, upon a generous one (*karīm*), whose hand was extended in giving goodness.

صَلِّ وَسَلِّم وَبَارِك يَا **مُغْنِي** عَلَى المُزَّمِّلِ بَحْرِ جُوْدِكَ الطَّاهِرِ المُغْنِي.

Send prayers, peace, and blessings, O Enricher, upon the wrapped one (*al-muzammil*), the ocean of Your generosity, the purified and giving one [i.e., the Prophet ﷺ].

صَلِّ وَسَلِّم وَبَارِك يَا **مَانِع** عَلَى نَبِي التَّوْبَةِ وَحَصِّنَّا بِحِصْنِهِ المَانِعِ.

Send prayers, peace, and blessings, O Preventer, upon the Prophet of repentance (*nabī l-tawba*) and safeguard us with his protective fortress.

صَلِّ وَسَلِّم وَبَارِك يَا **ضَارّ** عَلَى عِزِّ العَرَبِ نَاصِرِ الحَقِّ وَلِلأَعْدَاءِ ضَارّ.

Send prayers, peace, and blessings, O Distresser, upon the pride of the Arabs (*ʿizz al-ʿarab*), [who] brings victory to the truth and distress to the enemy.

صَلِّ وَسَلِّم وَبَارِك يَا **نَافِع** عَلَى صَاحِبِ الخَاتَم مَنْ حَلَا الأُجَاجُ بِرِيْقِهِ النَّافِعِ.

Send prayers, peace, and blessings, O Benefactor, upon the possessor of the Seal (*ṣāḥib al-khatam*), who sweetened the bitter with his healing saliva.

صَلِّ وَسَلِّم وَبَارِك يَا **نُوْر** عَلَى نُوْرٍ مَنْ لَا ظِلَّ لَهُ هُوَ مَنْبَعُ النُّوْر.

Send prayers, peace, and blessings, O Light, upon a light (*nūr*), which has no shadow and is the source of light.

صَلِّ وَسَلِّم وَبَارِك يَا **هَادِي** عَلَى صَحِيْحِ الإِسْلَام طَاهِرِ الأُمَّهَاتِ وَالأَجْدَاد.

Send prayers, peace, and blessings, O Guide, upon the one whose religion is sound (*ṣaḥīḥ al-Islām*), whose ancestors are pure.

صَلِّ وَسَلِّم وَبَارِك يَا **بَدِيع** عَلَى سَيِّدِ الكَوْنَين بَاهِي الجَمَالِ وَالحُسْنِ البَدِيْع.

Send prayers, peace, and blessings, O Absolute Cause, upon the master of the two worlds (*sayyid al-kawnayn*), who glows with beauty and exceptional brilliance.

صَلِّ وَسَلِّم وَبَارِك يَا **بَاقِي** عَلَى خَطِيْبِ الأُمَم مَا دَامَ البَاقِي.

Send prayers, peace, and blessings, O Everlasting, upon the speaker of the nations (*khaṭīb al-umam*), as long as eternity.

صَلِّ وَسَلِّم وَبَارِك يَا **وَارِث** عَلَى حَاشِرِ خَاتَمِ النَّبِيِّيْنَ وَ لِلْكِتَابِ وَارِث.

Send prayers, peace, and blessings, O Inheritor, upon the one who will be resurrected (*ḥāshir*), the seal of the prophets and the inheritor of the book.

صَلِّ وَسَلِّم وَبَارِك يَا **رَشِيد** عَلَى الْمَأْمُوْن الْهَادِي إِلَى الأَمْرِ الرَّشِيْد.

Send prayers, peace, and blessings, O Guide to the Right Path, upon the trustworthy (*al-maʾmūn*) guide to the sound path.

صَلِّ وَسَلِّم وَبَارِك يَا **صَبُور** عَلَى الْمَشْهُودِ الْمُبَلِّغ لِرِسَالَتَكَ الصَّبُور.

Send prayers, peace, and blessings, O Patient, upon the one who is testified (*al-mashhūd*) to, the conveyer of Your message and the endurer [of hardships].

صَلِّ وَسَلِّم وَبَارِك يَا **رَبَّ العَالَمِيْن** عَلَى مُحَمَّدٍ وَآلِهِ وَصَحْبِهِ أَجْمَعِيْن.

Send prayers, peace, and blessings, O Lord of the Worlds, upon Muḥammad, his family, and the entirety of his Companions.

The Muḥammadan Ode
(*al-Qaṣīdat al-Muḥammadiyya*)

القَصِيْدَة المُحَمَّدِيَّة

مُحَمَّدٌ أَشْرَفُ الأَعْرَابِ وَالعَجَمِ   مُحَمَّدٌ خَيْرُ مَنْ يَمْشِي عَلَى قَدَمِ
مُحَمَّدٌ بَاسِطُ الْمَعْرُوفِ جَامِعُهُ   مُحَمَّدٌ صَاحِبُ الإِحْسَانِ وَالكَرَمِ
مُحَمَّدٌ تَاجُ رُسْلِ اللهِ قَاطِبَةً   مُحَمَّدٌ صَادِقُ الأَقْوَالِ وَالكَلِمِ
مُحَمَّدٌ ثَابِتُ المِيْثَاقِ حَافِظُهُ   مُحَمَّدٌ طَيِّبُ الأَخْلَاقِ وَالشِّيَمِ
مُحَمَّدٌ جُبِلَت بِالنُّورِ طِيْنَتُهُ   مُحَمَّدٌ لَمْ يَزَلْ نُوْرًا مِنَ القِدَمِ
مُحَمَّدٌ حَاكِمٌ بِالعَدْلِ ذُو شَرَفٍ   مُحَمَّدٌ مَعْدِنُ الإِنْعَامِ وَالحِكَمِ
مُحَمَّدٌ خَيْرُ خَلْقِ اللهِ مِنْ مُضَرٍ   مُحَمَّدٌ خَيْرُ رُسْلِ اللهِ كُلِّهِمِ
مُحَمَّدٌ دِينُهُ حَقٌّ نَدِيْنُ بِهِ   مُحَمَّدٌ مُشْرِقٌ حَقًّا عَلَى عَلَمِ
مُحَمَّدٌ ذِكْرُهُ رُوحٌ لِأَنْفُسِنَا   مُحَمَّدٌ شُكْرُهُ فَرْضٌ عَلَى الأُمَمِ
مُحَمدٌ رَحِمَ اللهُ العِبَادَ بِهِ   مُحَمَّدٌ سَبَبُ الإِنْشَآءِ مِنْ عَدَمِ
مُحَمَّدٌ زِيْنَةُ الدُّنْيَا وَبَهْجَتُهَا   مُحَمَّدٌ كَاشِفُ الغُمَّاتِ وَالظُّلَمِ
مُحَمَّدٌ سَيِّدٌ طَابَت مَنَاقِبُهُ   مُحَمَّدٌ صَاغَهُ الرَّحْمٰنُ بِالنِّعَمِ
مُحَمَّدٌ شَرَّفَ البَارِي مَرَاتِبَهُ   مُحَمَّدٌ خَصَّهُ الرَّحْمٰنُ بِالنِّعَمِ
مُحَمَّدٌ صَفْوَةُ البَارِي وَخِيْرَتُهُ   مُحَمَّدٌ طَاهِرٌ مِنْ سَائِرِ التُّهَمِ
مُحَمَّدٌ ضَاحِكٌ لِلْضَّيْفِ مُكْرِمُهُ   مُحَمَّدٌ جَارُهُ وَاللهِ لَمْ يُضَمِ
مُحَمَّدٌ طَابَت الدُّنْيَا ببِعْثَتِهِ   مُحَمَّدٌ جَاءَ بِالآيَاتِ وَالحِكَمِ
مُحَمَّدٌ ظَهَرَتْ فِيْنَا هِدَايَتُهُ   مُحَمَّدٌ هَدْيُهُ نُوْرٌ لِكُلِّ عَمِي
مُحَمدٌ عَمَّنَا إِحْسَانُ نِعْمَتِهِ   مُحَمَّدٌ سِرُّ عِلْمِ اللَّوْحِ وَالْقَلَمِ
مُحَمَّدٌ غَيْثُ مَعْرُوْفٍ يَدُوْمُ لَنَا   مُحَمَّدٌ مَدْحُهُ يَشْفِي مِنَ السَّقَمِ

مُحَمَّدٌ فَاقَ كُلَّ الأَنْبِيَا شَـرَفاً   مُحَمَّدٌ قَدْ أَحَلَّ الدِّينَ فِيْ حَـرَمِ

مُحَمَّدٌ قَائِمٌ لِلّٰهِ ذُوْ هِمَـمِ   مُحَمَّدٌ كُلُّ إِحْسَانٍ إِلَيْهِ نُـمِي

مُحَمَّدٌ كُلُّ مَـا فِيْ الكَوْنِ مَظْهَرُهُ   مُحَمَّدٌ فِيْ البَرَايَا خَيْرُ مُـعْتَصِمِ

مُحَمَّدٌ لَمْ نَجِـدْ عَنْ حُبِّهِ بَدَلاً   مُحَمَّدٌ نَرْتَجِيْهِ عِنْدَ مُـضْطَرِمِ

مُحَمَّدٌ مَنْ رَجَـاهُ نَالَ غَايَتَهُ   مُحَمَّدٌ يُسْعِفُ الْمَلْهُوفَ عَنْ أَمَمِ

مُحَمَّدٌ نِعْمَةٌ كُبْرَى لَنَا شَمَـلَتْ   مُحَمَّدٌ مَنْشَأُ الخَيْرَاتِ وَالنِّعَـمِ

مُحَمَّدٌ وَاصَلَ الدُّنْيَا بِأَنْـعُمِهِ   مُحَمَّدٌ قَدْ تَسَامَى كُلَّ ذِي كَـرَمِ

مُحَمَّدٌ هَدْيُهُ فُزْنَا بِغَـايَتِهِ   مُحَمَّدٌ قَدْ وَافَى لِلّٰهِ مِنْ قِـدَمِ

مُحَمَّدٌ لَا نَرَى إِلَّا شَفَـاعَتَهُ   مُحَمَّدٌ خَيْرُ دَاعٍ عِنْدَ مُزْدَحَمِ

مُحَمَّدٌ يَوْمَ بَعْثِ النَّاسِ شَافِعُنَا   مُحَمَّدٌ خَاتَمٌ لِلرُّسْلِ كُلِّهِمِ

Muḥammad, the noblest of Arabs and non-Arabs.
  Muḥammad, the best of those who ever walked.

Muḥammad, the spreader of all goodness, who encompassed that goodness.
  Muḥammad, the possessor of excellence and generosity.

Muḥammad, crown of all God's messengers.
  Muḥammad, true in speech and words.

Muḥammad, always firm in keeping the pledge and protecting it.
  Muḥammad, of pure traits and qualities.

Muḥammad, his nature imprinted with light.
  Muḥammad, who remains a light from time immemorial.

Muḥammad, an arbitrator [who judges] with fairness and a possessor of honor.
  Muḥammad, a mine of bounties and wisdoms.

Muḥammad, the best of creation from Muḍar.
  Muḥammad, the best of all God's messengers.

Muḥammad, his religion is the truth, the religion we follow.
Muḥammad, truly more luminous than a mountain.

Muḥammad, mentioning and remembering him is a comfort to our souls.
Muḥammad, thanking him is incumbent on all nations.

Muḥammad, God showed mercy to His servants through him.
Muḥammad, the reason God brought existence out of nothingness.

Muḥammad, the adornment of the world and its delight.
Muḥammad, the remover of sorrows and darkness.

Muḥammad, a master whose qualities are virtuous.
Muḥammad, fashioned by the All-Merciful with bounties.

Muḥammad, the Creator gave honor to his ranks.
Muḥammad, the All-Merciful singled him out for his blessings.

Muḥammad, the elect of the Creator and His chosen one.
Muḥammad, free from all accusations.

Muḥammad, smiling and hospitable to his guests.
Muḥammad, by God his neighbor will never be wronged.

Muḥammad, the world became delightful with his being sent.
Muḥammad, he came with signs and wisdom.

Muḥammad, his guidance appeared among us.
Muḥammad, his guidance is a light to all who are blind.

Muḥammad, we are encompassed by the excellence of his bounty.
Muḥammad, secret of the Preserved Tablet and the Pen.

Muḥammad, a beneficial rain of goodness that lasts.
Muḥammad, his praise cures illnesses.

Muḥammad, he surpassed all the prophets in honor.
Muḥammad, he established religion in the Sacred Precinct.

Muḥammad, steadfast with God and possessing lofty aspirations.
Muḥammad, all excellence is ascribed to him.

Muḥammad, the object which everything is a manifestation of.
Muḥammad, he is the best refuge among all things created.

Muḥammad, we have not found any substitute for his love.
Muḥammad, we long for him in times of hardship.

Muḥammad, whoever hopes for him will attain his goal.
Muḥammad, he is the first to help the troubled one.

Muḥammad, a tremendous favor upon us, it is all-encompassing.
Muḥammad, the source of all good and blessings.

Muḥammad, he connected the world through his bounties.
Muḥammad, he surpassed all of those of nobility.

Muḥammad, his guidance has made us successful in our attaining his goal.
Muḥammad, he was loyal to God from earliest times.

Muḥammad, we see nothing other than his intercession.
Muḥammad, the best one to supplicate during the time of crowding.[14]

Muḥammad, our intercessor when humanity will be resurrected.
Muḥammad, the seal of all the messengers.

---

14 The day of crowding is the day all of humanity will be collected after the Resurrection. People will go to earlier prophets asking them to intercede on their behalf and each will say "myself, myself" (*nafsī, nafsī*) with the exception of Prophet Muḥammad, who will say: "my community, my community" (*ummatī, ummatī*).

Ode Sending Prayers upon the Prophet ﷺ

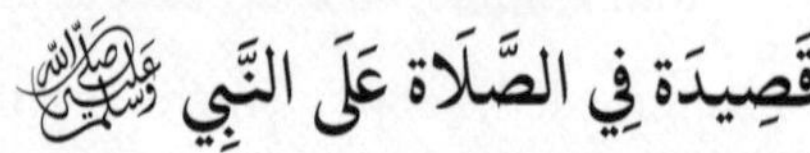

قَصِيدَة فِي الصَّلَاة عَلَى النَّبِي ﷺ

مَوْلَايَ صَلِّ وَسَلِّمْ دَائِماً أَبَداً ... عَلَى حَبِيْبِكَ خَيْرِ الخَلْقِ كُلِّهِمِ
يَارَبُّ يَا حَقُّ يَا رَحْمٰنُ يَا أَحَدُ ... يَا فَرْدُ يَامَنْ هُوَ الْمَوْصُوفُ بِالكَرَمِ
يَا أَكْرَمَ الكُرَمَا يَا أَلْطَفَ اللُّطَفَا ... الْطُفْ بِنَا وَاشْفِنَا يَا رَبِّ مِنْ سَقَمِ
وَامْنُنْ عَلَيْنَا بِقَصْدٍ أَنْتَ تَعْلَمُه ... وَلَيْسَ يَخْفَاكَ ما فِيْ القَلْبِ مِن وَخَمِ
إِنَّا اعْتَمَدْنَا عَلَيْكَ فِيْ حَوَائِجِنَا ... فَلَا تَكِلْنَا إِلَى عُرْبٍ وَلَا عَجَمِ
وَمِنْ عُلُومٍ لَدُنَّا هَبْ لَنَا مَدَداً ... وَافْتَحْ عَلَيْنَا بِمَا فِيْ الغَيْبِ مِنْ حِكَمِ
حَبِّبْ إِلَيْنَا حَبِيْباً ذِكْرُهُ فَرَحٌ ... نَفْدِيْهِ بِالنَّفْسِ وَالأَرْوَاحِ وَالرَّحِمِ
وَوَسِّعِ الرِّزْقَ يَأْتِيْنَا بِلَا نَصَبٍ ... رِزْقاً حَلَالاً كَثِيْراً غَيْرَ مُنْعَدِمِ
وَ بِالسَّعَادَةِ وَالتَّوْفِيْقِ تُسْعِدُنَا ... وَرَاعِنَا وَاكْفِنَا مِنْ كُلِّ ذِي نِقَمِ
بِبَرْدِ عَفوِكَ يَا مَوْلَايَ تَشْمَلُنَا ... وَالعَفْوُ أَوْسَعُ مِنْ تَقْصِيْرِ ذِيْ لَمَمِ
وَانْصُرْ إِلَهِي جُيُوْشَ الْمُسْلِمِيْنَ عَلَى ... أَعْدَائِهِمْ وَاكْفِهِمْ مِنْ كَيْدِ مَكْرِهِمِ
أَصْلِحْ وُلَاةَ أُمُورٍ وَاهْدِهِمْ سُبُلاً ... إِلَى الصَّلَاحِ وَإِخْلَاصاً لِشَعْبِهِمِ
وَاغْفِرْ لَنَا وَعِبَادِ اللهِ قَاطِبَةً ... وَوَالِدِيْنَا مَعَ الأَحْبَابِ كُلِّهِمِ
وَطَوِّلِ العُمْرَ فِيْ عِلْمٍ وَمَعْرِفَةٍ ... وَفِي سُرُوْرٍ وَفِي أُنْسٍ وَفِي نِعَمِ
يَارَبِّ عَبْدُكَ قَدْ ضَاقَتْ مَذَاهِبُهُ ... أَفِضْ عَلَيْهِ بِفَيْضِ الجُوْدِ وَالكَرَمِ
مُدَّتْ إِلَيْكَ يَدٌ يَارَبِّ رَاجِيَةً ... نَيْلَ الْمَقَاصِدِ فِي عِزٍّ وَفِي شَمَمِ
حَاشَا تَرُدَّنَّهَا يَا رَبِّ خَائِبَةً ... وَفَيْضُ بَحْرِكَ مِدْرَارٌ لِكُلِّ ظَمِي
إِنْ كَانَ عَفْوُكَ لِلأَحْبَابِ يَا أَمَلِي ... فَمَنْ لَنَا نَحْنُ أَهْلَ الذَّنْبِ وَاللَّمَمِ
وَانْظُرْ إِلَيْنَا بِعَيْنِ الوُدِّ فِي سَعَةٍ ... مِنْ رَحْمَةٍ سَبَقَتْ مِنْ حِكْمَةِ الحَكَمِ
وَكَمْ لَدَيْنَا ذُنُوبٌ لَيْس يَعْلَمُهَا ... إِلَّاكَ يَا ذَا العَطَا يَا كَاشِفَ الأَزَمِ
يَارَبِّ هَيِّءْ لَنَا سِرَّ الوُصُوْلِ إِلَى ... رُؤْيَا الرَّسُوْلِ عَلَيْنَا دَائِماً أَدِمِ

بِجَاهِهِ رَبَّنَا أَكْرِمْ بِـــرُؤْيَتِهِ   فِي يَقْظَةٍ إِنَّهَا مِنْ أَجْـــزَلِ النِّعَمِ
وَاكْتُبْ لَنَا الفَوْزَ فِي الدُّنْيَا وَيَوْمَ غَدِ   تَحْتَ اللِّوَاءِ بِلَا هَــمٍّ وَلَا نَدَمِ
وَاشْمُلْ جَمِيْعَ الوَرَى بِالفَضْلِ مَغْفِرَةً   وَتَوِّجِ العُمْرَ بِالإِيمَـــانِ فِي الخِتَمِ
جِوَارَ خَيْرِ عِبَادِ اللهِ قَـــاطِبَةً   مُسْتَودَعِ الحُسْنِ وَالإِحْسَانِ وَالـقِيَمِ
صَلِّ عَلَيْهِ صَلَاةً لَا انْـــفِصَامَ لَهَا   مَعَ السَّلَامِ دَوَاماً غَيْرَ مُـــنْصَرِمِ
وَالآلِ وَالصَّحْبِ مَا غَنَتْ مُـطَوَّقَةٌ   وَمَا تَرَنَّمَ حَادِيْ الشَّوْقِ لِلْـــحَرَمِ
يَارَبِّ بِالْمُصْطَفَى وَآلِهِ الـــشُّرَفَا   امْنُنْ لَنَا بِالشِّفَا وَالجُوْدِ وَالـــكَرَمِ
وَجُدْ لَنَا بِالرِّضَا وَاغْفِرْ لَنَا مَا مَضَى   وَامْلَأْ جَمِيْعَ الفَضَا مِنْ نُوْرِكَ الـعَمِمِ
أَنْزِلْ لَنَا الغَيْثَ وَاحْيِ الأَرْضَ أَجْمَعَهَا   فَرِّجْ عَنِ الكُلِّ قَدْ ضَاقَتْ عَلَى الأُمَـمِ
يَارَبِّ وَارْضَ عَنْ الصِّدِّيْقِ صَاحِبِهِ   وَعَنْ أَبِي حَفْصٍ الفَارُوْقِ ذِيْ الكَـرَمِ
وَجَامِعٍ لِكِتَابِ اللهِ سَــيِّدِنَا   عُـثْمَـانَ ثُـمَّ عَلِيٍّ عَالِيَ الهِمَـمِ
وَالأَحْسَنَيْنِ وَأَهْـلِ البَيْتِ أَجْمَعِهِمْ   وَمَا أَتَى هَلْ أَتَى إِلَّا لِأَجْـــلِهِمِ
وَالتَّابِعِيْنَ مِنَ الأَقْطَـابِ وَالبُدَلَا   وَالصَّالِحِيْنَ وَمَنْ يَسْعَى لِنَهْـــجِهِمِ
وَالْطُـفْ بِعَبْدٍ أَتَى بِالذَّنْبِ مُعْتَرِفاً   شَدَّادٍ شَدَّ بِحَبْلِ اللهِ مُـــعْتَصِمِ

My Lord, send prayers, greetings, and blessings perpetually and continuously,
upon Your beloved; the best of all creation.

O Lord, O Truth, O Compassionate, O One,
O Single One, O He who is described with generosity!

O most generous of the generous, O most kind of the kind;
show us kindness and cure us of ailments.

And grant us the [favors] which we seek and are known to You,
[even though] the sins that are in the hearts are not hidden from You.

We have relied upon You in our needs,
so leave us not [at the mercy of] any individual.

And grant us expanse in our worldly knowledge,
and grant us wisdom in the [matters of] the unseen.

Make dear to us the beloved whose remembrance is a joy,
[for whom] we would give our breaths, souls, and kin.

Grant us abundant provision without hardship,
provision that is lawful, plentiful, and not diminished.

Grant us joy in felicity and success,
and watch over us and protect us from every misfortune.

Envelope us in the coolness of Your forgiveness,
and Your forgiveness is vaster than the entirety of our shortcomings.

Grant victory to the armies of the Muslims,
against their enemies and protect them against the schemes of their plots.

Rectify those who are entrusted with governance and grant them the path,
of integrity and faithfulness to their people.

Forgive us and all of the servants of God,
and our parents along with all of our dear ones.

And lengthen our lives while we are [in a state of] knowledge and understanding,
and in happiness, friendship, and bounty.

O God, Your servant has become limited in his solutions,
bring down upon him the rains of abundance and generosity.

Hands are extended to You in hopefulness,
of attaining goals in a state of dignity and honor.

Do not turn them back empty [handed],
and Your ocean flows abundantly to each thirsty person.

If Your forgiveness was only for Your beloved ones, O One I put my hopes in;
then to whom do we sinful and blameworthy souls have [to turn]?

And look upon us with the eye of affection in that hour,
in which compassion takes precedence over the ruling of judgment.

How many sins do we have that are unknown to anyone,
except You, O Giver and Remover of Calamity.

O God enable us to obtain the secret of seeing
the Messenger always, perpetually.

By his stature, grant us the vision of him,
during wakefulness, for it is the best of blessings.

Write for us success in the world and tomorrow [afterlife],
under the flag [of Islam], without anxiety or regeret.

Encompass everyone with the favor of forgiveness,
and crown our lives with faith at their end.

Beside the unexceptionally best servant of God,
the source of excellence, perfection, and principles.

Send prayers upon him perpetually,
with greetings always and without diminishing.

And upon his family and Companions as long as the dove sings,
and as long as longing hearts venture to the Holy House resonate with song.

O God, by [the stature of] the Chosen One and his noble family,
bestow upon us healing, bounties, and favor.

And grant us Your pleasure with us and forgive us for what has passed;.
envelope all of the universe with Your comprehensive light.

Bring down the rain and bring life to the entirety of the earth
and resolve every [matter] that has troubled the nations.

O God, be pleased with his Companion Ṣiddīq (Abū Bakr)
and the noble Abū Hafṣa l-Fārūq (ʿUmar b. al-Khaṭṭāb).

And the gatherer of the Book of God,
our master ʿUthmān and then ʿAlī, whose aspirations were high.

And Ḥasan and Ḥusayn and all of the people of the Prophet's household.
Has not what has come, come except for their sake?

And the Followers (*tābiʿīn*), poles of the righteous, and upright people,
and the people of piety and those who follow their way.

And show kindness to Your sinful servant who has come acknowledging his sins,
holding fast, desperately, to the rope of God.

Closing Supplication in Gatherings of Prayers upon the Prophet ﷺ

دُعاء خَتم الصَّلاة عَلَى النَّبِي صَلَّى الله عَلَيهِ وَسَلم

اللَّهُمَّ اشْرَحْ بِالصَّلَاةِ عَلَيْهِ صُدُوْرَنَا، وَيَسِّرْ بِهَا أُمُوْرَنا، وَفَرِّجْ بِهَا هُمُومَنَا، وَاكْشِفْ بِهَا غُمُوْمَنَا، وَاغْفِرْ بِهَا ذُنُوْبَنَا، وَاقْضِ بِهَا دُيُونَنَا، وَأَصْلِحْ بِهَا أَحْوَالَنَا، وَبَلِّغْ بِهَا آمَالَنَا، وَتَقَبَّلْ بِهَا تَوْبَتَنَا، وَاغْسِلْ بِهَا حَوْبَتَنَا، وَانْصُرْ بِهَا حُجَّتَنَا، وَطَهِّرْ بِهَا أَلْسِنَتَنَا، وَآنِسْ بِهَا وَحْشَتَنَا، وَارْحَمْ بِهَا غُرْبَتَنَا، وَاجْعَلْهَا نُوْراً بَيْنَ أَيْدِينَا وَمِنْ خَلْفِنَا، وَعَنْ أَيْمَانِنَا، وَعَنْ شَمَائِلِنَا، وَمِنْ فَوْقِنَا وَمِنْ تَحْتِنَا، وَفِي حَيَاتِنَا وَمَوْتِنَا،

وَفِي قُبُوْرِنَا وَحَشْرِنَا وَنَشْرِنَا، وَظِلاًّ يَوْمَ الْقِيَامَةِ عَلَى رُؤُوْسِنَا، وَثَقِّلْ بِهَا مَوَازِيْنَ حَسَنَاتِنَا، وَأَدِمْ بَرَكَاتِهَا عَلَيْنَا، حَتَّى نَلْقَى نَبِيَّنَا وَسَيِّدَنَا مُحَمَّداً صَلَّى اللهُ عَلَيْهِ وَعَلَى آلِهِ وَسَلَّم، وَنَحْنُ آمِنُوْنَ مُطْمَئِنُّوْنَ، فَرِحُوْنَ مُسْتَبْشِرُوْنَ، وَلَا تُفَرِّقْ بَيْنَنَا وَبَيْنَهُ حَتَّى تُدْخِلَنَا مَدْخَلَهُ، وَتُؤْوِيَنَا إِلَى جِوَارِهِ الْكَرِيْمِ مَعَ الَّذِيْنَ أَنْعَمْتَ عَلَيْهِم مِنَ النَّبِيِّيْنَ وَالصِّدِّيْقِيْنَ وَالشُّهَدَاءِ وَالصَّالِحِيْنَ وَحَسُنَ أُوْلَئِكَ رَفِيْقاً.

Allāhumma ishraḥ bi-ṣalāti ʿalayhi ṣudūranā, wa-yassir bihā umūranā, wa-farrij bihā humūmanā, wa-kshif bihā ghumūmana, wa-ghfir bihā dhunūbanā, wa-qḍi bihā duyūnanā, wa-ṣliḥ bihā aḥwālanā, wa-balligh bihā āmālanā, wa-taqabbal bihā tawbatanā, wa-ghsil bihā ḥawbatanā, wa-nṣur bihā ḥujjatanā, wa-ṭahhir bihā alsinatanā, wa-ānis bihā waḥshatanā, wa-rḥam bihā ghurbatanā, wa-jʿalhā nūran bayna aydīnā, wa-min khalfinā, wa-ʿan aymāninā, wa-ʿan shamāʾilinā, wa-min fawqinā wa-min taḥtinā, wa-fī ḥayātinā wa-mawtinā, wa-fī qubūrinā wa-ḥashrinā wa-nashrinā, wa-ẓillan yawma al-qiyāmati ʿalā ruʾūsinā, wa-thaqqil bihā mawāzīna ḥasanātinā, wa-adim barakātihā ʿalaynā, ḥattā nalqā nabiyyanā wa-sayyidanā Muḥammadan ṣalla Allāhu ʿalayhi wa-sallam, wa-naḥnu āminūna muṭmaʾinnūna fariḥūna mustabshirūna, wa-lā tufarriq baynanā wa-baynahu ḥattā tudkhilanā madkhalahu, wa-tuʾwiyanā ilā jiwārihi al-karīmi maʿa alladhīna anʿamta ʿalayhim min al-nabiyyīna wa-l-ṣiddīqīna wa-shuhadāʾi wa-l-ṣāliḥīna wa-ḥasuna ulaʾika rafīqan.

O God, expand our hearts, facilitate our affairs, relieve our anxieties, and remove the darkness covering our [hearts] through our prayers upon him [the Prophet ﷺ]. [O God,] forgive our sins through them, repay our debts through them, rectify our states through them, enable us to attain our aspirations through them. [O God,] accept our repentance, cleanse us of our sins, grant us victory, purify our tongues, remove our sadness, and have mercy on our loneliness [through our prayers upon the Prophet ﷺ]. Make [our prayers upon him] a light within us, [a light] from behind us, [a light] from our right, from our left, from above us, and from below us. [Make them a light] after our death and during our lifetimes. [Make them a light] in our graves, when we are collected, and when we are dispersed. [O God, make our prayers upon him] a shade over our heads on the Day of Resurrection. Increase through them the weight of our good deeds. Bestow their blessings upon us until we meet our Prophet and master, Muḥammad, peace and blessing be upon him and his family, while we are secure, content, felicitous, and joyful. Do not separate us [from our Prophet ﷺ] until we are admitted into the same entrance as him and You have granted us his noble company alongside those whom You have blessed from among the prophets, upright people, martyrs, and people of righteousness. Indeed, they are the best of company.

اللَّهُمَّ إِنَّا آمَنَّا بِهِ صَلَّى اللهُ عَلَيْهِ وَسَلَّم وَلَمْ نَرَهُ، فَمَتِّعْنَا اللَّهُمَّ فِي الدَّارَيْنِ بِرُؤْيَتِهِ، وَثَبِّتْ قُلُوْبَنَا عَلَى مَحَبَّتِهِ وَاسْتَعْمِلْنَا عَلَى سُنَّتِهِ، وَتَوَفَّنَا عَلَى مِلَّتِهِ، وَاحْشُرْنَا فِي زُمْرَتِهِ النَّاجِيَةِ وَحِزْبِهِ الْمُفْلِحِيْنَ، وَانْفَعْنَا بِمَا انْطَوَتْ عَلَيْهِ قُلُوْبُنَا مِنْ مَحَبَّتِهِ ﷺ، يَوْمَ لَا جَدَّ وَلَا مَالَ وَلَا بَنِيْنَ، وَأَوْرِدْنَا حَوْضَهُ الأَصْفَى، وَاسْقِنَا بِكَأْسِهِ الأَوْفَى، وَيَسِّرْ لَنَا زِيَارَةَ حَرَمِكَ وَحَرَمِهِ مِنْ قَبْلِ أَنْ تُمِيْتَنَا، وَاجْعَلْ ذَلِكَ حُجَّةً وَقُرْبَةً لَنَا.

Allāhumma innā āmannā bihi ﷺ wa-lam narahu, fa-matti‘nā Allāhumma fī-l-dārayni bi-ru᾿yatihi, wa-thabbit qulūbanā ‘alā maḥabbatihi, wa-sta‘milnā ‘alā sunnatihi, wa-tawaffanā ‘alā millatihi, wa-ḥshurnā fī zumratihi al-nājiyati wa-ḥizbihi al-mufliḥīn. Wa-nfa‘nā bi-mā-nṭawat ‘alayhi qulūbunā min maḥabbatihi ﷺ yawma lā jadda wa-lā māla wa-lā banīn, wa-awridnā ḥawḍahu al-aṣfā, wa-sqinā bi-ka᾿sihi al-awfā, wa-yassir lanā ziyārata ḥaramika wa-ḥaramihi min qabli an tumītanā, wa-j'al dhālika ḥujjatan wa-qurbatan lanā.

O God, we have believed in him even though we have not seen him. So, O God, bestow on us the delight of seeing him in the two worlds.[15] Make our hearts firm in our love for him and use us to uphold his example. Make us die as a part of his nation and collect us [on the Day of Judgment] as a member of his saved community and successful group. Benefit us through the love that is in our hearts for him ﷺ on that day that ancestry, progeny, and wealth are of no avail. Grant us [the grace] to drink from his purest spring and let us drink from his most fulfilling cup. Enable us to visit Your Holy House (Kaʿba) and his Sacred Precinct before we die. Make this something that will be counted for us [on the Day of Judgment] and a source of increase in our closeness to You.

اللَّهُمَّ إِنَّا نَسْتَشْفِعُ بِهِ إِلَيْكَ إِذ هُوَ أَوْجَهُ الشُّفَعَاءِ إِلَيْكَ، وَنُقْسِمُ بِهِ عَلَيْكَ إِذ هُوَ أَعْظَمُ مَنْ أُقْسِمَ بِحَقِّهِ عَلَيْكَ، وَنَتَوَسَّلُ بِهِ إِلَيْكَ إِذ هُوَ أَقْرَبُ الوَسَائِلِ إِلَيْكَ، نَشْكُو إِلَيْكَ يَا رَبِّ قَسْوَةَ قُلُوبِنَا، وَكَثْرَةَ ذُنُوبِنَا، وَطُولَ آمَالِنَا، وَفَسَادَ أَعْمَالِنَا، وَتَكَاسُلَنَا عَنْ الطَّاعَاتِ، وَهُجُومَنَا عَلَى الْمُخَالَفَاتِ، فَنِعْمَ الْمُشْتَكَى إِلَيْهِ أَنْتَ. يَا رَبِّ بِكَ نَسْتَنْصِرُ عَلَى أَعْدَائِنَا وَأَنْفُسِنَا فَانْصُرْنَا، وَعَلَى فَضْلِكَ نَتَوَكَّلُ فِي صَلَاحِنَا فَلَا تَكِلْنَا إِلَى غَيْرِكَ يَا رَبَّنَا، وَإِلَى جَنَابِ رَسُولِكَ ﷺ نَنْتَسِبُ فَلَا تُبْعِدْنَا، وَبِبَابِكَ نَقِفُ فَلَا تَطْرُدْنَا، وَإِيَّاكَ نَسْأَلُ فَلَا تُخَيِّبْنَا.

Allāhumma innā nastashfi'u bihi ilayka idh huwa awjahu al-shufa'ā'i ilayka. Wa-nuqsimu bihi 'alayka idh huwa a'ẓamu man uqsima bi-ḥaqqihi 'alayka. Wa-natawassalu bihi ilayka

15 The two worlds are this world (e.g., one can see the Prophet in a dream) and the afterlife.

idh huwa aqrabu al-wasāʾili ilayka. Nashkū ilayka yā rabbi qaswata qulūbanā, wa-kathrata dhunūbanā, wa-ṭūla āmālinā, wa-fasāda aʿmālinā, wa-takāsulanā ʿan al-ṭāʿāti, wa-hujūmanā ʿalā al-mukhālafāti, fa-niʿma al-mushtaka ilayhi anta. Yā rabbi bika nastanṣiru ʿalā aʿdāʾinā wa-anfusinā fa-nṣurnā. Wa-ʿalā faḍlika natawakkalu fī ṣalāḥinā fa-lā takilnā ilā ghayrika yā rabbanā. Wa-ilā janābi raṣūlika ﷺ nantasibu fa-lā tubʿidnā, wa-bi-bābika naqifu fa-lā taṭrudnā, wa-iyyāka nasʾalu fa-lā tukhayyibnā.

O God, we seek his intercession on our behalf, for he is the most worthy person to intercede. We swear to You by [virtue of] his rank, as he is the greatest one by whose right is sworn to You. We seek to draw near [to You] through him, as he is the shortest path to You. O God, we complain to You of the hardness of our hearts, the abundance of our sins, our false hopes, the corruption of our deeds, our reluctance to do good works, and our eagerness for acts of disobedience, for You are the most generous One to bring our complaints to. O God, we ask You for victory over our enemies and our egos, so make us victorious. We rely upon Your favor for our well-being, do not allow us to rely on any other, our Lord. We attach ourselves to the Prophet's ﷺ side, do not distance us. We stand at Your doorstep, do not turn us away. We beg from none other than You, do not refuse us.

اللَّهُمَّ ارْحَمْ تَضَرُّعَنَا وَآمِنْ خَوْفَنَا، وَتَقَبَّلْ أَعْمَالَنَا وَأَصْلِحْ أَحْوَالَنَا، وَاجْعَلْ بِطَاعَتِكَ اشْتِغَالَنَا، وَإِلَى الخَيْرِ مَآلَنَا، وَحَقِّقْ بِالزِيَادَةِ آمَالَنَا، وَاخْتُمْ بِالسَّعَادَةِ آجَالَنَا. هَذَا ذُلُّنَا ظَاهِرٌ بَيْنَ يَدَيْكَ، وَحَالُنَا لَا يَخْفَى عَلَيْكَ، أَمَرْتَنَا فَتَرَكْنَا، وَنَهَيْتَنَا فَارْتَكَبْنَا، وَلَا يَسَعُنَا إِلَّا عَفْوُكَ فَاعْفُ عَنَّا يَا خَيْرَ مَأْمُولٍ وَأَكْرَمَ مَسْؤُوْلٍ، إِنَّكَ عَفُوٌّ رَؤُوْفٌ رَحِيمٌ يَا أَرْحَمَ الرَّاحِمِيْنَ، وَصَلَّى اللهُ عَلَى سَيِّدِنَا مُحَمَّدٍ وَعَلَى آلِهِ وَصَحْبِهِ وَسَلَّمَ

تَسْلِيماً. وَالحَمْدُ لله رَبِّ العَالَمِيْنَ، وَهُوَ حَسْبُنَا وَنِعْمَ الوَكِيْلُ، وَلَا حَوْلَ وَلَا قُوَّةَ إِلَّا بِاللهِ العَلِيِّ العَظِيْمِ.

Allāhumma irḥam taḍarru'anā wa-āmin khawfanā, wa-taqabbal a'mālanā wa-aṣliḥ aḥwālanā, wa-j'al bi-ṭā'atika ishtighālanā, wa-ilā al-khayri ma'ālanā, wa-ḥaqqiq bi-l-ziyādati āmālanā, wa-khtum bi-l-sa'ādati ājālanā. Hadha dhullunā ẓāhirun bayna yadayka, wa-ḥālunā lā yakhfā 'alayka. Amartanā fa-taraknā, wa-nahaytanā fa-rtakabnā. Wa-lā yasa'unā illa 'afwuka fa-'fu 'annā yā khayra ma'mūlin wa-akrama mas'ūlin. Innaka 'afuwwun ra'ūfun raḥīmun yā arḥama al-rāḥimīn, wa-ṣalla Allāhu 'alā sayyidinā Muḥammadin wa-'alā ālihi wa-ṣaḥbihi wa-sallama taslīman. Wa-l-ḥamduli-llāhi rabbi al-'ālamīn, wa-huwa ḥasbunā wa-ni'ma al-wakīlu, wa-lā ḥawla wa-lā quwwata illā bi-llahi l-'aliyyi l-'aẓīm.

O God, have mercy on our weakness and calm our anxieties. Accept our works, rectify our affairs, and preoccupy us with obedience to You. Make us prefer goodness. Grant us above and beyond what we hope for and make our end a fortunate one. This is our humiliation manifested in front of You and our wretched state is not concealed from You. You have commanded us and we have strayed. You forbade us and we disobeyed. We have no refuge other than Your forgiveness! So, forgive us, O best fulfiller of hopes, and the most generous of all those who are called upon. And send prayers, peace, and blessing upon the Prophet Muḥammad, his family, and [the entirety] of his Companions. Thanks be to God, the Lord of the worlds. He is sufficient for us and He is the best Protector. There is no power or strength except through God the Majestic and Exalted.

3

Remembrance Through the Noble Qurʾān

Gatherings to Recite and Complete the Entire Qurʾān

Gatherings of Qurʾānic study or recitation often consist of the distribution of a *juzʾ*[1] to each of the individuals in the gathering, who proceed to read these sections either aloud or quietly to themselves. Once the group completes a reading of the entire Qurʾān once or more (after accumulating all of the different sections read by the individuals in the gathering), the following supplication is often read.

Abū ʿAmr al-Dānī's Supplication upon a Complete Reading of the Glorious Qurʾān

دُعاء خَتَم القُرْآن الكَرِيم لِأَبِي عَمْرو الدَّاني

صَدَقَ اللهُ الَّذِي لَا إِلَهَ إِلَّا هُوَ الرَّحْمٰنُ الرَّحِيْمُ الحَيُّ القَيُّوْمُ، الَّذِي لَا

1 A section of the Qurʾān after it is divided into 30 segments of approximately 20 pages each.

يَمُوْتُ، ذُوْ الجَلَالِ وَالإِكْرَامِ، وَالأَسْمَاءِ العِظَامِ، وَبَلَّغَتِ الرُّسُلُ الكِرَامُ رِسَالَاتِ رَبِّنَا عَلَيْهِمُ السَّلَام. اللَّهُمَّ انْفَعْنَا بِالْقُرآنِ العَظِيْمِ وَ بِالآيَاتِ وَالذِّكْرِ الحَكِيْمِ. اللَّهُمَّ اجْعَلِ القُرآنَ رَبِيْعَ قُلُوْبِنَا، وَجَلَاءَ أَحْزَانِنَا، وَذَهَابَ هُمُوْمِنَا وَغُمُوْمِنَا، وَسَائِقَنَا وَقَائِدَنَا إِلَى جَنَّاتِكَ جَنَّاتِ النَّعِيْمِ.

Ṣadaqa Allāhu alladhī lā ilāha illā huwa al-raḥmānu l-raḥīmu l-ḥayyu l-qayyūm, alladhī lā yamūtu dhū al-jalāli wa-l-ikrām, wa-l-asmāʾi al-ʿiẓām, wa-balaghati al-rusulu al-kirāmu risālāti rabbinā ʿalayhimu al-salām. Allāhumma anfaʿnā bi-l-qurʾān al-ʿaẓīm, wa-bi l-āyāti wa-l-dhikri l-ḥakīm. Allāhumma ijʿali l-qurʾāna rabīʿa qulūbanā, wa-jalāʾa aḥzāninā, wa-dhahāba humūminā, wa-ghumūminā, wa-sāʾiqanā wa-qāʾidanā ilā jannātika jannāti al-naʿīm.

True are the words of God, whom there is no god but He. [He is] the Compassionate, the Merciful, the Living, Self-Existing, who does not die, Possessor of Might and Majesty, and the great names, and He conveyed the message to the noble prophets ﷺ, the message of our Lord. O God, enable us to benefit from the majestic Qurʾān, and from the verses of the Qurʾān and the wise remembrance. O God, make the Qurʾān the spring rain of our hearts, the remover of our anxieties and our sadness, and [make it] our vehicle and guide to Your bountiful Paradise.

اللَّهُمَّ لَا تَجْعَلِ القُرآنَ بِنَا مَاحِلاً، وَلَا الصِّرَاطَ بِنَا زَائِلاً، وَلَا مُحَمَّداً ﷺ عَنَّا فِي القِيَامَةِ مُوَلِّياً. اللَّهُمَّ اجْعَلْنَا مِمَن يُحِلُّ حَلَالَهُ، وَيُحَرِّمُ حَرَامَهُ، وَيَرْعَاهُ حَقَّ رِعَايَتِهِ. اللَّهُمَّ أَنْتَ عَلَّمْتَنَاهُ قَبْلَ عِلْمِنَا بِنَفْعِهِ، وَمَنَنْتَ بِهِ عَلَيْنَا قَبْلَ عِلْمِنَا بِمَعْرِفَتِهِ. اللَّهُمَّ وَإِنَّ ذَلِكَ مِن فَضْلِكَ لُطْفاً بِنَا، وَرَحْمَةً لَنَا، وَامْتِنَاناً عَلَيْنَا مِن غَيْرِ حَوْلِنَا، وَلَا حِيْلَتِنَا، وَلَا قُوَّتِنَا.

Allāhumma lā taj'ali al-qur'āna binā māḥilan, wa-lā al-ṣirāṭa binā za'ilan, wa-lā Muḥammadan ﷺ 'annā fī l-qiyāmati muwalliyā. Allāhumma ij'alnā mimman yuḥillu ḥalālahu wa-yuḥarrimu ḥarāmahu wa-yar'āhu ḥaqqa ri'āyatihi. Allāhumma anta 'allamtanāhu qabla 'ilminā bi-naf'ihi, wa-mananta bihi 'alaynā qabla 'ilminā bi-ma'rifatihi. Allāhumma wa-inna dhālika min faḍlika luṭfan binā, wa-raḥmatan lanā wa-mtinānan 'alaynā min ghayri ḥawlinā, wa-lā ḥīlatinā, wa-lā quwwatinā.

O God, do not make the Qurʾān absolved of us, [do not let] us slip on the bridge in the afterlife, or [let] Muḥammad ﷺ turn away from us on the Day of Judgment. O God, make us among those who establish what it permits, who forbid that which it forbids, and who follow its [injunctions] in the best way. O God, You have taught us its benefit before [we had] knowledge of it and You bestowed upon us our acquaintance with it before our knowledge of it. O God, this is from Your favor, kindness, and mercy toward us. And [this is] from Your grace upon us and not from our own efforts, ability, or power.

اللَّهُمَّ فَهَبْ لَنَا حُسْنَ تِلَاوَتِه، وَحِفْظَ آيَاتِهِ، وَإِيْمَاناً بِمُتَشَابِهِهِ، وَعَمَلاً بِمُحْكَمِهِ، وَعِبْرَةً فِي تَرْدِيْدِهِ، وَبَصِيْرَةً فِي تَرْجِيْعِهِ، وَيَقِيْناً ثَابِتاً عِنْدَ اسْتِفْهَامِهِ. اللَّهُمَّ اجْعَلْهُ لَنَا حِصْناً حَصِيْناً مِنْ عَذَابِكَ، وَحِرْزاً مَانِعاً مِنْ سَخَطِكَ، وَدَلِيْلاً عَلَى طَاعَتِكَ، وَنُوْراً يَوْمَ لِقَائِكَ نَسْتَضِيءُ بِهِ فِي خَلْقِكَ، وَنَجُوْزُ بِهِ عَلَى صِرَاطِكَ، وَنَهْتَدِي بِهِ إِلَى جَنَّتِكَ. اللَّهُمَّ إِنَّا نَعُوْذُ بِكَ مِنْ الشِّقْوَةِ فِي حَمْلِهِ، وَالعَمَى فِي عِلْمِهِ، وَالتَّقْصِيْرِ دُوْنَ حَقِّهِ. اللَّهُمَّ ارْزُقْنَا حَلَاوَةً فِي تِلَاوَتِهِ، وَنَشَاطاً عَلَى قِرَاءَتِهِ، وَوَجَلاً فِي تَرْدِيْدِهِ.

Allāhumma fa-hab lanā ḥusna tilāwatihi, wa-ḥifẓa āyātihi, wa-īmānan bi-mutashābihihi, wa-'amalan bi-muḥkamihi, wa-'ibratan fī tardīdihi, wa-baṣīratan fī tarjī'ihi, wa-yaqīnan thābitan ʿinda istifhāmihi. Allāhumma ijʿalhu ḥiṣnan ḥaṣīnan min ʿadhābika, wa-ḥirzan mānīʿan min sakhaṭika, wa-dalīlan ʿalā ṭāʿatik, wa-nūran yawma liqāʾika nastaḍīʾu bihi fī khalqika, wa-najūzu bihi ʿalā ṣirāṭika, wa-nahtadī bihi ilā jannatika. Allāhumma innā naʿūdhu bika min al-shiqwati fī ḥamlihi, wa-l-ʿamā fī ʿamalihi, wa-l-taqṣīri dūna ḥaqqihi. Allāhumma urzuqnā ḥalāwatan fī tilāwatihi, wa-nashāṭan ʿalā qirāʾatihi, wa-wajalan fī tardīdih.

O God, grant us the ability to recite it beautifully, retain its verses, have faith in its allegorical verses, practice its injunctions, acquire [new] lessons with its repetition, attain [new] insight with its review, and have firm belief in it upon understanding it. O God, make it a protecting fortress for us from Your punishment, an obstacle blocking Your wrath upon us, a guide to Your obedience, a light through which we are enlightened among Your creation, an assistant in crossing Your bridge, and a guide through which we are guided to Your Paradise. O God we seek refuge in You from becoming weary of reciting it, being blind to its wisdom, and being short in fulfilling its rights. O God, grant us sweetness in its recitation, keenness in its reading, and hearts that are moved by its repetition.

اللَّهُمَّ إِنَّا نَعُوْذُ بِكَ مِن تَخَلُّفِهِ فِي قُلُوبِنَا بِتَرْكِ تِلَاوَتِهِ بِأَلْسِنَتِنَا، وَتَوَسُّدِهِ عِنْدَ رِقَادِنَا، وَنَبْذِهِ وَرَاءَ ظُهُوْرِنَا، وَنَعُوْذُ بِكَ مِن قَسَاوَةِ قُلُوْبِنَا لِمَا بِهِ قَدْ وَعَظْتَنَا. اللَّهُمَّ انْفَعْنَا بِمَا صَرَّفْتَ فِيْهِ مِن الآيَاتِ، وَذَكِّرْنَا بِمَا ضَرَبْتَ فِيْهِ مِن الْمَثُلَاتِ، وَكَفِّر عَنَّا بِتِلَاوَتِهِ السَّيِّئَاتِ، وَضَاعِفْ لَنَا بِهِ الحَسَنَاتِ، وَلَقِّنَا بِهِ البُشْرَى عِنْدَ الْمَمَاتِ.

Allāhumma innā naʿūdhu bika min takhallufihi fī qulūbinā bi-tarki tilāwatihi bi-alsinatinā, wa-tawassudihi ʿinda riqādinā, wa-nabdhihi warāʾa ẓuhūrinā, wa-naʿūdhu bika min qasāwati qulūbinā limā bihi qad waʿaẓtanā. Allāhumma infaʿnā bimā ṣarrafta fīhi min al-āyāt, wa-dhakkirnā bi-mā ḍarabta fīhi min al-mathulāt, wa-kaffir ʿannā bi-tilāwatihi al-sayiʾāt, wa-ḍāʿif lanā bihi al-ḥasanāt, wa-laqqinā bihi al-bushrā ʿinda al-mamāt.

O God, we seek refuge in You, that its significance in our hearts not decline [because] we abandon its recitation on our tongues, let it not abandon us in the grave, or let us not forget the lessons You have taught us in it. And we seek refuge in You from the hardness of our hearts toward what you have instructed us in it. O God, benefit us through the verses You have included in it, remind us of the examples You have given in it, remove our sins through it, multiply our good deeds through it, and enable us to meet it with joy during our time of death.

اللَّهُمَّ إِنَّكَ جَعَلْتَهُ لَنَا بَرَكَةً فَزِدْنَا بِهِ مِنْ كُلِّ بَرَكَةٍ، اللَّهُمَّ إِنَّكَ جَعَلْتَهُ لَنَا نَجَاةً فَنَجِّنَا بِهِ مِنْ كُلِّ هَلَكَةٍ، وَجَعَلْتَهُ لَنَا عِصْمَةً فَاعْصِمْنَا بِهِ مِن كُلِّ شُبْهَةٍ وَكُلِّ بِدْعَةٍ أَوْ ضَلَالَةٍ أَوْ رِيَاءٍ. اللَّهُمَّ اجْعَلْهُ زَادَنَا إِلَى الْمَوْقِفِ، وَعِلْماً نَافِعاً نَشْكُرُ بِهِ نِعْمَاءَكَ، وَارْزُقْنَا بِهِ تَخَشُّعاً صَادِقاً نُسَبِّحُ بِهِ أَسْمَاءَكَ. اللَّهُمَّ إِنَّكَ اتَّخَذْتَهُ عَلَيْنَا حُجَّةً قَطَعْتَ بِهِ عُذْرَنَا، وَاصْطَنَعْتَ بِهِ نِعْمَةً عِنْدَنَا قَصُرَ عَنْهَا شُكْرُنَا.

Allāhumma innaka jaʿaltahu lanā barakatan, fa-zidnā bihi min kulli barakatin. Allāhumma innaka jaʿaltahu lanā najātan fa-najjinā bihi min kulli halakan. Wa-jaʿaltahu lanā ʿiṣmatan fa-ʿṣimnā bihi min kulli shubhin, wa-kulli bidʿatin, aw ḍalālatin, aw riyāʾin. Allāhumma ijʿalhu zādanā ilā al-mawqif, wa-ʿilman nāfiʿan nashkuru bihi niʿamāʾak, wa-arzuqnā bihi takhashshuʿan ṣādiqan nusabbiḥu bihi asmāʾak. Allāhumma innaka attakhadhtahu ʿalaynā ḥujjatan qaṭiʿta bihi ʿudhranā, wa-ṣṭanaʿta bihi niʿmatan ʿindanā qaṣura ʿanhā shukrunā.

O God, You have made it a blessing for us so increase us in every blessing through it. O God, You have made it a source of salvation for us, so save us, through it, from all forms of destruction. And You have made it a protection for us, so protect us, through it, from every doubtful matter, innovation, misguidance, and vanity. O God, make it our provision on the Day of Resurrection and a beneficial knowledge through which we thank You for Your bounties. And grant us through it a sincere God-fearing [heart] through which we praise Your names. O God, You have made it a proof for us, by which our excuses are suspended. And You have made it a blessing for us, for which our gratefulness for it falls short of its [supreme worth].

اللَّهُمَّ اجْعَلْهُ لَنَا شَافِعاً يَوْمَ اللِّقَاءِ، وَحَجِيْجاً يَوْمَ القَضَاءِ، وَنُوْراً يَوْمَ الظَّلْمَاءِ، يَوْمَ تُجْزَى كُلُّ نَفْسٍ بِمَا كَسَبَت، وَكُلُّ سَاعٍ بِمَا سَعَى، يَا رَبّ.. يَا رَبّ. اللَّهُمَّ لَا تُبْقِ لَنَا بِالقُرآنِ ذَنْباً إِلَا غَفَرْتَ، وَلَا دَيْناً إِلَا قَضَيْتَ، وَلَا مَأْسُوْراً إِلَا فَكَكْتَ، وَلَا غَازِياً إِلَّا غَنَّمْتَ، وَلَا غَائِباً إِلَّا رَدَدْتَ، وَلَا عَدُواً إِلَا كَفَيْتَ، وَلَا هَماً إِلَّا فَرَّجْتَ، وَلَا مَرِيْضاً إِلَّا شَفَيْتَ، وَلَا مَيِّتاً إِلَّا رَحِمْتَ، وَلَا شِدَّةً إِلَّا كَشَفْتَ، وَلَا مَعِيْشَةً إِلَّا وَسَّعْتَ، وَلَا بَرَكَةً إِلَا أَنْزَلْتَ، وَلَا سَعْراً إِلَّا أَرْخَصْتَ، وَلَا حَاجَةً مِنْ حَوَائِجِ الدُّنْيَا وَالآخِرَةِ لَكَ فِيْهَا رِضَى وَلَنَا فِيْهَا صَلَاحٌ إِلَّا أَعَنْتَ عَلَى قَضَائِهَا فِي يُسْرٍ مِنْكَ، وَعَافِيَةٍ يَا أَرْحَمَ الرَّاحِمِيْنَ.

Allāhumma ijʿalhu lanā shāfiʿan yawma al-liqāʾi, wa-ḥajījan yawma al-qaḍāʾi, wa-nūran yawma al-ẓalmāʾi, yawma tujzā kullu nafsin bi-mā kasabat, wa-kullu sāʿin bi-mā saʿā, yā rabb... yā rabb. Allāhumma lā tubqi lanā bi-l-qurʾāni dhanban illā ghafarta, wa-lā daynan illā qaḍayta, wa-lā maʾsūran illā fakkakta, wa-lā ghāziyan illā ghannamta, wa-lā ghāʾiban illā radadta, wa-lā ʿaduwwan illā kafayta, wa-lā hamman illā farrajta, wa-lā marīḍan illā shafayta, wa-lā mayyitan illā raḥimta, wa-lā shiddatan illā kashafta, wa-lā maʿīshatan illā wassaʿta, wa-lā barakatan illā anzalta, wa-saʿran illā arkhaṣta, wa-lā ḥājatan min ḥawāʾiji al-dunyā wa-l-ākhirati laka fīhā riḍā, wa-lanā fīhā ṣalāḥ illā aʿanta ʿalā qaḍāʾihā fī yusrin minka, wa-ʿāfiyatin yā arḥam al-rāḥimīn.

O God, make it an intercessor for us on the day we meet You, a light on a dark day in which each individual will be held to account for what they earned, and each person who has strived will receive what they strived [in this life] for. O Lord. O Lord! O God, do not leave for us our sins, except that You have forgiven us for it through the Qurʾān; a debt, except that you have fulfilled it; anyone fettered, except that You have freed him; any fighter for Your cause, except that You have granted him victory; anyone absent, except that You have returned him; any enemy, except that You have toppled him; any distress, except that You have relieved it; any ill person, except that You have cured him; any dead person, except that You have forgiven him; any hardship, except that You have resolved it; any earnings, except that You have made it sufficient; any blessing, except that You have granted it; any costly thing, except that you have made it affordable; and any need from any needs of the world and the hereafter that is for our benefit and pleases You, except that You have facilitated its fulfillment with ease and well-being, O most merciful of those who show mercy.

اللَّهُمَّ أَعِزَّنَا بِوِلَايَتِكَ، وَأَكْرِمْنَا بِكِفَايَتِكَ، وَجَمِّلْنَا بِبَرَكَاتِكَ وَزِيَادَتِكَ، وَامْنُنْ عَلَيْنَا بِعَفْوِكَ وَعَافِيَتِكَ وَأَيِّدْنَا بِحُسْنِ عِبَادَتِكَ. اللَّهُمَّ اجْعَلْنَا مِمَّنْ عَرَفَ نِعْمَتَكَ شُكْراً، وَأَقَامَ حُدُودَكَ احْتِسَاباً وَصَبْراً، وَلَا تَجْعَلْنَا مِنَ الَّذِيْنَ بَدَّلُوا نِعْمَتَكَ كُفْراً، وَاسْتَنْكَفُوا عَنْ عِبَادَتِكَ عُتُوّاً وَكِبْراً.

Allāhumma aʿizzanā bi-wilāyatika, wa-akrimnā bi-kifāyatika, wa-jammilnā bi-barakātika, wa-ziyādātika, wa-mnun ʿalaynā bi-'afwika wa-'āfiyatika, wa-ayyidnā bi-ḥusni 'ibādatika. Allāhumma ij'alnā mimman 'arafa ni'mataka shukran wa-aqāma ḥudūdaka iḥtisāban wa-ṣabran, wa-lā taj'alnā min alladhīna baddalū ni'mataka kufran, wa-stankafū 'an 'ibādatika 'utuwwan wa-kibran.

O God, honor us by making us Your select servants, bestow on us a state of sufficiency through You, ornament us with Your blessings and bounties, bestow on us Your forgiveness and well-being, and assist us to have excellence in worshipping You. O God, make us among those who know Your blessings and have gratitude. [Make us among those who] uphold Your commands with accountability and patience. Make us not from among those who deny Your blessings and abandon worshiping You out of obstinancy and arrogance.

اللّٰهُمَّ اجْعَلْنَا مِنْ أَهْلِ الْمَنَازِلِ الرَّفِيْعَةِ، وَثَبِّتْنَا عَلَى هَذِهِ الْمَقَامَاتِ الشَّرِيْفَةِ، وَاخْصُصْنَا مِنْهَا بِأَوْفَرِ الحَظِّ وَالنَّصِيْبِ، وَاجْعَلْ ذَلِكَ مَصْرُوفاً فِي رِضَاكَ فِي الدُّنْيَا، وَالثَّوَابِ فِي الآخِرَةِ يَا أَرْحَمَ الرَّاحِمِيْنَ. اللّٰهُمَّ اقْضِ عَنَّا دَيْنَكَ، وَدَيْنَ عِبَادِكَ، وَاغْفِرْ لَنَا مَا سَلَفَ مِنْ ذُنُوْبِنَا وَاحْفَظْنَا فِيْمَا بَقِيَ مِنْ أَعْمَارِنَا بِمَا تَحْفَظُ بِهِ عِبَادَكَ الصَّالِحِيْنَ. اللّٰهُمَّ وَمَنْ تَقَدَّمْنَا مِنْ أَسْلَافِنَا إِلَى القُبُوْرِ مِنَ الآبَاءِ وَالأُمَّهَاتِ، وَالإِخْوَةِ وَالأَخَوَاتِ وَجَمِيْعِ الأَهْلِ وَالقَرَابَاتِ، وَ إِخْوَانِنَا الَّذِيْنَ أَخْلَصُوا لَنَا الْمَحَبَّةَ فِيْكَ وَالْمَوَدَّاتِ، الَّذِيْنَ فَارَقُوا الأَحْبَابَ، وَسَكَنُوا التُّرَابَ، وَرَجَوْا بِتَوْحِيْدِكَ جَزِيْلَ الثَّوَابِ.

Allāhumma ij'alnā min ahli al-manāzili al-rafī'ati, wa-thabbitnā 'alā hādhihi al-maqāmāti al-sharīfati, wa-khṣuṣnā minhā bi-awfari al-ḥaẓẓi wa-l-naṣībi wa-j'al dhālika maṣrūfan fī riḍāka fī l-dunyā wa-l-thawābi fī l-ākhirati yā arḥama al-rāḥimīn. Allāhumma iqḍī 'annā daynaka wa-dayna 'ibādika, wa-ghfir lanā mā salafa min dhunūbinā, wa-ḥfaẓnā fī-mā baqā min aʿmārinā bi-mā taḥfaẓu bihi ʿibādaka al-ṣāliḥīn. Allāhumma wa-man taqaddamanā min aslāfinā ilā al-qubūri min al-ābāʾi wa-l-ummahāti wa-l-ikhwati wa-l-akhawāti, wa-jamīʿi al-ahli wa-l-qarābāti wa-ikhwāninā alladhīna akhlaṣū lanā al-maḥabbata fīka wa-l-mawaddāti alladhīna fāraqū al-aḥbāba, wa-sakanū al-turāba, wa-rajaw bi-tawḥīdika jazīl al-thawāb.

O God, make us of those of elevated rank. And make us firm in this lofty stature and grant us from it the best of shares and allocations. Make this a means of attaining Your pleasure with us in the world and reward in the hereafter, O most merciful of those who show mercy. O God, enable us to repay our debts to You and our debts to any of Your creation. Forgive our past sins and protect us in what remains of our lives, the way You protect Your righteous servants. O God, [grant the same] to those who preceded us to their graves from among our mothers and fathers, brothers and sisters, the entirety of our families and relatives, our brothers in the faith who love us sincerely for Your sake, as well as those dear to us who have left their loved ones, found their abode in the ground, and are hopeful by believing in Your oneness for the best of rewards.

اللَّهُمَّ وَأَهْلَ القُبُوْرِ مِنْ أَهْلِ مِلَّتِنَا كَافَّةً بَرِّدْ عَلَيْهِم مَضَاجِعَهُمْ، وافْسَحْ لَهُم فِي قُبُورِهِم، وَاجْعَلْ لَهُم فِي ثَوَابِنَا هَذَا أَوْفَرَ الحَظِّ وَالنَّصِيْبِ، اللَّهُمَّ وَ إِذَا صِرْنَا إِلَى مَا صَارُوا إِلَيْهِ فَكُنْ بِنَا رَؤُوْفاً رَحِيْماً يَا أَرْحَمَ الرَّاحِمِيْنَ.

Allāhumma wa-ahla al-qubūri min ahli millatinā kaffatan barrid ʿalayhim maḍājiʿahum, wa-fsaḥ lahum fī qubūrihim, wa-jʿal lahum fī thawābinā hadhā awfara al-ḥaẓẓi wa-l-naṣīb. Allāhumma wa-idhā ṣirnā ilā mā ṣārū ilayhi, fa-kun binā raʾūfan raḥīman yā arḥama al-rāḥimīn.

O God, make the resting place of all of those deceased Muslims cool and expand their graves for them. And grant them from a portion of our reward here the best of shares and allocations. O God, when what has happened to them also becomes our reality, then be gentle and merciful with us, O most merciful of those who show mercy!

اللَّهُمَّ ارْحَمْنَا بِرَحْمَتِكَ الوَاسِعَةِ وَارْحَمْ مَنْ قَرَأْنَا عَلَيْهِ، وَقَرَأَ عَلَيْنَا،
وَمَنْ تَعَلَّمْنَا مِنْهُ وَمَنْ تَعَلَّمَ مِنَّا، وَاجْعَل بَعْضَنَا عَلَى بَعْضٍ بَرَكَةً
وَرَحْمَةً يَا أَرْحَمَ الرَّاحِمِيْنَ. اللَّهُمَّ وَمَنْ سَأَلَنَا الدُّعَاءَ وَسَأَلْنَاهُ الدُّعَاءَ،
فَأَجِبْ دُعَاءَنَا فِيْهِ وَ دُعَاءَهُ فِيْنَا، وَاجْعَلِ السَّهْمَ اللَّهُمَّ بَيْنَنَا وَبَيْنَهُم
وَاحِداً، وَاقْضِ حَوَائِجَنَا وَحَوَائِجَهُمْ، وَحَوَائِجَ السَّائِلِيْنَ، رَبَّنَا لَا تُزِغْ
قُلُوبَنَا بَعْدَ إِذْ هَدَيْتَنَا وَهَبْ لَنَا مِن لَّدُنكَ رَحْمَةً إِنَّكَ أَنتَ ٱلْوَهَّابُ ﴿٨﴾
(سُورَةُ آلِ عِمْرَانَ)

Allāhumma irḥam bi-raḥmatika al-wāsiʿati wa-arḥam man qaraʾnā ʿalayhi wa-qaraʾa ʿalaynā, wa-man taʿallamnā minhu wa-man taʿallama minnā, wa-jʿal baʿḍanā ʿalā baʿḍin barakatan wa-raḥmatan yā arḥama al-rāḥimīn. Allāhumma wa-man saʾalanā al-duʿāʾa wa-saʾalnāhu al-duʿāʾ, fa-ajib duʿāʾanā fīhi wa-duʿāʾahu fīnā, wa-jʿal al-sahma Allāhumma baynanā wa-baynahum wāḥidan, wa-qḍi ḥawāʾijanā wa-ḥawāʾijahum wa-ḥawāʾij al-sāʾilīn. *Rabbanā lā tuzigh qulūbanā baʿda idh hadaytanā wa-hab lanā min ladunka raḥmatan innaka anta al-wahhābu.*

O God, have mercy upon us with Your expansive mercy and have mercy upon the one we have read [Qurʾān] for; what has been read for us, what we know of from it, and what we do not. Make us a source of blessings and mercy for others, O most merciful of those who show mercy. O God, of those who have asked us to pray for them and of those we have asked to pray for us, accept our prayers and their prayers for us. Unite our hearts with them, fulfill our needs and their needs, and [the needs] of those who beseech you. *Our Lord, let not our hearts deviate after You have guided us and grant us mercy from Yourself. Indeed, You are the Bestower [of bounties]*, [Āli ʿImrān, 3:8].

رَبَّنَا مَا خَلَقْتَ هَذَا بَاطِلاً سُبْحَانَكَ فَقِنَا عَذَابَ النَّارِ، رَبَّنَا إِنَّنَا سَمِعْنَا مُنَادِياً يُنَادِي لِلإِيْمَانِ أَنْ آمِنُوا بِرَبِّكُم فَآمَنَّا رَبَّنَا فَاغْفِرْ لَنَا ذُنُوبَنَا، وَكَفِّرْ عَنَّا سَيِّئَاتِنَا وَتَوَفَّنَا مَعَ الأَبْرَارِ، رَبَّنَا آمَنَّا بِمَا أَنْزَلْتَ، وَاتَّبَعْنَا الرَّسُوْلَ فَاكْتُبْنَا مَعَ الشَّاهِدِيْنَ. اللَّهُمَّ إِنَّا قَدْ دَعَوْنَاكَ كَمَا أَمَرْتَنَا، فَأَجِبْنَا كَمَا وَعَدْتَنَا إِنَّكَ لَا تُخْلِفُ الْمِيْعَادَ، رَبَّنَآ ءَاتِنَا فِي ٱلدُّنْيَا حَسَنَةً وَفِي ٱلْأَخِرَةِ حَسَنَةً وَقِنَا عَذَابَ ٱلنَّارِ ﴿٢٠١﴾ (سُورَةُ البَقَرَةِ)

Rabbanā mā khalaqta hādha bāṭilan subḥānaka faqinā ʿadhāba al-nār. Rabbanā innanā samiʿnā munādiyan yunādī li-l-īmāni an āminū bi-rabbikum fa-āmannā rabbanā fa-ghfir lanā dhunūbanā wa-kaffir ʿannā sayiʾātinā, wa-tawaffanā maʿa al-abrār, rabbanā āmannā bi-mā anzalta wattabaʿnā al-rasūla fa-ktubnā maʿa al-shāhidīn. Allāhumma innā qad daʿawnāka ka-mā amartanā fa-ajibnā ka-mā waʿadtanā innaka lā tukhlifu al-mīʿād. Rabbanā ātinā fī al-dunyā ḥasanatan wa-fī l-ākhirati ḥasanatan waqinā ʿadhāba al-nār.

O God, You have not created this [world] in vain, protect us from the punishment of Hellfire. Our Lord, we have heard the caller calling to faith and to "believe in your Lord" and we have believed, so O God forgive our sins. Remove our sins, and let us die among the upright ones. Our Lord, we have believed in what You have sent and we have followed the Messenger, so write us among those who witness [the truth of this message]. Our Lord, we have called upon You as You have commanded us, so answer us as You have promised us. You are never a breaker of oaths. *Our Lord, grant us goodness in this world and goodness in the hereafter. And protect us from the punishment of Hellfire* [al-Baqara, 2:201].

رَبَّنَا لَا تُؤَاخِذْنَآ إِن نَّسِينَآ أَوْ أَخْطَأْنَاۚ رَبَّنَا وَلَا تَحْمِلْ عَلَيْنَآ إِصْرًا كَمَا حَمَلْتَهُۥ عَلَى ٱلَّذِينَ مِن قَبْلِنَاۚ رَبَّنَا وَلَا تُحَمِّلْنَا مَا لَا طَاقَةَ لَنَا بِهِۦۖ وَٱعْفُ عَنَّا وَٱغْفِرْ لَنَا وَٱرْحَمْنَآۚ أَنتَ مَوْلَىٰنَا فَٱنصُرْنَا عَلَى ٱلْقَوْمِ ٱلْكَـٰفِرِينَ ﴿٢٨٦﴾ (سُورَةُ البَقَرَةِ)

Rabbanā lā tuʾākhidhnā in nasīnā aw akhṭaʾnā rabbanā wa-lā taḥmil ʿalaynā iṣran ka-mā ḥamaltahu ʿalā alladhīna min qablinā rabbanā wa-lā tuḥammilnā mā lā ṭāqata lanā bihi wa-aʿfu ʿannā wa-aghfir lanā wa-arḥamnā anta mawlānā fa-anṣurnā ʿalā al-qawmi al-kāfirīna.

Our Lord! Condemn us not if we forget or fall into error, our Lord! Lay not on us a burden like that which You gave those before us, Our Lord! Lay not on us a burden greater than we have strength to bear. Remove our sins, and grant us forgiveness. Have mercy on us. You are our Protector. Help us against those who stand against faith [al-Baqara, 2:286].

Additional Supplications

اللَّهُمَّ اجْمَعْ عَلَى الهُدَى أَمْرَنَا، وَاجْعَلِ التَّقْوَى زَادَنَا، وَاجْعَل الجَنَّةَ مآبَنَا، وَزِدْنَا وَلَا تَنْقِصْنَا، وَأَعْطِنَا وَلَا تَحْرِمْنَا، وَأَكْرِمْنَا وَلَا تُهِنَّا، وَآثِرْنَا وَلَا تُؤْثِرْ عَلَيْنَا، وَارْضَ عَنَّا وَرَضِّنَا، وَاغْفِرْ لَنَا وَلِوَالِدِيْنَا، وَلِأَئِمَّتِنَا وَلِمُعَلِّمِيْنَا، وَلِمَن سَبَقَنَا بِالإِيْمَانِ، مَغْفِرَةً عَزماً لَا تُغَادِر ذَنْباً، بِرَحْمَتِكَ يَا أَرْحَمَ الرَّاحِمِيْنَ.

Allāhumma ijma‘ ‘alā al-hudā amranā, wa-j‘ali al-taqwa zādanā, wa-j‘al al-jannata ma᾽ābanā, wa-zidnā wa-lā tanqisnā, wa-a‘ṭinā wa-lā taḥrimnā, wa-akrimnā wa-lā tahinnā, wa-āthirnā wa-lā tu᾽thir ‘alaynā, wa-arḍa ‘annā wa-raḍḍinā, wa-aghfir lanā wa-l-wālidīnā, wa-li-a᾽immatinā wa-li-mu‘allimīnā, wa-liman sabaqanā bi l-īmān, maghfiratan ‘azman lā tughādir dhanban, bi-raḥmatika yā arḥama al-rāḥimīn.

O God, combine all of our affairs on true guidance. Make the fear and awareness of You our provision and Paradise our destination. Increase for us [the good] and do not decrease it for us. Grant us and do not withhold from us. Honor us and do not humiliate us. Take retribution on our behalf and do not take retribution against us. Be pleased with us and make us pleased. Forgive us and our parents, leaders, teachers, and those who have preceded us in faith with a comprehensive forgiveness that does not miss any sin, by Your mercy, O most merciful of those who show mercy.

اللَّهُمَّ إِنَّنَا نَسْأَلُكَ إِخْبَاتَ الْمُخْبِتِيْنَ وَإِخْلَاصَ الْمُؤْمِنِيْنَ، وَمُرَافَقَةَ الأَبْرَار، وَاسْتِحْقَاقَ حَقَائِقِ الإِيْمَانِ وَالغَنِيْمَةَ مِنْ كُلِّ بِرٍّ، وَالسَّلَامَةَ مِنْ كُلِّ إِثْمٍ، وَوُجُوْبَ رَحْمَتِكَ وَعَزَائِمَ مَغْفِرَتِكَ، وَالفَوْزَ بِالجَنَّةِ، وَالنَّجَاةَ مِنَ النَّارِ. وَصَلَّى اللهُ عَلَى سَيِّدِنَا مُحَمَّدٍ خَاتَمَ النَّبِيِّيْنَ وَعَلَى آلِهِ الطَّيِّبِيْنَ الطَّاهِرِيْنَ، وَالحَمْدُ للهِ رَبِّ العَلَمِيْنَ.

Allāhumma innanā nas᾽aluka ikhbāta al-mukhbitīn, wa-ikhlāṣ al-mu᾽minīn, wa-murāfaqata al-abrār, wa-istiḥqāqa ḥaqā᾽iqi al-īmān, wa-l-ghanīmata min kulli birr, wa-l-salāmata min kulli ithm, wa-wujūba raḥmatik, wa-‘azā᾽ima maghfiratik, wa-l-fawza bi al-janna, wa-l-najāta min al-nār. Wa-ṣalla Allāhu ‘alā sayyidinā Muḥammadin khātama al-nabiyīn, wa-‘alā ālihi wa-l-ṭayyibīna al-ṭāhirīna wa-alḥamduli-llāhi rabbi al-‘ālamīn.

O God we ask you for the humility of the humble, the sincerity of the believers, the companionship of the upright, and the realization of the realities of faith. [O God, we ask You] for abundance in every goodness, immunity from every harm, the acquisition of Your mercy, the utmost of Your forgiveness, the attainment of Heaven, and salvation from Hellfire. Prayers be upon Muḥammad, the last of the prophets, and upon his pure and noble family. And thanks be to God, the Lord of the worlds.

Gatherings of Remembrance using Specific Qur'ānic Chapters

Some gatherings of recitation focus on the recitation of specific Qur'ānic chapters, such as al-Baqara, al-Anʿām, Yāsīn, or the last three chapters of the Qur'ān (*al-muʿwadhāt*), either individually or as a group.

Sūrat al-Anʿām with Its Supplication

According to the people of righteousness (*ṣāliḥīn*), the recitation of Sūrat al-Anʿām is praiseworthy for the fulfillment of needs. It is also mentioned that the recitation of this Qur'ānic chapter 70 times facilitates in curing the ill. One is encouraged to recite the following supplication in verse number 124 in between the two names of God: Allāh.

دُعَاء سُوْرَة الأَنْعَام

إِلَهِي مَنْ ذَا الَّذِي دَعَاكَ فَلَمْ تُجِبْهُ، وَمَنْ الَّذِي سَأَلَكَ فَلَمْ تُعْطِهِ، وَمَن الَّذِي اسْتَجَارَكَ فَلَم تُجِرْهُ، وَمَن الَّذِي اسْتَغَاثَ بِكَ فَلَم تُغِثْهُ، وَمَنْ الَّذِي تَوَكَّلَ عَلَيْكَ فَلَم تَكْفِهِ، واغَوْثَاه، واغَوْثَاه، وَاغوثَاه، أَغِثْنَا

يَامُغِيْث أَغِثْنَا، افْعَلْ بِنَا مَا أَنْتَ أَهْلُهُ، وَلَا تَفْعَلْ بِنَا مَا نَحْنُ أَهْلُهُ، فَإِنَّكَ أَهْلُ التَّقْوَى وَأَهْلُ الْمَغْفِرَة، يَاسَرِيْعَ الحِسَابِ.

Ilāhī man dhalladhī daʿāka fa-lam tujibhu wa-man alladhi saʾalaka fa-lam tuʿṭihi wa-man alladhi astajāraka fa-lam tujirhu wa-man alladhī istaghātha bika fa-lam tughithhu wa-man alladhi tawakkala ʿalayka fa-lam takfihi, wa-aghawthāh, wa-aghawthāh, wa-aghawthāh, aghithnā yā mughīth aghithnā. Ifʿal binā mā anta ahluhu, wa-lā tafʿal binā mā naḥnu ahluhu, fa-innaka ahlu al-taqwā wa-ahlu al-maghfira, yā sarīʿ al-ḥisāb.

O my Lord, who is there who does not supplicate to You, except that You answer him? Who is there who asks of You, except that You give him? Who is there who seeks Your protection, except that You grant it to him? Who is there who sought Your deliverance from adversity, except that You delivered him? Who is there who has relied upon You, except that You have protected him? O Savior! O Savior! Rescue us, O Savior [from the tribulations that have afflicted us]. Treat us in the way that is befitting [of Your grace] and do not treat us in the way we deserve to be treated. You are the most worthy of our fear and most oft to forgive.

بِسْمِ اللهِ الرَّحْمٰنِ الرَّحِيْم، والحَمْدُ للهِ رَبِّ العَالَمِيْن، وَصَلَّى اللهُ عَلَى سَيِّدِنَا مُحَمَّدٍ وَعَلَى آلِهِ وَصَحْبِهِ أَجْمَعِيْن. اللَّهُمَّ يَا سَرِيْعَ الحِسَاب، وَيَا شَدِيْدَ العِقَاب، يَا غَفُوْر، يَا رَحِيْم، يَا فَالِقَ الإِصْبَاح، يَا مُفَتِّحَ الأَبْوَاب، يَا مُسَبِّبَ الأَسْبَاب، يَا غَافِرَ الخَطَايَا، يَا سَاتِرَ العَوْرَات، يَا مَانِعَ البَلِيَّات، يَا مُقِيلَ العَثَرَات، يَا مُحْيَ الأَمْوَات، اقْضِ يَا إِلَهَ الأَوَّلِيْنَ وَالآخِرِيْنَ حَوَائِجَنَا . . . وَصَلَّى اللهُ عَلَى سَيِّدِنَا مُحَمَّدٍ وَعَلَى آلِهِ وَصَحْبِهِ وَسَلَّم.

Bismillāh al-Raḥmān al-Raḥīm, wa-alḥamduli-llāhi rabbi al-ʿālamīn, wa-ṣalla Allāhu ʿalā sayyidinā Muḥammadin wa-ʿalā ālihi wa-ṣaḥbihi ajmaʿīn. Allāhumma yā sarīʿa al-ḥisāb, wa-yā shadīd al-ʿiqāb, yā ghafūr, yā raḥīm, yā fāliqa al-iṣbāḥ, yā mufattiḥa al-abwāb, yā musabbib al-asbāb, yā ghāfira al-khaṭāyā, yā sātira al-ʿawrāt, yā māniʿa al-balliyyāt, yā muqīla al-ʿatharāt, yā muḥyi al-amwāt, iqḍi yā ilāh al-awwalīn wa-l-ākhirīn ḥawāʾijanā. Wa-ṣalla Allāḥu ʿalā sayyidinā Muḥammadin wa-ʿalā ālihi wa-ṣaḥbihi wa-sallam.

In the name of God, the Most Compassionate and Most Merciful. Thanks be to God, the Lord of the worlds. And may the prayers of God be upon our master Muḥammad, his family, and upon the entirety of his Companions. O God, the One of haste in His reckoning! O One of mighty punishment! O Forgiver! O Most Merciful! O Breaker of the dawn! O Opener of doors! O Cause of all causes! O Forgiver of wrong actions! O Concealer of flaws! O Averter of harm! O Diminisher of hardship! O Reviver of the dead, fulfill all of our needs! O Lord of all that has come before and all that will come after! Send prayers and peace upon our master Muḥammad, his family, and Companions.

Additional Supplications Seeking Divine Assistance

يَا مَن يَرَى مَا فِي الضَّمِيرِ وَيَسْمَعُ   أَنْتَ الْمُعَدُّ لِكُلِّ مَا يُتَوَقَّعُ

يَا مَن يُرَجَّى لِلشَّدَائِدِ كُلِّهَا   يَا مَن إِلَيْهِ الْمُشْتَكَى وَالْمَفْزَعُ

يَا مَن خَزَائِنُ رِزْقِهِ فِي قَوْلِ كُنْ   امْنُنْ فَإِنَّ الخَيْرَ عِنْدَكَ أَجْمَعُ

مَالِي سِوَى فَقْرِي إِلَيْكَ وَسِيْلَةً   فَبِالافْتِقَارِ إِلَيْكَ فَقْرِي أَدْفَعُ

مَالِي سِوَى قَرْعِي لِبَابِكَ حِيْلَةً   وَلَئِنْ رُدِدْتُ فَأَيَّ بَابٍ أَقْرَعُ

وَمَنْ الَّذِي أَدْعُو وَأَهْتِفُ بِاسْمِهِ   إِنْ كَانَ فَضْلُكَ عَنْ فَقِيرِكَ يُمْنَعُ

حَاشَا لِجُوْدِكَ أَنْ تُقَنِّطَ عَــاصِياً   الفَضْلُ أَجْزَلُ وَالْمَــواهِبُ أَوْسَعُ

ثُــــمَ الصَــــلاةُ عَلَى النَّبِيِّ وَآلِهِ   خَيْرِ الأَنَامِ وَمَــــــن بِهِ يَتَشَفَّعُ

O You who sees what is in the souls and hears,
You are the determiner of all that occurs.

O You to whom we turn in anticipation against all calamities;
O You to whom complaints and fears are brought forth;

O You in whose treasury of provisions is the word, "Be";
bestow upon us [what is beseeched], for all of goodness is in Your possession.

I have no means [to resolve my troubles], except by my dire need of You,
for it is through my poverty in Your presence that I stave off my poverty in the world.

I possess no solution [to my troubles], except knocking on Your door.
If I am turned away, then on which door can I knock?

And who else can I appeal to and call upon
if Your favor upon one in dire need of You is held back?

It is beyond [Your attribute of] generous mercy to turn away a sinner,
Your favors are overflowing in abundance and Your gifts are even greater.

And send prayers upon the Prophet and his family,
the best of creation and the one whose intercession we seek.

Additional Supplications

يَا فَارِجَ الهَمِّ فَرِّجْ كَرْبِيَ الدَّاجِي مَنْ لِي سِوَاكَ أَيَــا غَوْثِي وَيَا تَاجِي

يَا رَبِّ إِنَّ العِدَا يَسْعَوْنَ فِي تَلَفِي وَيَدَّعُونَ بِأَنِّي لَسْــــتُ بِالنَّاجِي

وَقَدْ قَصَدْتُكَ فِي إِحْـبَاطِ مَا زَعَمُوا فَأَنْتَ يَــا رَبِّ غَوْثُ الخَائِفِ الرَّاجِي

يَا قَاهِرَ الظُّلْمِ زَلْزِلْهُمْ بِــدَاهِيَةٍ يَكُـونُ إِهْلَاكُهُم فِيْهَا وَإِخْرَاجِي

O Reliever of anxieties, relieve my dark troubles.
I have none other than You; my Savior, my Master!

O my Lord, the enemies are striving for my destruction,
claiming that I will not be saved.

I turn to You to undermine what they claim,
as You are, O my Lord, the Deliverer of the frightened and hopeful.

O Destroyer of oppression, shake them with a calamity
that will be their demise and my salvation.

Supplication for Seeking the Fulfillment of Needs

اللَّهُمَّ إِنَّا نَسْأَلُكَ يَا مَنْ أَقَرَّ لَهُ بِالعُبُودِيَّةِ كُلُّ مَعْبُودٍ، يَامَنْ سَائِلُهُ مِنْ فَضْلِهِ غَيْرُ مَرْدُوْدٍ، يَا مَنْ بَابُهُ لِسُؤَالِهِ غَيْرُ مَسْدُودٍ، يَا مَنْ هُوَ غَيْرُ مَحْصُوْرٍ وَلَا مَحْدُوْدٍ، يَامَن عَطَاؤُهُ غَيْرُ مَمْنُوْنٍ وَلَا مَنْكُوْدٍ، يَا مَنْ هُوَ لِمَن دَعَاهُ دَائِماً مَقْصُوْدٌ، يَا مَنْ رَجَاءُ عِبَادِهِ بِحَبْلِهِ مَشْدُوْدٌ، يَا مَنْ لَيْسَ لَهُ شَبِيْهٌ وَلَا مَثِيْلٌ مَوْجُوْدٌ، يَا مَن لَيْسَ لَهُ وَالِدٍ وَلَيْسَ بِمَوْلُوْدٍ، يَا مَنْ لَا يُوْصَفُ بِقِيَامٍ وَلَا قُعُوْدٍ وَلَا حَرَكَةٍ وَلَا جُمُوْدٍ، يَا رَاحِمَ يَعْقُوْب، يَا كَاشِفاً ضُرَّ أَيُّوْب، يَا مُنَجِّيَ إِبْرَاهِيْمَ مِنْ نَارِ النَّمْرُود، يَا مَنْ لَا يُخْلِفُ

الوَعْدَ وَيَعْفُو عَنْ الْمَوْعُودِ، يَا مَنْ بِرُّهُ وَ رِزْقُهُ لِلْعَاصِيْنَ مَمْدُوْدٌ، يَا مَنْ هُوَ مَلْجَأُ كُلِّ مَلْهُوْفٍ وَمَطْرُوْدٍ، يَا مَنْ أَذْعَنَ لَهُ جَمِيْعُ خَلْقِهِ بِالسُّجُوْدِ، يَا مَنْ لَيْسَ عَنْ بَابِ جُوْدِهِ أَحَدٌ بِمَطْرُوْدٍ، يَا مَن يَحْلُمُ عَنِ الظَّالِمِ الجَحُوْدِ، ارْحَمْ عَبْداً ظَالِماً مُخْطِئاً لَمْ يُوَفِّ بِالْعُهُودِ، إِنَّكَ فَعَّالٌ لِمَا تُرِيْدُ وَأَنْتَ الْمَقْصُودُ، يَاللهِ... يَارَبُّ... يَارَحْمٰنُ... يَا رَحِيْمُ... يَاوَدُوْدُ... ارْحَمْنَا بِرَحْمَتِكَ يَا أَرْحَمَ الرَّاحِمِيْنَ يَارَبُّ يَامَعْبُوْدُ.

Allāhumma innā nas'aluka yā man aqarra lahu bi al-'ubūdiyati kullu ma'būdin, yā man sā'iluhu min faḍlihi ghayru mardūdin, yā man bābuhu li-su'ālihi ghayru masdūdin, yā man huwa ghayru maḥṣūrin wa-lā maḥdūdin, yā man 'aṭā'uhu ghayru mamnūnin wa-lā mankūdin, yā man huwa liman da'āhu dā'iman maqṣūdun, yā man rajā'u 'ibādihi bi-ḥablihi mashdūdun, yā man laysa lahu shabīhun wa-lā mathīlun mawjūdun, yā man laysa lahu wālidin wa-laysa bi-mawlūdin, yā man lā yūṣafu bi-qiyāmin wa-lā qu'ūdin wa-lā ḥarakatin wa-lā jumūdin, yā rāḥima ya'qūb, yā kāshifan ḍarra Ayyūb, yā munajjiya Ibrāhīma min nāri al-Namrūd, yā man lā yukhlifu al-wa'da wa-ya'fu 'an al-maw'ūdi, yā man birruhu wa-rizquhu li-l-'āṣīna mamdūdun, yā man huwa malja'ū kulli malhūfin wa-maṭrūdin, yā man adh'ana lahu jamī'ū khalqihi bi al-sujūdi, yā man laysa 'an bābi jūdihi aḥadun bi-maṭrūdin, yā man yaḥlumu 'an al-ẓālimi al-jaḥūd, irḥam 'abdan ẓāliman mukhṭi'an lam yuwaffi bi-al-'uhūdi. Innaka fa''ālun lima turīdu wa-anta al-maqṣudu. Yā Allāh. . .Yā Rabb. . .Yā Raḥmān. . .Yā Raḥīm. . .Yā Wadūd. . .irḥamnā bi-raḥmatika yā arḥama al-rāḥimīna yā rabbu yā ma'būdu.

O God, we beg You, [O One] to whom all worshipers submit in devotion. O You who does not turn away those who ask for Your favors! O You whose door for requests is never shut! O You who is neither limited nor restricted! O You whose gifts are not given begrudgingly or with bitterness! O You who is always sought by all who supplicate to Him! O You whose servants lay their hopes in His rope to which they hold fast! O You to whom none is likened, and none resembles! O You who has neither father nor progeny! O You who cannot be characterized by standing, sitting, movement, or stillness! O One who showed mercy on Yaʿqūb! O Remover of the pains of Ayyūb! O Savior of Ibrāhīm from the fire of Namrūd! O You who never breaks promises but forgives those who do! O You whose provisions and benevolence are constant, even to the disobedient ones! O refuge of every troubled and rejected one! O You to whom all of His creation submit in prostration! O You whose generous door no one is turned away from! O You who postpones [the punishment] of every oppressive transgressor! Have mercy on a servant who has transgressed, is full of shortcomings, and has not fulfilled what is expected of him! You do as You will and You are the one who is sought after. O Allāh! O Lord! O Most Compassionate! O Most Merciful! O All Loving! Have mercy on us, O most merciful of those who show mercy and the Lord who is worshiped.

اللّٰهُمَّ فَارِجَ الهَمِّ وَكَاشِفَ الغَمِّ وَمُجِيْبَ دَعْوَةِ الْمُضْطَرِّيْنَ رَحْمٰنَ الدُّنْيَا وَالآخِرَةِ وَ رَحِيْمَهُمَا، أَنْتَ تَرْحَمُنَا، فَارْحَمْنَا رَحْمَةً تُغْنِيْنَا بِهَا عَنْ رَحْمَةِ مَنْ سِوَاكَ.

Allāhumma fārija al-hammi wa-kāshifa al-ghammi wa-mujība daʿwati al-muḍṭarrīna raḥmāna al-dunyā wa-l-ākhirati wa-raḥīmahumā. Anta tarḥamunā fa-arḥamnā raḥmatan tughnīnā bihā ʿan raḥmati man siwāk.

O God, the Resolver of troubles, Remover of anxieties, the Answerer of the call of those in dire need, the most compassionate of this world and the next, and the one who is merciful to them! You are the one who shows us compassion, so bestow upon us a mercy that frees us of the need for mercy from anyone else.

اللَّهُمَّ اجْعَل لَنَا مِنْ كُلِّ هَمٍّ يَهُمُّنَا فَرَجاً وَمَخْرَجاً، وَارْزُقْنَا مِنْ حَيْثُ لَا نَحْتَسِب، يَا سَابِقَ الفَوْتِ، وَيَا سَامِعَ الصَّوْتِ، وَيَا كَاسِيَ العِظَامِ لَحْماً بَعْدَ الْمَوْتِ، صَلِّ عَلَى سَيِّدِنَا مُحَمَّدٍ وَآلِهِ، وَاجْعَلْ لَنَا مِنْ أَمْرِنَا فَرَجاً وَمَخْرَجاً، إِنَّكَ تَعْلَمُ وَلَا نَعْلَمُ، وَتَقْدِرُ وَلَا نَقْدِرُ وَأَنْتَ عَلَّامُ الغُيُوبِ، يَاغِيَاثَ الْمُسْتَغِيْثِيْنَ، يَا مُجِيْباً دُعَاءَ الْمُضْطَرِّيْنَ، وَجَّهْنَا وُجُوهَنَا إِلَيْكَ، وَتَوَكَّلْنَا عَلَيْكَ، وَلَا نَرْفَعُ حَاجَتِنَا إِلَّا إِلَيْكَ، خَاشِعِيْنَ بَيْنَ يَدَيْكَ، صِلِ اللَّهُمَّ حبَالَنَا بِحبَالِكَ، وَأَلْحِقْنَا بِالصَّالِحِيْنَ، وَأَيِّدْنَا بِجَلَالِكَ، وَاجْعَلْنَا مِنْ عِبَادِكَ الْمُتَّقِيْنَ، لَاتَصْرِفْ وُجُوهَنَا إِلَّا إِلَى جَنَابِكَ، وَلَا تَجْذُبْ قُلُوبَنَا إِلَّا إِلَى بَابِكَ، قَرِّبْنَا مِنْ أَحْبَابِكَ وَأَهْلِ وَلَائِكَ، وَاحْفَظْنَا مِنْ صُحْبَةِ ذَوِي الجَهْلِ وَ الْمَكْرِ مِنْ عْبَادِكَ، حَقِّقْنَا بِالمَعْرِفَةِ المُحَمَّدِيَّةِ، وَجَمِّلْنَا بِالصِّفَاتِ الْمَرْضِيَّةِ، وَأَطْلِقْ أَلْسِنَتَنَا بِشُكْرِكَ. رَبِّ إِنِّي مَسَّنِيَ الضرُّ وَ أنتَ أرحَمُ الرَّاحِمِينَ (ثلاث مرات).

Allāhumma ij'al lanā min kulli hammin yahummunā farajan wa-makhrajan, wa-arzuqnā min ḥaythu lā naḥtasib, yā ṣābiqa al-fawti, yā sāmi' al-ṣawti, wa-yā kāsiya al-'iẓāmi laḥman ba'da al-mawti, ṣalli 'alā sayyidinā Muḥammadin wa-ālihi, wa-aj'al lanā min amrinā farajan wa-makhrajan, innaka ta'lamu wa-lā na'lamu, wa-taqdiru wa-lā naqdiru, wa-anta 'allāmu al-ghuyūbi, yā ghiyātha al-mustaghīthīna, yā mujīban du'ā'a al-muḍṭarrīna, wajjahnā wujūhanā ilayka, wa-tawakkalnā 'alayk, wa-lā narfa'u ḥājātinā illā ilayka, khāshi'īna bayna yadayka, ṣalli Allāhumma ḥibālanā bi-ḥibālika, wa-alḥiqnā bi-al-ṣāliḥīn, wa-ayyidnā bi-jalālika, wa-aj'alnā min 'ibādika al-muttaqīn, lā taṣrif wujūhanā illā ilā janābika, wa-lā tajdhib qulūbanā illā ilā bābika, qarribnā min aḥbābika wa-ahli walā'ika wa-aḥfaẓnā min ṣuḥbati dhawi al-jahli wa-l-makri min 'ibādika, ḥaqqiqnā bi al-ma'rifati al-Muḥammadiyya wa-jammilnā bi al-ṣifāti al-marḍiyya, wa-aṭliq alsinatanā bi-shukrika. Rabbi innī massaniya al-ḍurru wa-anta arḥamu al-rāḥimīn (3 times).

O God, grant us a solution and a way out of every concern that troubles us. And grant us provision from where we do not anticipate it. O One who precedes all occurrences (*Yā sābiq al-fawt*)![2] O hearer of calls! O He who clothes the bones with flesh after death! Send prayers upon our master Muḥammad and upon his family. Grant us a resolution and a way out of our troubles. You are the One who knows and we know not, who is capable and we are incapable, and You are the knower of the unseen. O Savior of those who seek salvation! O Answerer of the call of those in desperate need! We have turned our faces toward You and we have submitted our affairs to You. We do not take our needs to anyone but You. We [stand] in humility in Your presence. Connect us, O God, to Yourself with Your rope. Grant us the company of the righteous. Continuously support us through Your majesty. And make us of Your devoted servants. Do not allow our faces to turn anywhere except to You. Do not allow our hearts to be drawn toward anything except Your door. Make us close to those whom You love, and who have been granted a most lofty rank. Protect us from keeping the company of the ignorant and treacherous ones among Your servants. Enable us to embrace the Muḥammadan teaching. Ornament us with the characteristics that please You and busy our tongues with thanking You. O my Lord, I have been afflicted with harm and You are the most merciful of the merciful (*Rabbī innī massaniya al-ḍurru wa-anta arḥama al-rāḥimīn*), [three times].

---

2 God precedes the occurrence of all events by being the One who determines their occurrence.

اللَّهُمَّ يَا مَوْضِعَ كُلِّ شَكْوَى، وَيَا سَامِعَ كُلِّ نَجْوَى، وَيَا كَاشِفَ كُلِّ بَلْوَى، يَا عَالِمَ كُلِّ خَفِيَّةٍ، وَيَا صَارِفَ كُلِّ بَلِيَّةٍ، يَا كَاشِفَ صِعَابِ الهُمُومِ، وَيَا مُفَرِّجَ الكُرُوْبِ، وَيَا سَاتِرَ العُيُوبِ، وَيَا مَن إِذَا أَرَادَ شَيْئاً فَحَسْبُهُ أَنْ يَقُوْلَ: كُنْ فَيَكُوْنُ.

Allāhumma yā mawḍiʿa kulli shakwā, wa-yā sāmiʿa kulli najwā, wa-yā kāshifa kulli balwā, yā ʿālima kulli khafiyyatin, wa-yā ṣārifa kulli baliyyatin, wa-yā kāshifa ṣiʿābi al-humūmi, wa-yā mufarrija al-kurūbi, wa-yā sātira al-ʿuyūbi, yā man idhā arāda shayʾan fa-ḥasbuhu an yaqūla kun fa-yakūn.

O God, to whom complaints are directed! O Hearer of every whisper! O Eliminator of every calamity! O Knower of every hidden matter! O Exterminator of every tribulation! O Resolver of the most complex concerns! O Remover of troubles! O Concealer of every shortcoming! O You who, if He wills a matter, says, "Be," and it is!

رَبَّاهُ.. رَبَّاه، لَا إِلَهَ إِلَّا أَنْتَ، الغَوْثَ.. الغَوْث، الرَّحْمَةَ.. الرَّحْمَةَ، العِنَايَةَ.. العِنَايَةَ، الرَّأْفَةَ.. الرَّأْفَةَ، إِنَّا نَتَوَسَّلُ إِلَيْكَ بِاسْمِكَ الأَعْظَم الَّذِي مَلَأَ بِنُوْرِ قُدْسِهِ أَرْكَانَ الأَكْوَانِ كُلِّهَا، إِلَا فَرَّجْتَ عَنَّا مَا أَصْبَحْنَا فِيْهِ وَ أَمْسَيْنَا. اسْتَجِبْ دُعَاءَنَا يَا اللهُ، فَإِنَّا نَدْعُوْكَ دُعَاءَ مَنِ اشْتَدَّتْ فَاقَتُهُ، وَقَلَّتْ حِيْلَتُهُ، وَضَعُفَتْ قُوَّتُهُ، دُعَاء الغَرِيْبِ الفَرِقِ الْمَلْهُوفِ الْمُضْطَرِّ الَّذِي يَعْلَمُ كُلَّ العِلْمِ أَنَّهُ لَا يَكْشِفُ عَنْهُ مَا هُوَ فِيْهِ إِلَّا أَنْتَ. يَا أَرْحَم الرَّاحِمِيْنَ، تَدَارَكْنَا بِإِغَاثَتِكَ، وَحُفَّنَا بِلُطْفِكَ، فَإِنَّ رَحْمَتَكَ وَاسِعَةٌ، وَمَوَاعِيدَكَ صَادِقَةٌ، وَأَيَادِيَكَ فَاضِلَةٌ مُتَوَاصِلَةٌ. فَالْطُفْ بِنَا فِي أُمُورِنَا كُلِّهَا وَالْمُسْلِمِيْنَ أَجْمَعِيْنَ، وَفَرِّجْ عَنَّا وَعَن أُمَّةِ سَيِّدِنَا مُحَمَّد ﷺ، وَثَبِّتْنَا عَلَى مَا يُرْضِيْكَ، وَقَرِّبْنَا مِمَّا يُوَالِيْكَ،

وَاجْعَلْ غَايَةَ حُبِّنَا وَبُغْضِنَا فِيكَ، وَلَا تُقَرِّبْنَا مِمَّن يُعَادِيْكَ. أَدِمْ عَلَيْنَا نِعْمَتَكَ وَبِرَّكَ وَإِحْسَانَكَ، وَاقْذِفْ فِي قُلُوبِنَا رَجَاءَكَ، وَاقْطَعْ رَجَاءَنَا عَمَّنْ سِوَاكَ، حَتَّى لَا نَرْجُو أَحَداً غَيْرَكَ، وَلَا تُنْسِنَا ذِكْرَكَ، وَأَلْهِمْنَا فِي كُلِّ حَالٍ شُكْـــرَكَ، وَعَـرِّفْنَا قَدْرَ النِّعَمِ بِدَوَامِهَا، وَقَدْرَ العَافِيَةِ بِاسْتِمْرَارِهَا، وَاجْعَلْنَا نَخْشَاكَ حَتَّى كَأَنَّنَـا نَرَاكَ، وَأَسْعِدْنَا بِتَقْوَاكَ، وَلَا تُشْقِنَا بِمَعْصِيَتِكَ، وَافْعَلْ بِنَا مَا أَنْتَ أَهْلُهُ، وَلَا تَفْعَلْ بِنَا مَا نَحْنُ أَهْلُهُ، فَإِنَّكَ أَهْلُ التَّقْوَى وَالْمَغْفِرَةِ.

Rabbāhu...rabbāh...lā ilāha illā anta, al-ghawtha...al-ghawtha, al-raḥma...al-raḥma, al-ʿināya...al-ʿināya, al-raʾfata...al-raʾfata, innā natawassalu ilayka bismika al-aʿẓam alladhī malaʾa bi-nūri qudsihi arkāna al-akwāni kullihā, illā farrajta ʿannā mā aṣbaḥnā fīhi wa-amsaynā. Istajib duʿāʾanā yā Allāh, fa-innā nadʿūka duʿāʾa man ishtaddat fāqatuhu, wa-qallat ḥīlatuhu, wa-ḍaʿufat quwwatuhu, duʿāʾa al-gharībi al-fariqi al-malhūfi al-muḍṭarri alladhī yaʿlamu kulla al-ʿilmi annahu lā yakshifu ʿanhu mā huwa fīhi illā anta. Yā arḥam al-rāḥimīna, tadāraknā bi-ighāthatika, wa-ḥuffanā bi-luṭfika, fa-inna raḥmataka wāsiʿatun, wa-mawāʿīdaka ṣādiqatun, wa-ayādīka fāḍilatun mutawāṣilatun. Fa-alṭuf binā fī umūrinā kullihā wa-l-muslimīna ajmaʿīn, wa-farrij ʿannā wa-ʿan ummati sayyidinā Muḥammad ﷺ, wa-thabbitnā ʿalā mā yurḍīka, wa-qarribnā mimmā yuwālīka, wa-ajʿal ghāyata ḥubbinā wa-bughḍinā fīka, wa-lā tuqarribnā mimman yuʿādīka. Adim ʿalaynā niʿmataka wa-birraka wa-iḥsānaka wa-aqdhif fī qulūbinā rajāʾaka, wa-aqṭaʿ rajāʾanā ʿamman siwāka ḥattā lā narjū aḥadan ghayraka, wa-lā tunsinā dhikraka, wa-alhimnā fī kulli ḥālin shukraka, wa-ʿarrifnā qadra al-niʿami bi-dawāmihā, wa-qadra al-ʿāfiyati bi-stimrārihā, wa-ajʿalnā nakhshāka ḥattā kaʾannanā naraka, wa-asʿidnā bi-taqwāka, wa-lā tushqinā bi-maʿṣiyatika, wa-afʿal binā mā anta ahluhu wa-lā tafʿal binā mā naḥnu ahluhu, fa-innaka ahlu al-taqwā wa-l-maghfirati.

O God! There is no god but You. [Grant us] salvation, mercy, special attention, and kindness. We beseech You through the means of Your greatest name, which has filled the entire universe with the light of its sanctity, that You remove from us [the troubles] with which we are afflicted. Answer our prayers, O God. We supplicate to You prayers of one whose capacity is overwhelmed, whose power is limited, and whose strength is weakened. [We supplicate to You] prayers of the lonely, fearful, troubled, and one in dire need; who knows with full certainty that no one can remove the calamity he is in but You. O most Merciful of the merciful! We implore You for Your assistance, deliverance; envelop us with Your gentleness! For Your mercy is vast, Your promises are true, and Your favors are superior and constant. So show us kindness in all of our affairs and the affairs of all of the Muslims. And relieve us and relieve the community of our master Muḥammad ﷺ. Make us firm in what pleases You. Enable us to attain the means of achieving the most elevated spiritual rank with You. Make our love and anger for Your sake and keep us far from that which invokes Your wrath. Bestow upon us Your blessings, benevolence, and favors. Place in our hearts a state of hopeful expectation from You; and remove from it any hope or expectation from anyone other than You. And do not allow us to forget Your remembrance. Inspire our hearts to be grateful to You in every situation. Make us aware of the value of Your blessings through their ceaseless continuation. [Make us aware of] the value of our well-being through its constancy; and give us a state of presence of heart with You until it is as though we see You. Facilitate us to become God-fearing. Do not allow us to approach sins. Deal with us in a way that befits Your grace and not what befits our [unworthy] state; for You are the one who grants a state of mindfulness of God; and You are the one who forgives.

اللَّهُمَّ يَا مُسَهِّلَ الصَّعْبِ الشَّدِيْدِ، يَا مُلَيِّنَ قَسْوَةِ الحَدِيْدِ، وَيَا مُنْجِزَ الأَمْرَيْنِ الوَعْدِ وَالوَعِيْدِ، يَا مَنْ هُوَ فِي كُلِّ يَوْمٍ بِأَمْرٍ وَشَأْنٍ جَدِيْدِ،

أَخْرِجْنَا مِنْ حِلَقِ الكَـــرْبِ وَالضِّـيْقِ إِلَى أَوْسَعِ الفَرَجِ وَأَبْلَجِ الطَّرِيْقِ، بِكَ نَدْفَعُ مَا نُطِيْقُ وَمَا لَا نُطِيْق، يَا مَوْلَانَا الشَّفِيْقُ، يَا رَبَّ البَيْتِ العَتِيْقِ، اكْشفْ عَنَّا كُلَّ شِدَّةٍ وَضِيْقٍ، وَلَا حَولَ وَلَا قُوَّةَ إِلَّا بِاللهِ العَلِيِّ العَظِيْمِ.

Allāhumma yā musahhila al-ṣaʿbi al-shadīdi, wa-yā mulayyina qaswati al-ḥadīdi, wa-yā munjiza al-amrayni al-waʿdi wa-l-waʿīdi, yā man huwa fī kulli yawmin bi-amrin wa-shaʾnin jadīdi, akhrijnā min ḥilaqi al-karbi wa-l-ḍīqi ilā awsaʿi al-faraji wa-ablaji al-ṭarīqi, bika nadfaʿu mā nuṭīqu wa-mā lā nuṭīq, yā mawlānā al-shafīqu, yā rabba al-bayti al-ʿatīqi, ikshif ʿannā kulla shiddatin wa-ḍīqin, wa-lā ḥawla wa-lā quwwata illā bi-llāhi al-ʿaliyyi al-ʿaẓīmi.

O God! O Facilitator of what is most difficult! O One who makes flexible the sturdy iron! O Implementer of punishment and reward! O You who is involved in a new affair and matter every day! Relieve us from the state of tribulation and hardship and [grant us] the easiest resolution [of our troubles] and the most felicitous way. Through You we stave off all that we have power to withstand and that which we have no power to withstand. O Compassionate Benefactor! O Lord of the emancipated house![3] Remove from us every hardship and tribulation. There is no strength or power except through You, the Most Exalted and Majestic.

اللَّهُمَّ يَا سَابِغَ النِّعَمِ، وِيَا دَافِعَ النِّقَمِ، وِيَا فَارِجَ الكُــرَبِ، يَا وَلِيَّ مَنْ ظُلِمَ يَا مُسَبِّبَ الأَسْبَابِ، يَا مُفَتِّحَ الأَبْوَابِ، يَا سَامِعَ الأَصْـوَاتِ، يَا مُجِيْبَ الدَّعْوَاتِ، يَا قَاضِيَ الحَــاجَاتِ، إِنَّـــنَا أَنْـزَلْـنَا بِكَ حَاجَاتِنَا كُلَّهَا، الظَّاهِرَةَ وَالبَاطِنَةَ، الدُّنْيَوِيَّةَ وَالأُخْرَوِيَّةَ، يَا حَيُّ يَا قَيُّومُ، بِحَوْلِكَ

3 The *Kaʿba*, which is known as, "*al-bayt al-ʿatīq*."

وَقُوَّتِكَ نَسْتَعِيْنُ وَنَسْتَجِيْرُ، فَارْحَمْنَا بِرَحْمَتِكَ، يَا أَرْحَمَ الرَّاحِمِيْنَ، وَفَرِّجْ عَنَّا وَعَنْ أُمَّةِ نَبِيِّنَا مُحَمَّدٍ ﷺ فَرَجاً عَاجِلاً قَرِيْباً إِنَّكَ أَنْتَ نِعْمَ الْمُجِيْبُ. اللَّهُمَّ إِنَّا نَنْتَظِرُ فَرَجَكَ وَنرقبُ لُطْفَكَ، فَأَجِبْ دُعَاءَنَا، وَلَا تَرُدَّنَا خَائِبِيْنَ، بِرَحْمَتِكَ يَا أَرْحَمَ الرَّحِمِيْنَ.

Allāhumma yā sābigha al-niʿami, wa-yā dāfiʿa al-niqami, wa-yā fārija al-kurabi, yā waliyya man ẓulima, yā musabbiba al-asbābi, yā mufattiḥa al-abwābi, yā sāmiʿa al-aṣwāti, yā mujība al-daʿwāti, yā qāḍiya al-ḥājāti, innanā anzalnā bika ḥājātinā kullahā, al-ẓāhirata wa-l-bāṭinata, al-dunyawiyyata wa-al-ukhrawiyyata, yā ḥayyu yā qayyūmu, bi-ḥawlika wa-quwwatika nastaʿīnu wa-nastajīru fa-arḥamnā bi-raḥmatika yā arḥama al-rāḥimīna, wa-farrij ʿannā wa-ʿan ummati nabiyyinā Muḥammadin ﷺ farajan ʿājilan qarīban innaka anta niʿma al-mujīb. Allāhumma innā nantaẓiru farajaka wa-narqabu luṭfaka fa-ajib duʿāʾanā wa-lā taruddanā khāʾibīn, bi-raḥmatika yā arḥama al-rāḥimīn.

O Granter of blessings! O Averter of harms! O Remover of troubles! O Guardian of the oppressed! O Cause of all causes! O Opener of doors! O Hearer of calls! O Answerer of prayers! O Fulfiller of needs! We have brought to You all of our needs: those that are inward and outward, and those that are related to this life and the next. O Living and Self-Subsistent! We seek assistance and refuge in Your ability and Your power. Shower us with Your mercy, O most merciful of the merciful. And relieve our [troubles] and the troubles of community of our Prophet Muḥammad ﷺ, through a relief which is soon. You are the best Answerer of calls! O God, we wait for Your relief and anticipate Your gentle favor. Answer our prayer and do not turn us back empty handed, by Your mercy, O most merciful of the merciful!

4

Seeking Repentance (*Tawba*) and Forgiveness (*Istighfār*)

The Merits of Seeking Forgiveness

God the Exalted says in the Qurʾān, *And turn to God in repentance, all of you, O believers, so that you might succeed* [al-Nūr, 24:31]. God also says, *And, O my people! Ask forgiveness of your Lord, then turn to Him repentant; He will cause the sky to rain abundance on you and will add to you strength to your strength. Turn not away, guilty* [al-Hūd, 11:52].

A man came to Ḥasan al-Baṣrī complaining of drought. He advised him, "Make *istighfār*." Another man came to him complaining of his inability to have children. He advised him, "Make *istighfār*." Another man came to him complaining of poverty. He advised him, "Make *istighfār*." When questioned about this he replied, "I make up nothing from myself. God the Exalted says in the chapter *Nūh*: "I said (to them): 'Ask forgiveness from your Lord; Verily, He is Oft-Forgiving; He will send rain to you in abundance. And give you increase in wealth and children, and bestow on you gardens and bestow on you rivers'" [Nūḥ, 71:10–12].

Gatherings of Seeking Forgiveness (*Istighfār*)

Sessions of *istighfār* are performed by saying the "Major *Istaghfār*" (*al-Istighfār al-Kabīr*) mentioned below, followed by 70,000 istighfārs in the following wording: *istaghfir Allāh al-ʿaẓīm* (I seek forgiveness from God the Magnificent). At the beginning of each round of 100 *istighfārs*, one should recite what is known as the *sayyid al-istighfār* (master of phrases of repentance), a practice that is derived from the following *ḥadīth*.

> It is reported on the authority of Shaddād b. Aws ﵁ that the Prophet ﷺ said: "The master of repentance (*istighfār*) is to say: 'O God You are my Lord, there is no god but You. You have created me and I am Your servant. I am faithful to my covenant and my promise to the best of my ability. I seek refuge with You from all the evil I have done. I acknowledge before You all the blessings You have bestowed on me, and I confess to You all my sins. So I beg You to forgive my sins, for nobody can forgive sins except You.' He said, 'Whoever recites this in the day while believing in it with certainty and then dies before the evening, then he will be from the people of Paradise. Whoever recites this at night while believing in it with certainty and then dies before the morning, he is from the people of Paradise.'"

The wording for the Master of *Istighfārs* is the following:

سَيِّد الإِاسْتِـغفَار

اللَّهُمَّ أَنْتَ رَبِّي لَا إِلَهَ إِلَّا أَنْتَ، خَلَقْتَنِي وَأَنَا عَبْدُكَ وَأَنَا عَلَى عَهْدِكَ وَوَعْدِكَ مَا اسْتَطَعْتُ، أَعُوذُ بِكَ مِنْ شَرِّ مَا صَنَعْتُ أَبُوءُ لَكَ بِنِعْمَتِكَ عَلَيَّ وَأَبُوءُ لَكَ بِذَنْبِي فَاغْفِرْ لِي فَإِنَّهُ لَا يَغْفِرُ الذُّنُوبَ إِلَّا أَنْتَ.

Allāhumma anta rabbi lā ilāha illā anta. Khalaqtanī wa-ana ʿabduka. Wa-ana ʿalā ʿahdika wa-waʿdika mā astaṭaʿtu. Aʿūdhu bika min sharri mā ṣanaʿtu. Abūʿu laka bi niʿmatika ʿalayya wa-abūʿu laka bi-dhanbī faghfirlī fa-innahu lā yaghfiru al-dhunūba illa anta.

O God You are my Lord, there is no god but You. You have created me and I am Your servant. I am faithful to my covenant and my promise to the best of my ability. I seek refuge with You from all the evil I have done. I acknowledge before You all the blessings You have bestowed on me, and I confess to You all my sins. So I beg You to forgive my sins, for nobody can forgive sins except You.

This is then followed by the following supplication:

The Supplication of Repentance

دُعَاء الإِسْتِغْفَار

بِسْمِ اللهِ الرَّحْمٰنِ الرَّحِيْم، وَصَلَّى اللهُ تَعَالَى عَلَى سَيِّدِنَا مُحَمَّدٍ وَعَلَى آلِهِ وَصَحْبِهِ وَسَلَّم، أَسْتَغْفِر الله (ثلاثا) وَأَتُوْبُ إِلَى اللهِ مِمَّا يَكْرَهُ اللهُ قَوْلاً وَفِعْلاً وَخَاطِراً، وَبَاطِناً وَظَاهِراً، أَسْتَغْفِرُ الله العَظِيْمَ الَّذِي لَا إِلَهَ إِلَّا هُوَ الحَيُّ القَيُّوْمُ وَأَتُوْبُ إِلَيْه.

Bismillāh al-raḥmān al-raḥim wa-ṣalla Allāhu taʿāla ʿalā sayyidinā Muḥammadin wa-ʿalā ālihi wa-ṣaḥbihi wa-sallam, astaghfir Allāh (3 times), wa-atūbu ilā Allāhi mimmā yakrahu Allāhu qawlan wa-faʿlan wa-khāṭiran, wa-bāṭinan wa-ẓāhiran. Astaghfirullāh al-ʿaẓīma alladhi lā ilāha illa huwa al-ḥayyu al-qayyūmu wa-atūbu ilayh.

In the name of God, the most Compassionate, the most Merciful. Send prayers and the blessings of God, the Most High, upon our master Muḥammad, his family, and all of his Companions. I seek forgiveness from God ("*astaghfir Allāh*" is said 3 times) and I turn to God, away from all that He dislikes: from words, deeds, or thoughts, both inward and outward. I seek forgiveness from God the Majestic, there is no god but God, the Living and Self-Subsistent, and I turn to him.

اللَّهُمَّ إِنِّي أَسْتَغْفِرُكَ لِمَا قَدَّمْتُ وَمَا أَخَّرْتُ وَمَا أَسْرَرْتُ وَمَا أَعْلَنْتُ، وَمَا أَنْتَ أَعْلَمُ بِهِ مِنِّي، أَنْتَ الْمُقَدِّمُ وَأَنْتَ الْمُؤَخِّرُ، وَأَنْتَ عَلَى كُلِّ شَيْءٍ قَدِيْرٌ.

Allāhumma innī astaghfiruka limā qaddamtu wa-mā akhrajtu, wa-mā asrartu wa-mā aʿlantu, wa-mā anta aʿlamu bihi minnī. Anta al-muqaddimu wa-anta al-muʾākhkhiru, wa-anta ʿalā kulli shayʾin qadīrun.

O God, I seek forgiveness from all I have hastened to do and all I delayed, what I made public and what I kept secret, and what You are most knowledgeable of [in my affairs]. You are the First and You are the Last, and You have power over all things.

أَسْتَغْفِرُ اللهَ ذَا الجَلَالِ وَالإِكْرَامِ، مِنْ جَمِيْعِ الذُّنُوْبِ وَالآثَامِ، أَسْتَغْفِرُ اللهَ لِذُنُوبِي كُلِّهَا وَسِرِّهَا وَجَهْرِهَا وَصَغِيْرِهَا وَكَبِيْرِهَا وَقَدِيْمِهَا وَجَدِيْدِهَا، وَأَوَّلِهَا وَآخِرِهَا وَظَاهِرِهَا وَبَاطِنِهَا وَأَتُوْبُ إِلَيْه.

Astaghfir Allāh dha al-jalāli wa-l-ikrāmi, min jamīʿ al-dhunūbi wa-l-āthām. Astaghfir Allāh li-dhunūbī kullihā, sirrihā wa-jahrihā, wa-ṣaghīrihā wa-kabīrihā wa-qadīmihā wa-jadīdihā, wa-awwalihā wa-ākhirihā, wa-ẓahirihā wa-bāṭinihā, wa-atūbu ilayh.

I seek forgiveness from God, the Lord of Grace and Majesty, for all sins and immoralities. I seek forgiveness from God for all of my sins: secret and public, small and large, old and new, first and last, outward and inward; and I turn to him.

اللَّهُمَّ إِنِّي أَسْتَغْفِرُكَ لِمَا أَرَدْتُ بِهِ وَجْهَكَ الكَرِيْم فَخَالَطُهُ مَا لَيْسَ لَكَ فِيْهِ رِضَى، وَأَسْتَغْفِرُكَ لِمَا دَعَانِي إِلَيْهِ الهَوَى مِن قِبَلِ الرُّخصِ، مِمَّا اشْتَبَهَ عَلَيَّ وَهُوَ عِنْدَكَ حَرَامٌ، وَأَسْتَغْفِرُكَ يَا مَن لَا إِلَهَ إِلَّا أَنْتَ، يَا عَالِمَ الغَيْبِ وَالشَّهَادَةِ مِن كُلِّ سَيِّئَةٍ عَملْتُهَا، فِي بَيَاضِ النَّهَارِ وَسَوَادِ اللَّيْلِ، فِي مَلَاءٍ وَخَلَاءٍ، وَسِرٍّ وَعَلَانِيَةٍ وَأَنْتَ نَاظِرٌ إِلَيَّ إِذَا ارْتَكَبْتُهَا، فَأَتُوْبُ إِلَيْكَ يَا حَلِيْمُ يَا كَرِيْمُ يَا رَحِيْمُ. أَسْتَغْفِرُكَ مِن النِّعَمِ الَّتِي أَنْعَمْتَ بِهَا عَلَيَّ فَتَقَوَّيْتُ بِهَا عَلَى مَعْصِيَتِك.

Allāhumma innī astaghfiruka limā aradtu bihi wajhaka al-karīm al-karīm fa-khālaṭuhu mā laysa laka fīhi riḍā. Wa-astaghfiruka limā daʿānī ilayhi al-hawā min qibali al-rukhaṣi, mimmā ishtabaha ʿalayya wa-huwa ʿindaka ḥarāmun, wa-astaghfiruka yā man lā ilāha illā anta, yā ʿālima al-ghaybi wa-al-shahādati min kulli sayyiʾatin ʿamaltuhā fī bayāḍ al-nahāri wa-sawādi al-layli, fī malaʾin wa-khalāʾin, wa-sirrin wa-ʿalāniyatin wa-anta nāẓirun ilayya idhā artakabtuhā, fa-atūbu ilayka yā ḥalīmu yā karīmu yā raḥīmu. Astaghfiruka min al-niʿami allatī anʿamta bihā ʿalayya fa-taqawwaytu bihā ʿalā maʿṣiyatik.

O God, I seek forgiveness for all that I have done seeking Your favor and then associated it with that which displeases You. I seek forgiveness from You of what my whims invited me to without [prior] permission [to perform] and from what was doubtful to me even though it was [clearly determined] prohibited by You. And I seek forgiveness, O You, there is no god but You, the Knower of the unseen and seen, from every sin I committed; in broad daylight and the darkness of the night, in open places and in closed spaces, in secret and in public, and You are the Seer of it if I committed it. So I turn to You, O Generous and Forbearing One! I seek forgiveness for the provisions You have bestowed upon me and that I have [used] to gain strength to disobey You.

أَسْتَغْفِرُكَ مِن الذُّنُوب الَّتِي لَا يَعْرِفُهَا أَحَدٌ غَيرُك وَلَا يَطَّلِعُ عَلَيْهَا أَحَدٌ سِوَاكَ، وَلَا يَسَعُهَا إِلَّا حِلْمُكَ وَلَا يُنَجِّينِي مِنْهَا إِلَّا عَفْوُكَ. وَأَسْتَغْفِرُكَ لِكُلِّ يَمِيْنٍ سَلَفَتْ مِنِّي فحنثتُ فِيْهَا وَ أَنَا عِنْدَكَ مُؤَاخَذٌ بِهَا. أَسْتَغْفِرُكَ يَامَنْ لَا إِلَهَ إِلَّا أَنْتَ سُبْحَانَكَ إِنِّي كُنْتُ مِن الظَّالِمِيْنَ، رَبِّ اغْفِرْ وَارْحَمْ وَأَنْتَ خَيْرُ الرَّاحِمِيْنَ.

Astaghfiruka mina al-dhunūbi allatī lā ya'rifhā aḥadun ghayruka wa-lā yuṭṭali'u 'alayhā aḥadun siwāka wa-lā yasa'uhā illā ḥilmuka wa-lā yunajjinī minhā illā 'afwuka wa-astaghfiruka li-kulli yamīnin salafat minnī fa-ḥanathtu fīhā wa-anā 'indaka mu'ākhidhun bihā. Astaghfiruka yā man lā ilāha illā anta subḥānaka innī kuntu min al-ẓālimīn. Rabbi ighfir wa-arḥam wa-anta khayru al-rāḥimīn.

I seek refuge in You from sins that nobody knows of but You and nobody has seen but You. None can tolerate them except Your forbearance. None can save [me] from them except Your forgiveness. I seek forgiveness for every oath that I have taken and I have breached, while still being held to account for it in front of You. I seek forgiveness from You, there is no god but You. Praise be to You! I was of the wrongdoers. My Lord, forgive and show mercy. You are the Most Merciful of the merciful.

أَسْتَغْفِرُكَ مِنْ كُلِّ فَرِيْضَةٍ أَوْجَبْتَهَا عَلَيَّ آنَاءِ اللَّيْلِ وَأَطْرَافَ النَّهَارِ فَتَرَكْتُهَا خَطَأً أَوْ عَمْداً أَوْنِسْيَاناً أَوْ تَهَاوُناً أَوْ جَهْلاً وَأَنَا مُعَاقَبٌ بِهَا وَأَسْتَغْفِرُكَ مِن كُلِّ سُنَّةٍ مِنْ سُنَنِ سَيِّدِ الْمُرْسَلِيْنَ، وَخَاتَمِ النَّبِيِّيْنَ نَبِيِّكَ مُحَمَّد ﷺ فَتَرَكْتُهَا غَفْلَةً أَوْ سَهواً أَوْ نِسْيَاناً أَوْ تَهَاوُناً أَوْ جَهْلاً أَوْ قِلَّةَ مُبَالَاةٍ بِهَا. وَأَسْتَغْفِرُكَ يَا مَنْ لَا إِلَهَ إِلَّا أَنْتَ وَحْدَكَ لَا شَرِيْكَ لَكَ، وَأَنَّ سَيِّدِنَا مُحَمَّداً عَبْدُكَ وَرَسُولُكَ سُبْحَانَكَ يَا رَبَّ

الْعَالَمِيْنَ، لَكَ الْمُلْكُ وَلَكَ الحَمْدُ، وَأَنْتَ حَسْبُنَا وَنِعْمَ الوَكِيْلُ، نِعْمَ الْمَوْلَى وَنِعْمَ النَّصِيْرِ، وَلَاحَوْلَ وَلَا قُوَّةَ إِلَّا بِاللهِ العَلِيِّ العَظِيْمِ . . . يَا جَابِرِ كُلِّ كَسِيْرٍ، وَيَا مُؤْنِسَ كُلِّ وَحِيْدٍ وَيَا صَاحِبَ كُلِّ غَرِيْبٍ، وَيَا مُيَسِّرَ كُلِّ عَسِيْرٍ، يَا مَنْ لَا يَحْتَاجُ إِلَى البَيَانِ وَالتَّفْسِيْرِ، وَأَنْتَ عَلَى مَا تَشَاءُ قَدِيْرٌ. وَصَلَّى اللهُ عَلَى سَيِّدِنَا مُحَمَّدٍ وَعَلَى آلِهِ وَصَحْبِهِ وَسَلَّم بِعَدَدِ مَن صَلَّى عَلَيْهِ، وَبِعَدَدِ مَن لَمْ يُصَلِّ عَلَيْهِ، لَقَدْ جَآءَكُمْ رَسُولٌ مِّنْ أَنفُسِكُمْ عَزِيزٌ عَلَيْهِ مَا عَنِتُّمْ حَرِيصٌ عَلَيْكُم بِٱلْمُؤْمِنِينَ رَءُوفٌ رَّحِيمٌ ﴿١٢٨﴾ فَإِن تَوَلَّوْاْ فَقُلْ حَسْبِيَ ٱللَّهُ لَآ إِلَٰهَ إِلَّا هُوَ عَلَيْهِ تَوَكَّلْتُ وَهُوَ رَبُّ ٱلْعَرْشِ ٱلْعَظِيمِ ﴿١٢٩﴾ (سُورَةُ التَّوْبَةِ)

Astaghfiruka min kulli farīḍatin awjabtahā ʿalayya ānāʾa al-layli wa-aṭrāfa al-nahāri fa-taraktuhā khaṭaʾan aw ʿamdan aw nisyānan aw tahāwunan aw jahlan wa-ana muʿāqabun bihā wastaghfiruka min kulli sunnatin min sunani sayyidi al-mursalīna, wa-khātam al-nabiyīna nabiyyika Muḥammadin ﷺ fa-taraktuhā ghaflatan aw sahwan aw nisyānan aw tahāwunan aw jahlan aw qillata mubālātin bihā. Wa-astaghfiruka yā man lā ilāha illā anta waḥdaka lā sharīka laka, wa-anna sayyidinā Muḥammadan ʿabduka wa-rasūluka. Subḥānaka yā rabba al-ʿālamīna laka al-mulku wa-laka al-ḥamdu, wa-anta ḥasbunā wa-niʿma al-wakīlu, wa-niʿma al-mawlā wa-niʿma al-naṣīr, wa-lā ḥawla wa-lā quwwata illā bi-llāhi al-ʿaliyyi al-ʿaẓīm...yā jābir kulli kasīr, wa-yā muʾannisa kulli waḥīdin, wa-yā ṣāḥiba kulli gharīb, wa-yā muyassira kulli ʿasīrin, yā man lā yaḥtāju ilā al-bayāni wa-l-tafsīri, wa-anta ʿalā mā tashāʾu qadīrun. Wa-ṣalla Allāhu ʿalā sayyidinā Muḥammadin wa-ʿalā ālihi wa-ṣaḥbihi wa-sallam bi-ʿadadi man ṣalla ʿalayhi wa-bi-ʿadadi man lam yuṣalli ʿalayhi. *Laqad jāʾakum rasūlun min anfusikum ʿazīzun ʿalayhi mā ʿanittum ḥarīṣun ʿalaykum bi al-muʾminīna raʾūfun raḥīmun. Fa-in tawallaw faqul ḥasbiya Allāhu lā ilāha illa huwa 'alayhi tawakkaltu wa-huwa rabbu al-'arshi al-'aẓīmi.*

I seek forgiveness from You for every prayer that was required of me in the day or in the night, those I left by mistake, negligence, forgetfulness, will, or out of ignorance, and I am held accountable for. I seek forgiveness from You for every *sunna* from the example of the master of the messengers, Muḥammad ﷺ and the seal of the prophets, which I left out of heedlessness, forgetfulness, will, ignorance, or out of a lack of enthusiasm. I seek forgiveness from You, there is no god but You, [who are] the Unique One and without any partners, and [I testify] that Muḥammad is Your servant and Messenger. Praise be to You, O Lord of the worlds! To You belongs the dominion and to You do we give thanks. You suffice us and [You] are our best disposer of affairs, the best protecter, and the best of victors. There is no power or strength except by that of God the Exalted and Majestic. O Mender of every broken heart! O Intimate Companion of every lonely person! O Master of every alienated person! O Facilitator of every difficult matter! O One who needs no clarification or interpretation and You possess full power over anything You will. Prayers and peace be upon our master Muḥammad, his family, and his Companions; to the extent of those who send prayers upon him and to the extent of those who do not send prayers upon him. "There has certainly come to you a Messenger from among yourselves. Grievous to him is what you suffer; [he is] concerned for you and to the believers he is kind and merciful. But if they turn away [O Muḥammad], say, 'Sufficient for me is Allah; there is no deity except Him. On Him I have relied, and He is the Lord of the Great Throne'" [al-Tawba, 9:128–9].

5

REMEMBRANCE THROUGH GOD'S BEAUTIFUL NAMES

God says in the Qur'ān, *Say, "Call upon Allah or call upon the Most Merciful. Whichever [name] you call—to Him belong the beautiful names"* [al-Isrā', 17:110]. God also says, *And to Allah belong the beautiful names, so invoke Him by them* [al-Aʿrāf, 7:180].

The Messenger of God ﷺ said: God has ninety-nine names, one hundred minus one. No one memorizes them except that they enter Paradise. And He is odd (in number), and loves [what is] odd."[1] In Tirmidhī's transmission the wording is, "whoever realizes (*aḥṣāhā*) them, enters Paradise."[2] The word used here "*aḥṣāhā*" means to memorize the names while contemplating their meanings in a state of belief in them, their secrets, and lights; and to embody their good qualities.

1 *Ṣaḥīḥ al-Bukhārī*, vol. 4, Kitāb al-daʿwāt: bāb Allāh mi'at ism ghayr wāḥid, no. 6047.

2 *Sunan al-Tirmidhī*, vol.5, Kitāb al-daʿwāt, no. 3506.

Formula of Remembrance using God's Beautiful Names

One begins by saying: "*Allāhumma innī atawajjahu bi-asmāʾika al-ḥusnā yā man huwa Allāhu alladhī lā ilāha illā hū* (O God I turn to You through Your beautiful names, O He who is Allāh, there is no other god but He)." Then one proceeds to recite each of God's ninety-nine names as follows.

الرَّحْمٰنُ	*al-Raḥmān*	The Compassionate
الرَّحِيْمُ	*al-Raḥīm*	The Most Merciful
المَلِكُ	*al-Malik*	The King
القُدُّوْسُ	*al-Quddūs*	The Holy
السَّلَامُ	*al-Salām*	The Source of Peace
الْمُؤْمِنُ	*al-Muʾmin*	The Granter of Safety
المُهَيْمِنُ	*al-Muhaymin*	The Guardian
العَزِيْزُ	*al-ʿAzīz*	The Eminent
الجَبَّارُ	*al-Jabbār*	The Compeller
المُتَكَبِّرُ	*al-Mutakabbir*	The Majestic
الخَالِقُ	*al-Khāliq*	The Creator
البَارِئُ	*al-Bāriʾ*	The Originator
الْمُصَوِّرُ	*al-Muṣawwir*	The Giver of Form
الغَفَّارُ	*al-Ghaffār*	The Forever Forgiving
القَهَّارُ	*al-Qahhār*	The Subjugator
الوَهَّابُ	*al-Wahhāb*	The Bestower
الرَزَّاقُ	*al-Razzāq*	The Provider

الفَتَّاحُ	*al-Fattāḥ*	The Opener
العَلِيْمُ	*al-ʿAlīm*	All-Knowing
القَابِضُ	*al-Qābiḍ*	The Constrainer
البَاسِطُ	*al-Bāsiṭ*	The Expander
الخَافِضُ	*al-Khāfiḍ*	The Abaser
الرَّافِعُ	*al-Rāfiʿ*	The Exalter
المُعِزُّ	*al-Muʿizz*	The One who Honors
المُذِلُّ	*al-Mudhill*	The One who Humbles
السَّمِيْعُ	*al-Samīʿ*	The All-Hearing
البَصِيْرُ	*al-Baṣīr*	The All-Seeing
الحَكَمُ	*al-Ḥakam*	The Arbitrator, Judge
العَدْلُ	*al-ʿAdl*	The Just
اللَّطِيْفُ	*al-Laṭīf*	The Benevolent
الخَبِيْرُ	*al-Khabīr*	The All-Aware
الحَلِيْمُ	*al-Ḥalīm*	The Mild, Forbearing
العَظِيْمُ	*al-ʿAẓīm*	The Tremendous
الغَفُوْرُ	*al-Ghafūr*	The All-Forgiving
الشَّكُوْرُ	*al-Shakūr*	The One who Rewards
العَلِيُّ	*al-ʿAlī*	The Most High
الكَبِيْرُ	*al-Kabīr*	The Great
الحَفِيْظُ	*al-Ḥafīẓ*	The Protector
المُقِيْتُ	*al-Muqīt*	The Nourisher

الحَسِيْبُ	*al-Ḥasīb*	The Reckoner
الجَلِيْلُ	*al-Jalīl*	The Sublime
الكَرِيْمُ	*al-Karīm*	The Generous
الرَّقِيْبُ	*al-Raqīb*	The All-Observant
المُجِيْبُ	*al-Mujīb*	The One who Answers
الوَاسِعُ	*al-Wāsiʿ*	The Vast, Limitless
الحَكِيْمُ	*al-Ḥakīm*	The Wise
الوَدُوْدُ	*al-Wadūd*	The Loving
المَجِيْدُ	*al-Majīd*	The All-Glorious
البَاعِثُ	*al-Bāʿith*	The Raiser of the Dead
الشَّهِيْدُ	*al-Shahīd*	The Universal Witness
الحَقُّ	*al-Ḥaqq*	The Truth
الوَكِيْلُ	*al-Wakīl*	The Trustee
القَوِيُّ	*al-Qawī*	The Almighty
المَتِيْنُ	*al-Matīn*	The Invincible
الوَلِيُّ	*al-Walī*	The Patron
الحَمِيْدُ	*al-Ḥamīd*	The Praiseworthy
المُحْصِي	*al-Muḥṣī*	The Keeper of Accounts
المُبْدِئُ	*al-Mubdiʾ*	The Originator
المُعِيْدُ	*al-Muʿīd*	The Restorer of Life
المُحْيِي	*al-Muḥyī*	The Giver of Life
المُمِيْتُ	*al-Mumīt*	The Giver of Death

الحَيُّ	*al-Ḥayy*	The Living
القَيُّومُ	*al-Qayyūm*	The Self-Existing
الوَاجِدُ	*al-Wājid*	The Resourceful
المَاجِدُ	*al-Mājid*	The Magnificent
الوَاحِدُ	*al-Wāḥid*	The Unique
الأَحَدُ	*al-Aḥad*	The One
الصَّمَدُ	*al-Ṣamad*	The Eternal
القَادِرُ	*al-Qādir*	The All-Powerful
المُقْتَدِرُ	*al-Muqtadir*	The Determiner of All
المُقَدِّمُ	*al-Muqaddim*	The Promoter
المُؤَخِّرُ	*al-Muʾakhkhir*	The Postponer
الأَوَّلُ	*al-Awwal*	The First
الآخِرُ	*al-Ākhir*	The Last
الظَّاهِرُ	*al-Ẓāhir*	The Manifest
البَاطِنُ	*al-Bāṭin*	The Hidden
الوَالِي	*al-Wālī*	The Ruler
المُتَعَالِي	*al-Mutaʿālī*	The Exalted
البَرُّ	*al-Barr*	The Perfect Doer of Good
التَّوَّابُ	*al-Tawwāb*	The Accepter of Repentance
المُنْتَقِمُ	*al-Muntaqim*	The Avenger
العَفُوُّ	*al-ʿAfuww*	The Forgiver
الرَّؤُوفُ	*al-Raʾūf*	The Most Kind

مَالِكُ المُلْكِ	*Mālik al-Mulk*	The King of Sovereignty
ذُو الجَلالِ وَالإِكْرَام	*Dhū l-Jalāli wa-l-Ikrām*	The Possessor of Majesty and Honor
المُقْسِطُ	*al-Muqsiṭ*	The Equitable
الجَامِعُ	*al-Jāmiʿ*	The Gatherer, Uniter
الغَنِيُّ	*al-Ghanī*	The Self-Sufficient
المُغْنِي	*al-Mughnī*	The Enricher
المَانِعُ	*al-Mānīʿ*	The Protector, Preventer
الضَّارُّ	*al-Ḍārr*	The One who Afflicts
النَّافِعُ	*al-Nāfiʿ*	The One who Benefits
النُّوْرُ	*al-Nūr*	The Light
الهَادِي	*al-Hādī*	The Guide
البَدِيْعُ	*al-Badīʿ*	The Absolute Cause
البَاقِي	*al-Bāqī*	The Everlasting
الوَارِثُ	*al-Wārith*	The Inheritor
الرَّشِيْدُ	*al-Rashīd*	The Right Guide
الصَّبُوْرُ	*al-Ṣabūr*	The Patient

The nintey-nine names should be read 1,000 times. At the beginning of each tenth time the following supplication should be recited.

Supplication through God's Beautiful Names

دُعَاء أَسْمَاء اللهِ الحُسْنى

اللَّهُمَّ إِنِّي عَبْدُكَ وَابْنُ عَبْدِكَ وَابْنُ أَمَتِكَ نَاصِيَتِي بِيَدِكَ مَاضٍ فِيّ حُكْمُكَ عَدْلٌ فِيّ قَضَاؤُكَ أَسْأَلُكَ بِكُلِّ اسْمٍ هُوَ لَكَ سَمَّيْتَ بِهِ نَفْسَكَ أَوْ أَنْزَلْتَهُ فِي كِتَابِكَ أَوْ عَلَّمْتَهُ أَحداً مِنْ خَلْقِكَ أَوْ اسْتَأْثَرْتَ بِهِ فِي عِلْمِ الغَيْبِ عِنْدَكَ أَنْ تَجْعَلَ القُرآنَ رَبِيْعَ قَلْبِي وَنُوْرَ صَدْرِي وَجَلَاءَ حُزْنِي وَذَهَابَ هَمِّي.

Allāhumma innī ʿabduka wa-ibnu ʿabdika wa-ibnu ammatika naṣiyatī bi-yadika māḍin fiyya ḥukmuka ʿadlun fiyya qaḍāʾuka asʾaluka bi-kulli ismin huwa laka sammayta bihi nafsaka aw anzaltahu fī kitābika aw ʿallamtahu aḥadan min khalqika aw istaʾtharta bihi fī ʿilmi al-ghaybi ʿindaka an tajʿala al-qurʾān al-ʿaẓīm rabīʿa qalbī wa-nūra ṣadrī wa-jalāʾa ḥuznī wa-dhahāba hammī.

O God, I am Your servant, the son (or daughter) of Your male and female servant. My destiny is in Your hand. My past is Your determination and Your determination with me is just. I ask You by all of Your names with which You have named Yourself, revealed in Your Book, taught any of Your creation, or bestowed its knowledge in the unseen world, that You make the exalted Qurʾān the spring rain of my heart, light in my breast, eliminator of my sadness, and remover of my worries.

بِسْمِ اللهِ الرَّحْمٰنِ الرَّحِيْمِ، سَيِّدِي. أَدْخِلْنِي فِي رِيَاضِ أَسْمَائِكَ، وَأَطْلِقْ بِي فِي نَيْلِ النِّعْمَةِ وَارْزُقْنِي رِزْقَ كُلِّ مَرْزُوْقٍ، حَتَّى أَكُوْنَ لَكَ فِيْكَ، وَأَكُوْنَ فِيْكَ لَكَ، مُبْتَهِجاً بِحَلَاوَةِ ذَلِكَ مِنْكَ، إِنَّكَ لَطِيْفٌ عَطُوْفٌ

كَرِيْم. اللَّهُمَّ أَنْتَ لَهَا وَلِكُلِّ معضلةٍ مِثْلِهَا بِحَقِّ مَّا يَفْتَحِ ٱللَّهُ لِلنَّاسِ مِن رَّحْمَةٍ فَلَا مُمْسِكَ لَهَا وَمَا يُمْسِكْ فَلَا مُرْسِلَ لَهُۥ مِنۢ بَعْدِهِۦ وَهُوَ ٱلْعَزِيزُ ٱلْحَكِيمُ ۝٢ (سُورَةُ فَاطِرٍ)

Bismillāh al-raḥmān al-raḥīm, sayyidī! Adkhilnī fī riyāḍi asmā'ika wa-aṭluq bī fī nayli al-ni'mati wa-arzuqnī rizqa kulli marzūq, ḥattā akūna laka fīka wa-akūna fīka laka, mubtahijan bi-ḥalāwati dhālika minka, innaka laṭīfun 'aṭūfun karīm. Allāhumma anta lahā wa-li-kulli mu'ḍilatin mithlihā bi-ḥaqqi: *Mā yaftaḥi Allāhu li-l-nāsi min raḥmatin fa-lā mumsika lahā wa-mā yumsik fa-lā mursila lahu min ba'dihi wa-huwa al-'azīzu al-ḥakīmu.*

In the name of God, the Most Merciful and Most Compassionate, my Master! Grant me entrance into the garden of Your names. Bestow upon me Your bounties and provide for me a sufficient provision, so that I may devote myself entirely to You and rejoice in the sweetness of Your blessings. You are the Subtle, Kind, and Generous one! O God, You have said in truth, *Whatever God grants to people of mercy—none can withhold it; and whatever He withholds—none can release it thereafter. And He is the Exalted in Might, the Wise* [Fāṭir, 35:2].

يَا سَامِعَ كُلِّ صَوْت، وَيَا سَابِقَ كُلِّ فَوْت وَيَا كَاسِي العِظَامَ لَحْماً مُنشِرَهَا بَعْدَ الْمَوْت، أَسْأَلُكَ بِأَسْمَائِكَ العِظَام، وَ بِاسْمِكَ الأَعْظَم الأَكْبَر الْمَخْزُون الْمَكْنُوْن الَّذِي لَم يَطَّلِع عَلَيْهِ أَحَد مِن الْمَخْلُوقِيْن. يَا حَلِيْماً ذَا أَنَاة، يَا ذَا الْمَعْرُوف الَّذِي لَا يَنْقَطِع أَبَداً، وَلَا نُحْصِي لَهُ عَدَداً. .فَرِّج عَنِّي.

Yā sāmi'a kulli ṣawt, wa-yā sābiqa kulli fawt wa-yā kāsiya al-'iẓāma laḥman munshirahā ba'd al-mawt, as'aluka bi-asmā'ika al-'iẓām, wa-bismika al-a'ẓam al-akbar al-makhzūn al-maknūn alladhī lam yaṭṭali' 'alayhi aḥad min al-makhlūqīn. Yā ḥalīman dhā anā, yā dhā al-ma'rūf alladhī lā yanqaṭi'u abadan, wa-lā nuḥṣī lahu 'adadan. . .farrij 'annī.

O Hearer of every call! O Determiner of each occurrence! O Clother of bones with flesh and their disperser after death! I beseech You by Your great names, and by Your greatest and most magnificent name, which is hidden, enclosed, and unseen by creation. O Mild and Forbearing one! O Bestower of endless bounties which can never be enumerated! Relieve me of my troubles!

اللَّهُمَّ إِنِّي أَعْزِمُ بِاسْمِكَ العَظِيْمِ الأَعْظَمِ الحَيِّ القَيُّوْمِ الأَحَدِ الصَّمَدِ عَلَى قَلْبِ (فُلان) وَسَمْعِهِ وَبَصَرِهِ وَلِسَانِهِ وَيَدِهِ، حَتَّى لَا يَجْرِي عَلَيَّ إِلَّا مَا هُوَ خَيْرٌ لِي فِي دِيْنِي وَدُنْيَايَ وَعَوَاقِبَ أَمْرِي. اللَّهُمَّ ارْزُقْنِي خَيْرَهُ وَاصْرِفْ عَنِّي شَرَّهُ، وَاكفنيهِ بِمَا شِئْتَ وَكَيْفَ شِئْتَ يَا أَرْحَمَ الرَّحِمِيْن.

Allāhumma innī a'zamu bi-ismika al-'aẓīmi al-a'ẓami al-ḥayyi al-qayyūmi li-aḥadi al-ṣamadi 'alā qalbi [name the individual] wa-sam'ihi wa-baṣarihi wa-lisānihi wa-yadihi, ḥattā lā yajrī 'alayya illā mā huwa khayrun lī fī dīnī wa-dunyāya wa-'awāqiba amrī. Allāhumma urzuqnī khayrahu wa-aṣrif 'annī sharrahu, wa-akfinīhi bimā shi'ta wa-kayfa shi'ta yā arḥama al-rāḥimīn.

O God, I swear by Your greatest name, the Living, the Self-Existing, the One, the Eternal, upon the heart of [name the individual] and upon his ears, sight, tongue, and hands. Until what is best for me in my religion, my material life, and the end of my affairs reaches me. O God, grant me the best from him and avert from me his harms. Protect me from his [harms] with what You see fit and in the way You see fit, O Most Merciful of the merciful!

The Magnificent Ode in Seeking Assistance through God's Beautiful Names

Compiled by Shaykh Yūsuf al-Nabahānī (1849–1932)

الْمُزْدَوِجَة الحَسناء في الاِسْتِغَاثَة بِأَسْمَاءِ اللهِ الحُسْنى
لِلعَلامَة يُوسُف بن اسماعيل النَبَهَاني

رَحِمَهُ الله تَعَالَى

الحَمْـــــدُ للهِ الَذِي تَحَمَّدَا　　　كَلَّمَ مُوْسَى وَاصْطَفَى مُحَـــمَّدَا

ثُمَّ الصَّلاةُ والسَّـلامُ تُهْتَدَى　　　لِخَيرِ مُرْسَلٍ هَدَى وسَـــدَّدا

وَالْآلِ وَالصَّحْبِ وَمَنْ يَهْدِيْنَا

بِاسْـــمِ الإِلهِ وَبِهِ بَدَيْنَا　　　وَلَو عَـــبَدْنَا غَيْرَهُ شَقِيْنَا

يَاحَبَّذَا رَبّاً وَحَـــبَّ دِيْنَا　　　وَحَبَّـــذَا مُحَمَّدٌ هَـــادِيْنَا

لَولاَهُ مَا كُنَّا وَلاَ بَقِيْنَا

اللهُـــمَّ لَوْلاَ أَنْتَ مَااهْتَدَيْنَا　　　وَلاَ تَصَّدقْنَا وَلاَ صَـــلَّيْنَا

فَأَنْزِلَنْ سَـــكِيْنَةً عَلَيْنَا　　　وَثَبِّتِ الأَقْـــدَامَ إِنْ لاَقَيْنَا

نَحْنُ الأُلَى جَاؤُوْكَ مُسْلِمِيْنَا

وَالمُـــشْرِكُونَ قَدْ بَغَوا عَلَيْنَا　　　إِذَا أَرَادُوا فِتْـــنَةً أَبَيْنَا

وَقَدْ تَدَاعَى جَمْعُهُـــمْ عَلَيْنَا　　　طِبْقَ الأَحَـــادِيْثِ الَتِي رَوَيْنَا

فَارْدُدْهُمُ اللَّهُمَ خَاسِرِيْنَا

اللهُ يَـــا رَحْمَنُ يا رَحِيْمُ　　　اللهُ يَا حَيُّ وَيَا قَـــيُّومُ

اللهُ يَا قَـــوِيُّ يَا قَدِيْمُ　　　اللهُ يَا عَلِيُّ يَا عَـــظِيْمُ

لاَ يَنْبَغِي لِلظُّلْمِ أَنْ يَعْلُونَا

اللهُ يا لَـــــطِيْفُ يا عَلِيْمُ   اللهُ يا رَؤُوْفُ يا حَـــكِيْمُ

اللهُ يا تَوَّابُ يا حَـــلِيْمُ   اللهُ ياوَهَّـــابُ يا كَـــرِيْمُ

هَبْنَا العُلا وَاجْعَل عِدَانَا الدُّوْنَا

اللهُ يا مَالِكُ يا مُـــنِيْرُ   اللهُ يا مَـلِيْكُ يا قَـــدِيْرُ

اللهُ يا مَوْلَى وَيا نَـــصِيْرُ   اللهُ أنتَ الْمَـــلِكُ الكَبِيْرُ

لَيْسَ عِدَانَا لَكَ مُعْجِزِيْنَا

اللهُ يَا شَاكِرُ يَا شَـــكُورُ   اللهُ يَا عَـــفُوُّ يَا غَـفُوْرُ

اللهُ يَا عَالِمُ يَا خَـــبِيْرُ   اللهُ يَا فَتَّـــاحُ يَا بَصِـــيْرُ

لا تَحْرِمَنَّا فَتْحَكَ الْمُبِيْنَا

اللهُ يا ظَاهِرُ يا جَـــلِيْلُ   اللهُ يا بَاطِـــنُ يا وَكِـــيلُ

اللهُ يا صَـــادِقُ ياجَمِيْلُ   اللهُ يا حَـــافِظُ يا كَـفِيْلُ

كُن حَافِظاً لَنَا وكُنْ مُعِيْناً

اللهُ يَا غَـــنِيُّ يَا حَمِيْدُ   اللهُ يا مُـغْنِي وَيَا رَشِـــيْدُ

اللهُ يَا مُبْدِئُ يَا مُـــعِيْدُ   اللهُ يا عَـــزِيْزُ يَا مَجِـــيْدُ

لِعِزِّكَ التَّوْحِيْدُ يَشْكُو الهُوْنَا

اللهُ يَا قَادِرُ يَا مُـــقْتَدِرُ   اللهُ يَا قَـاهِرُ يَا مُـــؤَخِّرُ

اللهُ يَا فَـــاطِرُ يَا مُـــصَوِّرُ   اللهُ يَا مُحصِي وَيَا مُـــدَبِّرُ

دَبِّرْ لَنَا وَدَمِّرِ العَادِيْنَا

اللهُ يَا دَائِـــمُ لاَ يَمُـــوْتُ   اللهُ يَا قَـــائِمُ لاَ يَفُوْتُ

اللهُ يَا مُحْيِي وَيَا مُـــمِيتُ   اللهُ يَا مُغِيْثُ يَـــا مُقِيتُ

كُنْ غَوْثَنَا وَحِصْنَنَا الحَصِيْنَا

اللهُ يَا بَاسِطُ أَنْتَ الوَاسِـعُ   اللهُ يَا قَـــابِضُ أَنْتَ الْمَانِعُ

اللهُ يَا خَالِقُ أَنْتَ الجَـامِعُ   اللهُ يَا خَـــافِضُ أَنْتَ الرَّافِعُ

ارْفَعْ مَعَالِيْنَا لِعِلِّيِّينَا

اللهُ ذُو المَـعَارِجِ الرَّفِيعُ   اللهُ يَا وَافِي وَيَا سَــرِيْعُ

اللهُ يَا كَافِي وَيَا سَـمِيْعُ   يَا نُوْرُ يَا هَادِي وَيَا بَـدِيْعُ

أَدَّبْتَنَا بِمَا جَرَى يَكْفِينَا

اللهُ ذُو الجَـلَالِ وَالْإِكْرَامِ   اللهُ ذُو الطَّوْلِ عَلَى الـدَّوَامِ

اللهُ يَـا ذَا الفَضْلِ وَالإِنْعَامِ   والسَّيِّدُ الْمُـطْلَقُ لِلأَنَامِ

إِرْحَم عَبِيْداً لَكَ عَابِدِيْنَا

اللهُ يَـا أَوَّلُ أَنْتَ الوَاحِدُ   اللهُ يَا آخِرُ أَنْتَ الرَّاشِـدُ

يَا وِتْرُ يَا مُتَكَبِّرُ يَـا وَاجِدُ   يَا بَرُّ يَا مُتَفَضِّلُ يَا مَاجِـدُ

بِفَضْلِكَ اقْبَلْنَا عَلَى مَا فِينَا

اللهُ يَا مُبِيْنُ يَـا وَدُوْدُ   اللهُ يَا مُحِيْطُ يَا شَهِيْـدُ

اللهُ يَا مَتِيْنُ يَا شَـدِيْدُ   يَا مَنْ هُوَ الفَعَّالُ مَا يُرِيْـدُ

إِنَّا ضِعَافٌ لَكَ قَدْ لَجِيْنَا

اللهُ يَا مُعِزُّ يَا مُـقَدِّمُ   اللهُ يَا مُذِلُّ يَا مُنْتَقِـمُ

البَادِئُ البَاقِي فَلاَ يَنْعَـدِمُ   المُحْسِنُ الوَالِي الحَفِيْظُ الأَكْرَمُ

لَيْسَ لَنَا سِوَاكَ مَنْ يَحْمِينَا

اللهُ يَـا وَارِثُ أَنْتَ الأَبَدُ   اللهُ يَا بَاعِثُ أَنْتَ الأَحَـدُ

يَا مَالِكَ المُلْكِ الإِلَهُ الصَّمَدُ   لَا كُفُؤٌ لا وَالِدٌ لا وَلَـدُ

كُفَّ الْعِدَا عَنَّا فَقَدْ أُوذِيْنَا

اللهُ يَا غَالِبُ يَا قَهَّارُ   اللهُ يَا نَافِعُ أَنْتَ الضَّارُّ
اللهُ يَا بَارِئُ يَا غَفَّارُ   يَا رَبُّ يَا ذَا القُوَّةِ الجَبَّارُ

قَوِّمْ لَنَا الدُّنْيَا وَقَوِّ الدِّيْنَا

اللهُ رَبُّ العِزَّةِ السَّلَامُ   الْمُؤْمِنُ الْمُهَيْمِنُ العَلَّامُ
ذُوْ الرَّحْمَةِ الأَعْلَى الأَعَزُّ التَّامُّ   مَنْ دِيْنُهُ الحَقُّ هُوَالإِسْلَامُ

قَيِّضْ لَهُ اللَّهُمَّ نَاصِرِيْنَا

اللهُ أَنْتَ الْمُتَعَالِي الحَكَمُ   الفَرْدُ ذُو الْعَرْشِ الوَلِيُّ الأَحْكَمُ
الغَافِرُ الْمُعطِي الجَوادُ الْمُنْعِمُ   العَادِلُ العَدْلُ الصَّبُوْرُ الأَرْحَمُ

مَكِّنْ لَنَا فِي أَرْضِنَا تَمْكِيْنَا

اللهُ يَا قُدُّوسُ يَا بُرْهَانُ   يَا بَرُّ يَا حَنَّانُ يَا مَنَّانُ
يَا حَقُّ يَا مُقْسِطُ يَا دَيَّانُ   تَبَارَكَتْ أَسْمَاؤُكَ الحِسَانُ

بِهَا قَرَعْنَا بَابَكَ الْمَصُونَا

اللهُ يَا خَلَّاقُ يَا مُنِيْبُ   اللهُ يَا رَزَّاقُ يَا حَسِيْبُ
اللهُ يَا قَرِيْبُ يَا رَقِيْبُ   الْمُسْتَعَانُ السَّامِعُ الْمُجِيْبُ

إِنَّا دَعَوْنَاكَ اسْتَجِبْ آمِيْنَا

Thanks be to the One who is praised,
and [the One who] spoke to Moses and chose Muḥammad.
Then may prayers and greetings of peace be bestowed,
upon the best Messenger who guided and directed,
and to his family, Companions, and those who guide us.

We begin with His name and through Him we start.
Were we to worship other than Him, we would be of the wretched.
How great is the Lord and beloved [His] religion,

and how great is Muḥammad our guide!
Were it not for Him we would not have existed or endured.

O God, were it not for You, we would not have been guided,
nor would we have given in charity or prayed.
So put serenity in our [hearts]
and make our feet firm when we are confronted.
We are of those who have come to You as Muslims!

The disbelievers have transgressed against us,
and if they seek conflict we turn away.
They have assembled their groups against us,
as the narratives [of old] do tell.
So turn them back, O God, in deprivation!

Allāhu, O Compassionate, O Merciful.
Allāhu, O Living, O Self-Existing.
Allāhu, O Strong, O Timeless.
Allāhu, O Exalted, O Tremendous.
Oppression must not triumph over us!

Allāhu, O Benevolent, O All-Knowing.
Allāhu, O Kind, O Wise.
Allāhu, O Accepter of Repentance, O Forbearing.
Allāhu, O Bestower, O Generous.
Grant us [of what is] lofty and make our enemies abased.

Allāhu, O King, O Luminous.
Allāhu, O Sovereign, O Powerful.
Allāhu, O Master, O Victor.
Allāhu, You are the Great King.
Our enemies cannot overpower You!

Allāhu, O Giver of Reward [for deeds], O Grateful One.
Allāhu, O Effacer of Sin, O All-Forgiving.
Allāhu, O Ominiscient, O All-Aware.
Allāhu, O Opener, O All-Seeing.
Do not deprive us of Your manifest victory!

Allāhu, O Manifest, O Majestic.
Allāhu, O Hidden, O Guardian.
Allāhu, O True, O Beautiful.
Allāhu, O Protector, O Guarantor.
Be our Protector and be our Helper!

Allāhu, O Self-Sufficient, O Praiseworthy.
Allāhu, O Granter of Wealth, O Director [to the right way].
Allāhu, O Beginner [of causes], O Restorer.
Allāhu, O Eminent, O Magnificent.
Divine unity complains to Your Majesty of its belittlement!

Allāhu, O All-Powerful, O All-Determiner.
Allāhu, O Subduer, O Postponer.
Allāhu, O Originator, O Fashioner.
Allāhu, O Accounter, O Planner.
Plan on our behalf and destroy our enemies!

Allāhu, O Eternal who does not perish.
Allāhu, O Vigilant who is not bypassed.
Allāhu, O Giver of Life, O Causer of Death.
Allāhu, O Helper, O Sustainer.
Be our Helper and our protected fortress!

Allāhu, O Expander, You are the Vast.
Allāhu, O Constricter, You are the Withholder.
Allāhu, O Creator, You are the Gatherer.
Allāhu, O Abaser, You are the Exalter.
Raise the lofty in us to [great] heights!

Allāhu, O Possessor of Lofty Ascensions.
Allāhu, All-Encompassing, O Swift.
Allāhu, O Sufficient, O All-Hearing.
Allāhu, O Light, O Guide, O Initiator.
You have disciplined us with what came before and it suffices us!

Allāhu, O Lord of Majesty and Honor.
Allāhu, O Constantly Giving One.

Allāhu, O Possessor of Favors and Blessings,
And the Ultimate Master of all beings.
Have mercy on Your servants who worship You!

Allāhu, O First, You are the One.
Allāhu, O Last, You are the Truth.
O Unequaled, O Majestic, O Resourceful.
O Source of All Goodness, O Superior, O Magnificent.
By Your Grace, accept us despite [the sinful state] which we are in!

Allāhu, O Manifest, O Most-Loving.
Allāhu, O All-Encompassing, O Universal Witness.
Allāhu, O Firm, O Mighty.
O One who is the Doer of what He wills.
We are weak and in You we seek refuge!

Allāhu, O Honorer, O Expediter.
Allāhu, O Abaser, O Avenger.
The Eternal Initiator who does not cease to exist,
The Benevolent, the Patron, the Most-Generous Protector,
We have none other than You to protect us!

Allāhu, O Inheritor, You are the Everlasting.
Allāhu, O Resurrector, You are the One.
O King of Sovereignty, the Absolute Lord;
who has none like Him, no father, no son.
Turn the enemy away from us, for we have been afflicted with harm!

Allāhu, O Dominator, O Subjugator.
Allāhu, O Benefactor, You are the Afflicter.
Allāhu, O Maker, O Full of Forgiveness.
O Lord of Irresistible Might,
Set our worldly affairs straight and strengthen the faith!

Allāhu, O Lord of Majesty and Peace.
The Guardian of Faith, the Preserver, the All-Knower,

Possessor of Utmost Mercy and Full Grandeur,
from whose true religion is Islam,
assign to it, O God, a victor!

Allāhu, You are the Most-Exalted, the Judge,
the Singular, the Possessor of the Throne, the Most Just Protector,
the Forgiver, the Giver, the Generous, the Bountiful One,
the Fair, the Justice, the Most Forbearing, the Most-Merciful.
Make us unwaveringly firm on our ground!

Allāhu, O Most Holy, O Clear Proof.
O Benefactor, O Compassionate, O Beneficent,
O Truth, O Equitable One, O Judge,
Blessed are Your beautiful names.
Through them we knock on Your fortified door!

Allāhu, O Creator, O Oft-Turning One [to his worshipers].
Allāhu, O Provider, O Reckoner.
Allāhu, O Near, O Watchful.
The Helper, All-Hearer, the Answerer,
We have called upon You, so accept our supplication! *Amīn!*

Remembrance through the Repetition of *Bismillāh al-Raḥmān al-Raḥīm*

Many of the people of righteousness have found reciting the *basmala* 786 times along with the divine attributes facilitates the fulfillment of all needs. This is known as the "Minor *Basmala*" (*al-basmala al-ṣughrā*). The "Grand *Basmala*" (*al-basmala al-kubrā*) entails the recitation of *bismillāh al-Raḥmān al-Raḥīm* 101,000 times.

The Supplication of the *Basmala*

دُعَاء البَسْمَلَة

إِنِّي أَسْأَلُكَ بِعَظَمَةِ بِسْمِ اللهِ الرَّحْمَنِ الرَّحِيمِ

وَأَسْأَلُكَ بِجَلَالِ بِسْمِ اللهِ الرَّحْمَنِ الرَّحِيمِ

وَأَسْأَلُكَ بِجَمَالِ بِسْمِ اللهِ الرَّحْمَنِ الرَّحِيمِ

وَأَسْأَلُكَ بِكَمَالِ بِسْمِ اللهِ الرَّحْمَنِ الرَّحِيمِ

وَأَسْأَلُكَ بِسَنَاءِ بِسْمِ اللهِ الرَّحْمَنِ الرَّحِيمِ

وَأَسْأَلُكَ بِبَهَاءِ بِسْمِ اللهِ الرَّحْمَنِ الرَّحِيمِ

وَأَسْأَلُكَ بِثَنَاءِ بِسْمِ اللهِ الرَّحْمَنِ الرَّحِيمِ

وَأَسْأَلُكَ بِبَهَاءِ بِسْمِ اللهِ الرَّحْمَنِ الرَّحِيمِ

وَأَسْأَلُكَ بِآلَاءِ بِسْمِ اللهِ الرَّحْمَنِ الرَّحِيمِ

وَأَسْأَلُكَ بِنُوْرِ بِسْمِ اللهِ الرَّحْمَنِ الرَّحِيمِ

وَأَسْأَلُكَ بِفَضَائِلِ بِسْمِ اللهِ الرَّحْمَنِ الرَّحِيمِ

وَأَسْأَلُكَ بِتَصْرِيْفِ بِسْمِ اللهِ الرَّحْمَنِ الرَّحِيمِ

وَأَسْأَلُكَ بِخَصَائِصِ بِسْمِ اللهِ الرَّحْمَنِ الرَّحِيمِ

وَأَسْأَلُكَ بِمَقَامِ بِسْمِ اللهِ الرَّحْمَنِ الرَّحِيمِ

وَأَسْأَلُكَ بِلَطَائِفِ بِسْمِ اللهِ الرَّحْمَنِ الرَّحِيمِ

وَأَسْأَلُكَ بِأَسْرَارِ بِسْمِ اللهِ الرَّحْمَنِ الرَّحِيمِ

وَأَسْأَلُكَ بِهَيْبَةِ بِسْمِ اللهِ الرَّحْمَنِ الرَّحِيمِ

وَأَسْأَلُكَ بِرَقَائِقِ بِسْمِ اللهِ الرَّحْمَنِ الرَّحِيمِ

وَأَسْأَلُكَ بِدَقَائِقِ بِسْمِ اللهِ الرَّحْمَنِ الرَّحِيمِ

وَأَسْأَلُكَ بِمُلُوكِ بِسْمِ اللهِ الرَّحْمَنِ الرَّحِيمِ

وَأَسْأَلُكَ بِحُرُوفِ بِسْمِ اللهِ الرَّحْمَنِ الرَّحِيمِ
وَأَسْأَلُكَ بِابْتِدَاءِ بِسْمِ اللهِ الرَّحْمَنِ الرَّحِيمِ
وَأَسْأَلُكَ بِانْتِهَاءِ بِسْمِ اللهِ الرَّحْمَنِ الرَّحِيمِ
وَأَسْأَلُكَ بِإمْدَادِ بِسْمِ اللهِ الرَّحْمَنِ الرَّحِيمِ
وَأَسْأَلُكَ بِإِحَاطَة بِسْمِ اللهِ الرَّحْمَنِ الرَّحِيمِ

أَنْ تُدْخِلَنِي فِي كَنَفِهَا وَتَمُدَّنِي مِن مَدَدِهَا وَتَرزُقَنِي بِحَقِهَا لَكَ الحَمدُ
يَا بَادِئَ كُلِّ بِدَايَةٍ، لَكَ الشُّكرُ يَا بَاقِيَ عَلَى كُلِّ نِهايةٍ، أَنتَ البَاعِثُ
لِكُلِ خَيرٍ، بَالِغَ آيَاتِ الأُمُورِ كلِّهَا، بَاسِطِ أرزَاقِ العَالَمِينَ. إلهي أَسْأَلُكَ
بِبِسمِ اللهِ الرَّحمَنِ الرَّحِيمِ وَبِجَاهِ سَيِّدِنَا مُحَمَدٍ أَن تَفعَلَ لِي كَذَا وَكَذَا
(وتدعو بما تشاء ثم تختم بقولك: انك على كل شيءٍ قدير).

Innī as'aluka bi-'aẓamati bismillāh al-raḥmān al-raḥīm
Innī as'aluka bi-jalāli bismillāh al-raḥmān al-raḥīm
Innī as'aluka bi-jamāli bismillāh al-raḥmān al-raḥīm
Innī as'aluka bi-kamāli bismillāh al-raḥmān al-raḥīm
Innī as'aluka bi-sanā'i bismillāh al-raḥmān al-raḥīm
Innī as'aluka bi-bahā'i bismillāh al-raḥmān al-raḥīm
Innī as'aluka bi-thanā'i bismillāh al-raḥmān al-raḥīm
Innī as'aluka bi-ālā'i bismillāh al-raḥmān al-raḥīm
Innī as'aluka bi-ḍiyā'i bismillāh al-raḥmān al-raḥīm
Innī as'aluka bi-nūri bismillāh al-raḥmān al-raḥīm
Innī as'aluka bi-faḍā'ili bismillāh al-raḥmān al-raḥīm
Innī as'aluka bi-taṣrīfi bismillāh al-raḥmān al-raḥīm
Innī as'aluka bi-khaṣā'iṣi bismillāh al-raḥmān al-raḥīm
Innī as'aluka bi-maqāmi bismillāh al-raḥmān al-raḥīm
Innī as'aluka bi-laṭā'ifi bismillāh al-raḥmān al-raḥīm

Innī as'aluka bi-asrāri bismillāh al-raḥmān al-raḥīm
Innī as'aluka bi-haybati bismillāh al-raḥmān al-raḥīm
Innī as'aluka bi-raqā'iqi bismillāh al-raḥmān al-raḥīm
Innī as'aluka bi-daqā'iqi bismillāh al-raḥmān al-raḥīm
Innī as'aluka bi-mulūki bismillāh al-raḥmān al-raḥīm
Innī as'aluka bi-ḥurūfi bismillāh al-raḥmān al-raḥīm
Innī as'aluka bi-ibtidā'i bismillāh al-raḥmān al-raḥīm
Innī as'aluka bi-intihā'i bismillāh al-raḥmān al-raḥīm
Innī as'aluka bi-imdādi bismillāh al-raḥmān al-raḥīm
Innī as'aluka bi-iḥāṭati bismillāh al-raḥmān al-raḥīm

An tadkhulanī fī kanafihā, wa-tamuddanī min madadihā, wa-tarzuqnī bi-ḥaqqihā. Laka alḥamdu yā bādi'a kulli bidāyat. Laka al-shukru yā bāqī 'alā kulli nihāya. Anta al-bā'ithu li-kulli khayrin, bāligh āyāt al-umūri kullihā, bāsiṭi arzāqi al-'ālamīna. Ilāhī as'aluka bi-bismillāh al-raḥmān al-raḥīm wa-bi-jāhi sayyidinā Muḥammadin ﷺ an taf'ala lī (insert what one is praying for). This is to be followed by a personal supplication which is ended with the phrase: innaka 'alā kulli shay'in qadīr.

I implore You by the magnificence (*'aẓama*) of *bismillāh al-Raḥmān al-Raḥīm*

I implore You by the majesty (*jalāl*) of *bismillāh al-Raḥmān al-Raḥīm*

I implore You by the beauty (*jamāl*) of *bismillāh al-Raḥmān al-Raḥīm*

I implore You by the perfection (*kamāl*) of *bismillāh al-Raḥmān al-Raḥīm*

I implore You by the radiance (*sanā'*) of *bismillāh al-Raḥmān al-Raḥīm*

I implore You by the splendor (*bahā'i*) of *bismillāh al-Raḥmān al-Raḥīm*

I implore You by the praise (*thanāʾ*) of *bismillāh al-Raḥmān al-Raḥīm*

I implore You by the highness (*ālāʾ*) of *bismillāh al-Raḥmān al-Raḥīm*

I implore You by the illumination (*ḍiyāʾ*) of *bismillāh al-Raḥmān al-Raḥīm*

I implore You by the light (*nūr*) of *bismillāh al-Raḥmān al-Raḥīm*

I implore You by the favors (*faḍāʾil*) of *bismillāh al-Raḥmān al-Raḥīm*

I implore You by the facilitation (*taṣrīf*) of *bismillāh al-Raḥmān al-Raḥīm*

I implore You by the specialties (*khaṣāʾiṣ*) of *bismillāh al-Raḥmān al-Raḥīm*

I implore You by the rank (*maqām*) of *bismillāh al-Raḥmān al-Raḥīm*

I implore You by the subtleties (*laṭāʾif*) of *bismillāh al-Raḥmān al-Raḥīm*

I implore You by the secrets (*asrār*) of *bismillāh al-Raḥmān al-Raḥīm*

I implore You by the awe (*hayba*) of *bismillāh al-Raḥmān al-Raḥīm*

I implore You by the intricacies (*raqāʾiq*) of *bismillāh al-Raḥmān al-Raḥīm*

I implore You by the particulars (*daqāʾiq*) of *bismillāh al-Raḥmān al-Raḥīm*

I implore You by the domains (*mulūk*) of *bismillāh al-Raḥmān al-Raḥīm*

I implore You by the letters (*ḥurūf*) of *bismillāh al-Raḥmān al-Raḥīm*

I implore You by the beginning (*ibtidāʾ*) of *bismillāh al-Raḥmān al-Raḥīm*

I implore You by the end (*intihāʾ*) of *bismillāh al-Raḥmān al-Raḥīm*

I implore You by the succor (*imdād*) of *bismillāh al-Raḥmān al-Raḥīm*

I implore You by the comprehensiveness (*iḥāṭa*) of *bismillāh al-Raḥmān al-Raḥīm*

[I implore] that You allow me entrance into its shade, under its protection. Grant me the full extent of its assistance and give me provision by its stature. To You is all thanks, O Beginner of every beginning. To You is our gratitude, O Everlasting One after all has ended. You are the Sender of all good, Knower of all the details of every matter, and the distributor of provision to humanity!

O God, I beseech You by *bismillāh al-raḥmān al-raḥīm* that you grant me such and such. One supplicates for whatever they wish and then ends their prayer with: "And You have power over all things" (*wa-innaka ʿalā kulli shayʾin qadīr*).

Shaykh Abū l-Ḥasan al-Shādhilī's Litany of Victory (*Ḥizb al-Naṣr*)

حِزْب النَّصْر لِلشَّيْخ الشَّاذِلِي رضي الله عنه

اللَّهُمَّ بِسَطْوَةِ جَبَرُوْتِ قَهْرِكَ، وَ بِسُرْعَةِ إِغَاثَةِ نَصْرِكَ، وبِغِيْرَتِكَ لانْتِهَاكِ حُرُمَاتِكَ، وَبِحِمَايَتِكَ لِمَنِ احْتَمَي بِآيَاتِكَ، نَسْأَلُكَ يَااللهُ، يَاسَمِيْعُ، يَاقَرِيْبُ، يَامُجِيْبُ، يَاسَرِيْعُ، يَامُنْتَقِمُ، يَاشَدِيْدَ البَطْشِ، يَاجَبَّارُ، يَاقَهَّارُ، يَامَنْ لَايُعْجِزُهُ قَهْرُ الجَبَابِرَةِ، وَلَايَعْظُمُ عَلَيْهِ هَلَاكُ الْمُتَمَرِّدَةِ مِنَ الْمُلُوكِ الأَكَاسِرَةِ، أَنْ تَجْعَلَ كَيْدَ مَنْ كَادَنَا فِي نَحْرِهِ، وَمَكْرَ مَنْ مَكَرَ بِنَا عَائِداً عَلَيْهِ، وَحُفْرَةَ مَنْ حَفَرَ لَنَا وَاقِعاً فِيْهَا، وَمَنْ نَصَبَ لَنَا شَبَكَةَ الخِدَاعِ اجْعَلْهُ يَا سَيِّدِي مُسَاقاً إِلَيْهَا، وَمُصَاداً فِيْهَا وَأَسِيْراً لَدَيْهَا.

Allāhumma bi saṭwati jabarūti qahrik, wa-bi-sur'ati ighāthati naṣrik, wa-bi ghīratika bi-intihāki ḥurumātik, wa-bi-ḥimāyatika liman iḥtamā bi-āyātik, nas'aluka yā Allāh, yā samī', yā qarīb, yā mujīb, yā sarī', yā muntaqim, yā shadīd al-baṭsh, yā jabbār, yā qahhār, yā man lā yu'jizuhu qahru-l jabābira, wa-lā ya'ẓumu 'alayhi halāku al-mutamarridati min al-mulūk al-akāsira, an taj'al kayda man kādanā fī naḥrih, wa-makra man makara binā 'ā'idan 'alayhi, wa-ḥufrata man ḥafara lanā wāqi'an fīhā, wa-man naṣaba lanā shabakat al-khidā' ij'alhu yā sayyidī musāqan ilayhā, wa-muṣādan fīhā, wa-asīran ladayhā.

O God, by the subjugating power of Your authority! By the speed of the relief of Your Victory! By Your protective wrath over the violation of what You have prohibited! And by Your shelter of whomever seeks Your protection through Your verses of the Qur'ān! We beg You! O Allāh! O All-Hearing! O Near One! O Answerer! O Swift One! O Avenger! O Mighty Assailer!

O Subjugator! O Compeller! O You who are not overcome by the domination of tyrants! [O You] for whom the destruction of tyrants is no significant challenge! We ask You to make the trap of he who plots against us entrap him, and the plot of he who plots against us make him fall prey to his own snare! And [we beg You] to cause he who digs a hole for us to fall into it [himself] and he who sets up a net of deception for us, be driven into it, trapped by it, and imprisoned by it!

اللَّهُمَّ بِحَقِّ كٓهيعٓصٓ اكْفِنَا هَمَّ العِدَا، وَلَقِّهِمُ الرَّدَى، وَاجْعَلْهُمْ لِكُلِّ حَبِيْبٍ فِدَا، وَسَلِّطْ عَلَيْهِمْ عَاجِلَ النِّقْمَةِ فِي اليَوْمِ وَالغَدَا.

Allāhumma bi-ḥaqqi kāf-hā-yā-ʿayn-ṣād ikfinā hamma al-ʿidā, wa-laqqihimu al-radā, wa-ajʿalhum li-kulli ḥabībin fidā, wa-salliṭ ʿalayhim ʿājil al-naqmati fī l-yawmi wa-l-ghadā.

O God, by the right of *Kāf-Hā-Yā-ʿAyn-Ṣād*, relieve us from the fear of [our] enemies! Oppose them with subjugation, make them a ransom for all that is dear, and overpower them with a swift defeat, today and tomorrow.

اللَّهُمَّ بَدِّدْ شَمْلَهُمْ.. اللَّهُمَّ فَرِّقْ جَمْعَهُمْ..اللَّهُمَّ أَقْلِلْ عَدَدَهُمْ..اللَّهُمَّ فِلَّ حَدَّهُمْ..اللَّهُمَّ اجْعَلِ الدَّائِرَةَ عَلَيْهِمْ..اللَّهُمَّ أَرْسِلِ العَذَابَ إِلَيْهِمْ.. اللَّهُمَّ أَخْرِجْهُمْ عَنْ دَائِرَةِ الحِلْمِ، وَاسْلُبْهُمْ مَدَدَ الإِمْهَالِ، وَغُلَّ أَيْدِيْهِمْ وَأَرْجُلَهُمْ، وَارْبُطْ عَلَى قُلُوبِهِمْ، وَلَا تُبَلِّغْهُمُ الآمَالَ. اللَّهُمَّ مَزِّقْهُمْ كُلَّ مُمَزَّقٍ مَزَّقْتَهُ لِأَعْدَائِكَ انْتِصَاراً لأَنْبِيَائِكَ وَرُسُلِكَ وَأَوْلِيَائِكَ. اللَّهُمَّ انْتَصِرْ لَنَا انْتِصَارَكَ لِأَحْبَابِكَ عَلَى أَعْدَائِكَ. اللَّهُمَّ لَا تُمَكِّنِ الأَعْدَاءَ فِينَا، وَلَا تُسَلِّطْهُمْ عَلَيْنَا بِذُنُوبِنَا حم حم حم حم حم حم حُمَّ الأَمْرُ وَجَاءَ النَّصْرُ فَعَلَيْنَا لَا يُنْصَرُونَ. حم عٓسٓقٓ حِمَايَتُنَا مِمَّا نَخَافُ. اللَّهُمَّ قِنَا شَرَّ الأَسْوَاءِ، وَلَا تَجْعَلْنَا مَحَلاً لِلْبَلْوَى.

Allāhumma baddid shamlahum. Allāhumma farriq jamʿahum. Allāhumma aqlil ʿadadahum. Allāhumma filla ḥaddahum. Allāhumma ajʿal al-dāʾirata ʿalayhim. Allāhumma arsil al-ʿadhāba ilayhim. Allāhumma akhrijhum ʿan dāʾirati al-ḥilm, waslubhum madada al-imhāl. Wa-ghulla aydīhim wa-arjulahum. Warbuṭ ʿalā qulūbihim. Wa-lā tuballighhum al-āmāl. Allāhumma mazziqhum kulla mumazzaqin mazzaqtahu li-aʿdāʾika intiṣāran li-anbiyāʾika, wa-rusulika, wa-awliyāʾik. Allāhumma antaṣir lanā intiṣāraka li-aḥbābika ʿalā aʿdāʾik. Allāhumma lā tumakkin al-aʿdāʾa fīnā. Wa-lā tusalliṭhum ʿalaynā bi dhunūbinā. Ḥā-mīm, ḥā-mīm, ḥā-mīm, ḥā-mīm, ḥā-mīm! Ḥumma al-amru wa-jāʾa al-naṣru fa-ʿalaynā lā yunṣarūn. Ḥā-mīm, ʿayn-sīn-qāf! Ḥimāyatunā mimmā nakhāf. Allāhumma qinā shar al-aswāʾ, wa-lā tajʿalnā maḥallan li-l-balwā.

O God, divide their unity! O God, disperse their assembly! O God, lessen their numbers! O God, blunt their edge! O God, make them shackled by their own ring [of fetters]! O God, bring retribution upon them! O God, exclude them from the shade of leniency! And deprive them of the support of sufficient time! Shackle their hands and feet, tie up their hearts, and do not enable them to reach their goals! O God, tear them apart in the way you make Your enemies perish in order to grant victory to Your prophets, messengers, and Your dearest servants (*awliyāʾ*). O God, grant us the victory of Your beloved ones over Your enemies. O God, do not allow the enemy to overpower us and do not give them authority over us as a result of our sins. *Ḥā-Mīm*, *Ḥā-Mīm*, *Ḥā-Mīm*, *Ḥā-Mīm*, *Ḥā-Mīm!* Matters have become intense, victory has arrived, and they will not overpower us. *Ḥā-Mīm*, *ʿAyn-Sīn-Qāf*, [grant us] protection from what we fear! O God, avert the evils of the malicious [enemies]. Do not make us a source of tribulation.

اللَّهُمَّ أَعْطِنَا أَمَلَ الرَّجَاءِ وَفَوْقَ الأَمَلِ، يَاهُوْ يَاهُوْ يَاهُوْ يَامَنْ بِفَضْلِهِ لِفَضْلِهِ نَسْأَلُ، نَسْأَلُكَ العَجَلَ.. العَجَلَ إِلٰهِي الإِجَابَةَ.. الإِجَابَةَ يَامَنْ أَجَابَ نُوْحاً فِي قَوْمِهِ، يَامَنْ نَصَرَ إِبْرَاهِيمَ عَلَى أَعْدَائِهِ، يَامَنْ رَدَّ يُوسُفَ عَلَى يَعْقُوبَ، يَامَنْ كَشَفَ ضُرَّ أَيُّوبَ، يَامَنْ أَجَابَ دَعْوَةَ زَكَرِيَّا، يَامَنْ قَبِلَ تَسْبِيحَ يُونُسَ بْنِ مَتَّى..نَسْأَلُكَ اللَّهُمَّ بِأَسْرَارِ أَصْحَابِ هَذِهِ الدَّعْوَاتِ أَنْ تَتَقَبَّلَ مَا بِهِ دَعَوْنَاكَ، وَأَنْ تُعْطِيَنَا مَا سَأَلْنَاكَ، وَأَنْجِزْ لَنَا وَعْدَكَ الَّذِي وَعَدْتَهُ لِعِبَادِكَ الْمُؤْمِنِينَ، لَّآ إِلَٰهَ إِلَّآ أَنتَ سُبْحَٰنَكَ إِنِّي كُنتُ مِنَ ٱلظَّٰلِمِينَ ﴿٨٧﴾ (سُورَةُ الأَنبياءِ) انْقَطَعَتْ آمَالُنَا وَعِزَّتِكَ إِلَّا مِنْكَ، وَخَابَ رَجَاؤُنَا وَحَقِّكَ إِلَّا فِيْكَ

Allāhumma aʿṭinā amal al-rajāʾi wa-fawq al-amal. Yā-Hū, Yā-Hū, Yā-Hū! Yā man bi-faḍlihi li-faḍlihi nasʾal! Nasʿaluka al-ʿajal, al-ʿajal! Ilāhī l-ijāba! al-Ijābata Yā man ajāba Nūḥan fī qawmih! Yā man naṣara Ibrāhīma ʿalā aʿdāʾih! Yā man radda Yūsufa ʿalā Yaʿqūb! Yā man kashafa ḍurra Ayyūb! Yā man ajāba daʿwata Zakariyyā! Ya man qabila tasbīḥa Yūnus bin Mattā! Nasʿaluka Allāhumma bi-asrāri aṣḥābi hādhihi al-daʿwāt an tataqabbala mā bihi daʿawnāk, wa-an tuʿṭīnā mā saʿalnāk, wa-anjiz lanā waʿdaka alladhī waʿadtahu li-ʿibādika al-muʾminīn. *"Lā ilāhā illā anta subḥānaka innī kuntu min al-ẓālimīn!"* Inqaṭaʿat āmālunā wa-ʿizzatika illā minka, wa-khāba rajāʾunā wa-ḥaqqika illā fīk!

O God, grant us what we hope [for] and beyond what we hope for. *Yā-Hū*, *Yā-Hū*, *Yā-Hū!* O One through whose favors we ask for His favors! We ask You for haste, haste! O God, answer [us]! Answer [us]! O One who answered Nūḥ among his people! O One who gave victory to Ibrāhīm over his enemies! O One who returned Yūsuf to Yaʿqūb! O One who removed the tribulation of Ayyūb! O One who answered the call of

Zakariyyā! O One who answered the prayers of Yūnus b. Mattā! We implore You, O God, through the secrets of the sources of these supplications, accept what we call upon You for, grant us what we ask for, and manifest for us the promise which You have promised the believers! *Lā ilāha illā anta subḥānaka innī kuntu min al-ẓālimīn!* There is no god but You. All praises are to You. I have been of those who have transgressed! By Your majesty, all our hopes have been lost except [our hope] in You! By Your truth, all of our expectations have diminished except for our expectations from You!

إِنْ أَبْطَأَتْ غَارَةُ الأَرْحَامِ وَابْتَعَدَتْ   فَأَقْرَبُ الشَّيْءِ مِنَّا غَارَةُ اللهِ
يَا غَارَةَ اللهِ جِدِّي السَّيْرَ مُسْرِعَــةً   فِي حَلِّ عُقْدَتِنَا يَــاغَارَةَ اللهِ

In abṭaʾat ghārat al-arḥāmi wa-abtaʿadat.
Fa-aqrabu shayʾi minnā ghāratu-llāh
Yā ghārata-llāhi jiddī sayra musriʿatan
Fī ḥallī ʿuqdatinā yā ghārata-llāh

When the might of our kin has become unresponsive,
the closest thing to us is the might of God!
O might of God, intensify Your coming with haste,
and unravel our knots, O might of God!

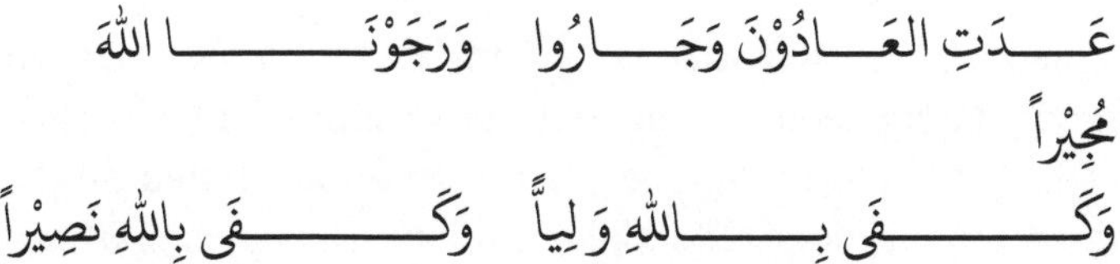
عَـــدَتِ العَـــادُوْنَ وَجَـــارُوا   وَرَجَوْنَـــــــا اللهَ مُجِيْراً
وَكَـــــــفَى بِـــــاللهِ وَلِياًّ   وَكَـــــــفَى بِاللهِ نَصِيْراً

ʿAdat al-ʿādūna wa-jārū   Wa-rajawnā Allāha mujīran
Wa-kafā bi-llāhi waliyyan   Wa-kafā bi-llāhi naṣīran

The enemy has antagonized and violated,
and we have turned to God seeking refuge.

God is the most sufficient guardian.

God is the most sufficient victor.

وَحَسْبُنَا اللهُ وَنِعْمَ الوَكِيْلُ، وَلَا حَوْلَ وَلَا قُوَّةَ إِلَّا بِاللهِ العَلِيِّ العَظِيْمِ، اسْتَجِبْ لَنَا آمِيْنَ فَقُطِعَ دَابِرُ القَوْمِ الَّذِيْنَ ظَلَمُوا وَالْحَمْدُ للهِ رَبِّ العَالَمِيْنَ، وَصَلَّى اللهُ عَلَى سَيِّدِنَا مُحَمَّدٍ النَّبِيِّ الأُمِّيِّ وَعَلَى آلِهِ وَصَحْبِهِ وَسَلَّم تَسْلِيْماً.

Wa-ḥasbuna Allāhu wa-niʿma al-wakīl. Wa-lā ḥawla wa-lā quwwata illā bi-llāhi al-ʿaliyyi al-ʿaẓīm. Istajib lanā, amīn! Fa-quṭiʿa dābiru al-qawmi alladhīna ẓalamū wa-l-ḥamdu li-llāhi rabbi al-ʿālamīn. Wa-ṣallā Allāhu ʿalā sayyidinā Muḥammadin al-nabiyy al-ummī wa-ʿalā ālihi wa-ṣaḥbihi wa-sallam taslīman.

God is sufficient for us and He is the best of guardians. And there is no power, nor strength except through God the Exalted and Magnificent. Answer our prayers! *Amīn!* The plan of the oppressors has failed. All thanks are to God, Lord of the worlds. May prayers and peace be upon Muḥammad, the unlettered prophet, upon his family, and the entirety of his Companions.

Remembrance with the Divine Name *Laṭīf*

Remembrance using the name, *Laṭīf*, is commonly practiced among the righteous throughout the Muslim world. It is often categorized into three types of remembrance based on the amount that is done. The Major Laṭīfiyya (*laṭīfiyyat al-akbar*) consists of 116,487 mentions of "*Yā Laṭīf*" while the Grand Laṭīfiyya (*laṭifiyya al-kabīr*) has 16,641 and the Minor Laṭīfiyya (*laṭifiyya al-saghīr*) has 129 repetitions of "*Yā Laṭīf*." One prays two *rakaʿa*s reciting the *fātiḥa* and Chapter 112 (*Sūrat al-ikhlāṣ*) from the Qurʾān ten times in each unit of prayer (*rakaʿa*). Then one makes 100 *istighfār*s. After this one says, *Yā Laṭīf* while facing the direction of prayer and saying the following at the beginning of every 129 times:

أَلَا يَعْلَمُ مَنْ خَلَقَ وَهُوَ ٱللَّطِيفُ ٱلْخَبِيرُ ﴿١٤﴾

Alā ya'lamu man khalaqa wa-huwa al-laṭīf al-khabīr.

Does He who created not know, while He is the Subtle, the All-Aware? [al-Mulk, 67:14].

ٱللَّهُ لَطِيفٌۢ بِعِبَادِهِۦ يَرْزُقُ مَن يَشَآءُ ۖ وَهُوَ ٱلْقَوِىُّ ٱلْعَزِيزُ ﴿١٩﴾

Allāhu laṭīfun bi-'ibādihi, yarzuqu man yashā'u wa-huwa al-qawiyyu al-'azīz.

Allah is Subtle with His servants, He gives provisions to whom He wills. And He is the Powerful, the Exalted in Might [al-Shūrā, 42:19].

يَا لَطِيْفاً فِي الأَزَلِ أَنْتَ الحَقُّ لَمْ تَزَلْ، الْطُفْ بِعِبَادِكَ الْمُسْلِمِيْنَ فِيْمَا بِهِم نَزَل، بِحُرْمَةِ القُرآنِ العَظِيْمِ وَمَنْ عَلَيْهِ نَزَل.

Yā laṭifan fī l-azal, anta al-ḥaqqu lam tazal. Ulṭuf bi 'ibādika al-muslimīna fīmā bihim nazal, bi ḥurmati al-qur'ān al-'aẓīm wa-man 'alayhi nazal.

O Subtle one in eternity, You are the unchanging reality! Be gentle with Your Muslim servants in what comes down to them, by the sanctity of the Qur'ān and the one to whom [revelation] was revealed.

This is followed by the next well-known supplication.

The *Laṭīfiyya* Supplication

دُعَاء اللَّطِفِيَّة

اللَّهُمَّ يَا مَنْ سَخَّرَ السَّمَوَاتِ السَّبْعَ وَمَنْ فِيْهِنَّ، والأَرَضِيْنَ السَّبْعَ وَمَنْ عَلَيْهِنَّ، سَخِّرْ لِي كُلَّ شَيْءٍ مِنْ عِبَادِكَ مِمَّا فِي بَرِّكَ وَبَحْرِكَ، حَتَّى لَا يَكُوْنَ لِي فِي الكَوْنِ شَيْءٌ مُتَحَرِّكٌ أَوْ سَاكِنٌ، صَامِتٌ أَوْ نَاطِقٌ، ظَاهِرٌ أَوْ بَاطِنٌ، إِلَّا سَخَّرْتَهُ لِي بِبَرَكَةِ اسْمِكَ اللَّطِيْفِ الْمَكْنُوْنِ، يَا حَيُّ يَا قَيُّومُ يَا بَدِيْعُ السَّمَاوَاتِ وَالأَرْضِ يَا ذَا الجَلَالِ وَالإِكْرَامِ يَا الله: إِنَّمَآ أَمْرُهُۥٓ إِذَآ أَرَادَ شَيْـًٔا أَن يَقُولَ لَهُۥ كُن فَيَكُونُ ﴿٨٢﴾ (سُورَةُ يسٓ) إِلَهِي جُودُكَ دَلَّنِي عَلَيْكَ وَإِحْسَانُكَ قَرَّبَنِي إِلَيْكَ، أَشْكُو إِلَيْكَ مَالَا يَخْفَى عَلَيْكَ، وَأَسْأَلُكَ مَالَا يَعْسُرُ عَلَيْكَ، عِلْمُكَ بِحَالِي يُغْنِي عَنْ سُؤَالِي، يَا مُفَرِّجاً عَنْ الْمَكْرُوبِ كَرْبَهُ فَرِّجْ عَنِّي مَا أَنَا فِيْهِ، يَا مَنْ لَيْسَ بِغَائِبٍ فَأَنْتَظِرُهُ، وَلَا بِنَائِمٍ فَأُوْقِظُهُ، وَلَا بِغَافِلٍ فأُنبِّهُهُ، ولا بناسٍ فَأُذَكِّرُهُ، وَلَا بِعَاجِزٍ فَأُمْهِلُهُ، يَا عَالِماً بِالْجُمْلَةِ وَغَنِيّاً عَنْ التَفْصِيْلِ، كَفَى عِلْمُكَ عَنْ الْمَقَالِ، وَكَفَى كَرَمُكَ عَنْ السُّؤَالِ، انْقَطَعَ الرَّجَاءُ إِلَّا مِنْكَ، وَخَابَتِ الآمَالُ إِلَّا فِيْكَ، وَانْسُدَّتِ الطُّرُقُ إِلَّا إِلَيْكَ، يَا اللهُ. . يَااللهُ. . . يَا سَمِيْعُ. . يَا سَمِيْعُ. . . يَا بَصِيْرُ. . . يَا بَصِيْرُ. . . يَاقَرِيْبُ، يَامُجِيْبُ، يَا اللهُ اغْفِرْ لِي، وَارْحَمْنِي بِرَحْمَتِكَ يَا أَرْحَمَ الرَّاحِمِين، وَصَلى اللهُ عَلى سَيِّدِنَا مُحَمَّد وَعَلى آلِهِ وَصَحبِهِ وَسَلِّم.

Allāhumma yā man sakhkhara al-samāwāti al-sabʿa wa-man fīhinna wa-l-araḍīna al-sabʿa wa-man ʿalayhinna, sakhkhir lī kulla shayʾin min ʿibādika mimmā fī barrika wa-baḥrika ḥattā lā yakūna lī fī al-kawni shay'un mutaḥarrikun aw sākinun, ṣāmitun aw nāṭiqun, ẓāhirun aw bāṭinun, illā sakhkhartahu lī bi-barakati ismika al-laṭīfi al-maknūni. Yā ḥayyu yā qayyūmu yā badī'u al-samawāti wa-l-arḍi yā dhā al-jalāli wa-l-ikrāmi yā Allāh: Innamā amruhu idhā arāda shay'an an yaqūla lahu kun fa-yakūnu. Ilāhī jūduka dallanī 'alayka wa-iḥsānuka qarrabanī ilayka ashkū ilayka mā lā yakhfā 'alayka. Wa-as'aluka mā lā ya'suru 'alayka. Ilmuka bi-ḥālī yughnī 'an su'ālī, yā mufarrijan 'an al-makrūbi karbahu farrij 'annī mā ana fīhi, yā man laysa bi-ghā'ibin fa-antaẓiruhu, wa-lā bi-nā'imin fa-ūqiẓuhu, wa-lā bi-ghāfilin fa-unabbihuhu, wa-lā bi-nāsin fa-adhkuruhu, wa-lā bi-'ājizin fa-umhiluhu, yā 'āliman bi al-jumlati wa-ghaniyyan 'an al-tafṣīli, kafā 'ilmuka 'an al-maqāli, wa-kafā karamuka 'an al-su'āli, inqaṭa'a al-rajā'u illā minka, wa-khābati al-āmālu illā fīka, wa-ansaddati al-ṭuruqu illā ilayka, yā Allāh... yā Allāh... yā Samī'... yā Samī'... yā Baṣīr... yā Baṣīr... yā Qarīb... yā Mujīb... yā Allāh ighfir lī wa-arḥamnī bi-raḥmatika yā arḥama al-rāḥimīn, wa-ṣalla Allāhu 'alā sayyidinā Muḥammadin wa-'alā ālihi wa-ṣaḥbihi wa-sallam.

O God! O One who has made the seven heavens and all that is in them; as well as the seven lands and all that is on them! Make all of Your servants on land and water submit to me until there is nothing in the universe—anything that moves or remains still, is silent or speaks, manifest or hidden, except that You have made it submit to me by the blessing of Your name, the subtle name, *Lāṭīf.* O Living and Self-Existing! O Initiator of the heavens and the earth! O Lord of Majesty and Honor! *Verily, when He intends a thing, His Command is: "Be!" and it is* [Yāsīn, 38:82]. O my God! It is Your bounty that has led me to You and Your favor upon me that has brought me near to You. I complain to You of what is not hidden from You and I ask You for what is not difficult for You. Your knowledge of my affairs has made my asking unnecessary for You. O Reliever of the troubles of troubled ones, relieve [the troubles] I am in! O You who is not absent that I would need to await Him, nor asleep that I must awake Him! Your knowledge of my states makes my words inessential. And Your generosity makes my asking not necessary. All of my hopes [in all else] are severed, except [my hope] in You. And all of my expectations are lost, except [my expectation] from You. All paths have become closed, except the path to You. O Allāh! O Allāh! O All-Hearing! O All-Hearing! O All-Seeing! O All-Seeing! O One who is near! O Answerer! O God, forgive me and have mercy upon me through Your compassion, O Most Merciful of those who show mercy. And send prayers and peace upon our master Muḥammad, his family, and the entirety of his Companions.

The Supplication for Divine Assistance and Rain by Shaykh ʿUmar al-Yāfī (1759–1818)

دُعَاء وَ إِسْتِغَاثَة لِنُزُول الغَيْث

لِلشَّيْخ عُمَر اليَافِي العثماني رَحِمَهُ الله

يَا مَنْ يُغِيْثُ الْمُـــسْتَغِيْث   إِنْ لَمْ تُغِثْنَا مَنْ يُغِيْـــث
وَمَـــا لَنَا رَبٌ مُغِيْـــث   سِوَاكَ يَارَبَّ الْعِبَـــاد
فِيْنَا صِـــغَارٌ رُضَّـــعُ   فِيْنَـــا شُيُوخٌ رُكَّـــعُ
كَذَا بَهَـــائِمُ رُتَّـــعُ   وَأَنْـــتَ لِلْكُلِّ مُـــرَادُ
جَهْـــدُ الْبَلاَ حَلَّ بِنَـــا   ضَاقَ الفَلَا مِنْ كَـــرْبِنَا
وَكُلُّ ذَا مِـــنْ ذَنْبِنَـــا   فَهُوَ الَّذِي طَمَسَ الْـــفُؤَاد
إِنْ كُنْتَ غَيْثَ الْطَّـــائِعِيْن   فَمَنْ يُغِيْثُ الْـــمُذْنِبِيْنَ
رَحْمَةُ خَـــيْرِ الْـــرَّاحِمِيْن   مُطْلَقَـــةٌ بِلَا قِيَـــادِ
إِنْ كَانَ لَايَـــرْجُو عَطَـــاك   إِلاَّ الْمُطِيْعُ إِلَى هُـــدَاك
بِمَنْ يَلُـــوْذُ مَنْ عَصَـــاك   أَنْتَ لِمَنْ قَدْ ضَـــلَّ هَاد
يَا رَبِّ عَامِـــلْنَا بِمَـــا   أَنْتَ لَهُ أَهْـــلٌ كَمَـــا
عَوَّدْتَ هَـــذَا كَرَمَـــا   عَبِيْدَ جُـــوْدِكَ يَاجَـــوَاد
يَا رَبِّ قُـــلْتَ اسْتَغْـــفِرُوْا   رَبَّكُـــمُ فَيَـــغْفِرُ
يَأْتِي السَّـــحَابُ الْـــمُمْطِرُ   يَرْوِي العِبَـــادَ وَالْبِـــلاَدَ
فَـــيَا رَحِـــيْمَ الرُّحَمَـــا   وَيَا كَـــرِيْمَ الكُـــرَمَا
أَفِـــضْ أَفِضْ غيثَ السَّمَـــا   فِي الأَرْضِ فَهْيَ لَنَا مِهَـــاد
رَحْمَةُ رَبِّي وَسِـــعَت   لِـــكُلِّ شَيْءٍ جَمَـــعَتْ

عَادَاتُهَا مَا انْقَطَعَتْ   وَلَمْ تَزَلْ بِالإِزْدِيَاد
بِالْمُصْطَفَى جُدْ يَا كَرِيْمُ   فَهْوَ الرَّؤُوْفُ بِنَا الرَّحِيْم
مَنْ كَانَ فِي العِلْمِ القَدِيْم   مِنْهُ الوُجُوْدُ مُسْتَفَاد
صَلَّى عَلَيْهِ اللهُ مَا   غَيْثُ السَّمَاءِ انْسَجَمَا
وَقَدْ هَمَا فَعَمَّمَا   كُلَّ الأَبَاطِحِ وَالوِهَادِ
وَآلِهِ وَصَحْبِهِ   وَرَهْطِهِ وَحِزْبِهِ
فَهُمْ غُيُوْثُ سُحْبِهِ   لِلْخَلْقِ فِي نَهْجِ السَّدَاد
فَاغْفِرْ لِلْنَّاظِمِ يَا تَوَّاب   أَيْضاً وَالنَّاشِرِ يَا وَهَّاب
عَبْدٌ وَقِيْعٌ فِي الأَعْتَاب   يَرْجُو النَّجَاةَ فِي الْمِعَاد

O Helper of those who seek succor,
    if You do not assist us who else can help us?
We have no other Lord who can relieve us,
    other than You, O Lord of the worshipers.
Among us are suckling infants,
    and among us are the hunchbacked elderly.
As are the grazing beasts,
    for You are [the One] desired by all.
The pains of tribulations have afflicted us,
    the [vast] plains have become constricted with our troubles.
And these are all a consequence of our sins,
    for they are indeed what destroys the hearts.
If you are the Helper of only those who are obedient,
    who will then help those [of us] who are sinful?
The mercy of the Most-Merciful,
    is absolute without any restriction.
If none could hope for Your provision,
    other than those who are obedient on Your path,
in whom can those [of us] who disobey You seek refuge?

For You are the Guide for the one who is astray.
O God, deal with us in the way, which is worthy of Your [Grace].
In the way which You have been generous,
[with] Your servants [dependent upon] Your bounty, O Profusely Generous.
My Lord, You have said: "Repent,
and your Lord will forgive."
And the rain-filled clouds of the sky will come,
and pour [rain] over all [Your] servants and lands.
So O Most-Merciful of all those who are merciful,
and Most-Generous of all those who are generous,
bring down, bring down the rain from the sky
upon the earth, for it is where we lie.
The mercy of my Lord is all encompassing,
and it includes everything.
Its vastness does not cease,
and still continues to increase.
By virtue of the [rank of the] Chosen one, grant us bounty,
for he is kind and compassionate toward us.
[The] one whose timeless knowledge
benefitted existence.
God, send prayers upon him,
whenever the rain of the sky forms.
And come down and disperse throughout
all the plains and valleys.
And to his family and Companions
and his people and allies.
For they are the 'rains of his cloud,'
and the best guide for creation to the path [of success].
Forgive the compiler (of this poem), O Accepter of Repentance,
also, the distributor, O Bestower of Gifts.
[I am but] a servant who stands at Your doorstep,
seeking salvation on the Promised Day.

Bibliography

Abū Dāwūd, Sulaymān b. al-Ashʿath al-Sijastānī. *Sunan*. Beirut: Dār Ibn Ḥazm, 1997.

al-Bayhaqī, Aḥmad b. al-Ḥusayn. *Shuʿab al-īmān*. Beirut: Dār al-Kutub al-ʿIlmiyya, 1410/1990.

al-Bukhārī, Muḥammad b. Ismāʿīl b. Ibrāhīm. *al-Jāmiʿ al-ṣaḥīḥ*. Beirut: Dār Ṭawq al-Najā, 1422/2002.

al-Dāraquṭnī, ʿAlī b. ʿUmar. *Sunan*. Beirut: Dār al-Maʿrifa, 1966.

al-Ḥākim, Muḥammad b. ʿAbd Allāh. *al-Mustadrak ʿalā al-Ṣaḥiḥayn*. Beirut: Dār al-Maʿrifa, 1335/1917.

al-Ḥaythamī, ʿAlī b. Abū Bakr. *Majmaʿ al-zawāʾid wa-manbaʿ al-fawāʾid*. Beirut: Dār Kitāb al-ʿArabī, 1982.

Ibn Māja, Muḥammad b. Yazīd al-Qazwīnī. *Sunan*. Edited by Muḥammad Fuʾād ʿAbd al-Bāqī. Beirut: Dār Iḥyāʾ al-Kutub al-ʿArabiyya, 1954.

Muslim, Ibn al-Ḥajjāj al-Qushayrī al-Nīsābūrī. *al-Jāmiʿ al-ṣaḥīḥ*. Edited by Muḥammad Fuʾād ʿAbd al-Bāqī. Beirut: Dār Iḥyāʾ al-Kutub al-ʿArabiyya, 1954.

al-Nasāʾī, Aḥmad b. Shuʿayb *al-Sunan al-kubrā*. Beirut: Dār al-Maʿrifa, 1356/1938.

al-Tirmidhī, Muḥammad b. ʿĪsā. *al-Jāmiʿ al-ṣaḥīḥ*. Edited by Aḥmad Shākir and Muḥammad Fuʾād ʿAbd al-Bāqī. Beirut: Dār Iḥyāʾ al-Turāth al-ʿArabī, 1938.

Nur Foundation
FOR SACRED SCIENCES
PUBLICATIONS

7030078R00096

Printed in Great Britain
by Amazon.co.uk, Ltd.,
Marston Gate.